To all who follow their heart — and move on...

CONTENTS

Chapter   Page

1   Two Childhoods   7
2   Borstal: End of Innocence   16
3   Flight from Fascism   27
4   How Behar Became Blake   38
5   Secret Service in Korea   61
6   Captive of the Communists   68
7   The Conversion of George Blake   79
8   How GB became KGB   92
9   Bourke —The Missing Years   104
10   Blake — Making of a Double Agent   109
11   Berlin — Swamp of Espionage   118
12   Two Lives Converge   139
13   Trials and Punishment   154
14   Life in 'The Scrubs'   168
15   Over One Wall…   182
16   …and another Wall   192
17   Privileges of Communism   203
18   Fear in the Forest   219
19   Parting is Such Sweet Sorrow…   230
20   Bourke: Home is the Hero   240
21   Blake — a New Life   253
22   Bourke — The Downward Slope…   273
23   Bourke — Under an Open Sky…   288
24   Outing The Conspirators   307
25   A Shock to the System   320
26   The End Of Empires   337

Acknowledgements & Sources   348
Chapter Notes   351
Select Bibliography   363
Index   368

CHAPTER ONE

TWO CHILDHOODS

Within yards of the Bourke household, in the lane-ways off Little Gerald Griffin Street, stood the disintegrating walls of the old siege city — 12 feet thick. Everybody growing up in that district knew of the walls and especially of the legends of the Cromwellian and Williamite sieges. The city of Limerick had fallen only when the walls were breached.

From the time he could scamper to play, the bulky, jutting — and unsafe walls were a totem of Sean Bourke's streetscape. Quite simply, walls came into his perspective. When his father moved the family of seven boys to the new home in Bengal Terrace, it was along the mile length of Mulgrave Street, which was marked, successively, by the perimeter walls of the gaol, lunatic asylum and cemetery. There was no other street like it in the city. The high walls to these institutions were uniformly of limestone blocks, cut and dressed by local stonemasons. Limerick was a city of tradesmen's guilds rooted in baronial Medievalism. Stonemasons were among the oldest and most respected of the city's guilds; their prowess stood exalted in the great stretching walls of Mulgrave Street.

Sean Bourke moved back and forth along this stone conduit in his daily trek to school, going by gaol, asylum and graveyard, 'the bad, the mad and the dead'.

School was within more high walls, again of grey limestone. Here, in Sexton Street, the Christian Brothers taught the children of the north city, within a regime of religious discipline. A teaching order given carte blanche by the fledgling state to impose values in accord with De Valera's Ireland of the late 1930s, the teachers at Sexton Street were monks who lived lives of intense discipline in communal house, rising early for personal prayer, to equip themselves for the exhausting daily ritual of confrontation with classes of schoolboys, each class with a minimum of fifty pupils. Not surprisingly, many of the teachers lost their tempers trying to keep order.

Sean Bourke grew up in De Valera's Ireland, upon which the ascetic visionary had stamped a version of Gaelic apartheid, in an attempt to fill a philosophical vacuum in the aftermath of British colonial withdrawal. It was an uneasy grafting that never quite took in the cities; the external imposition of Gaelic values from an imagined rural utopia was resisted by those whom it was intended to convert. The education storm troopers were the Christian Brothers. Recruited in their teens, confined to all male seminaries, 'The Brothers' saw themselves as front-line enforcers of the New Ireland, which, in the year before Sean Bourke went to school, had been officially promulgated as Gaelic-speaking, family-based and Catholic[*]. Yet, the majority of its citizens were English speaking, their Catholicism was automatic — and family life was often matriarchal, with the male parent spending many of his years in England.

The Irish Constitution made much of family life, specifically in relation to education. The family unit was declared to be '…the natural, primary and fundamental unit group of Society — a moral institution possessing inalienable and imprescriptible rights, antecedent and superior to all positive law.'

Another tenet laid down; 'The State acknowledges that the primary and natural educator of the child is the Family.' And warned: 'In exceptional cases, where the parents for physical and moral reasons fail in their duty towards their children, the State as guardians of the common good, by appropriate means shall endeavour to supply the place of parents, but always with due regard for the natural and imprescriptible rights of the child.'

I quote these edicts because the gap between the high-minded rhetoric and actual practice was to show, in the life of Sean Bourke, the harsh reality that made hollow such promises. Crucial to his later attitudes, and to how he lived

---

[*] Bunracht Na hÉireann, (Constitution of Ireland) 1937.

his life, was an abiding detestation of State institutions. Specifically, as it turned out, when any of the 'isms' of 20th century life were tied to State institutions. Catholicism, Capitalism, even Communism, were all to embrace him, with an apparent benevolence which his individual spirit eventually kicked against.

It is difficult to know quite where such rebelliousness began. Perhaps as early as age five, when he explored the hinterland of the new house. Bengal Terrace lay on the outskirts of Limerick. Owned and administered by the British Army, in a Republican Ireland, the terrace teemed with anomalies of colonialism. Occupied by Irish families whose men-folk had served in the forces, named to honour a siege of the Indian sub-continent in the heyday of The British Raj, the cluster of houses gave off a whiff of its own siege mentality in a city that was culturally riven between past and present. In Bengal Terrace, the stamp of De Valera's Ireland lay uneasily upon a lost settlement of the British Empire.

These tensions were driven early into the awareness of Sean Bourke. He left a home full of British army insignia to attend a school where such trophies were objects of abuse, meted out in harsh scorn by monks infected with the proselytising of the New Gaelic Ireland. An Ireland laden with the contradictions of post-colonial uncertainty. De Valera, architect and symbol of the new 'Gaelic' Ireland appeared from a Rolls Royce on formal occasions, dressed in a frock coat, saluted by officers of the fledgling Irish Army whose dress and ceremony was innately British.

Such ceremonial imitation was replicated across the declining British Empire, from Cairo to Delhi, in what the novelist V.S. Naipul termed 'the mimic men'.

Schoolbooks denigrated England's past in Ireland, while the Irish Government assiduously wooed British industrialists to invest in the new state, whose population was haemorrhaging from unemployment into emigration to England. 'Remember The Bull, John Bull looked after us', admonished Mrs. Bourke when the boy told of being harassed by ruffians from nearby Garryowen, jealous of the

9

new houses provided for veterans of British Armed Forces. The Bourke boys ran the gauntlet of jeers from Garryowen:

'Toora-loo, a loo, aloo
I saw the monkey up in the zoo
If I had a face like yours
I'd join the British Army.'

Early on, young Bourke learned life was tough. From the house, where his mother was the only buffer against the blows of a severe father, he foraged out in the streets where fights and catcalls were a daily hazard, trekking to a school that was unsympathetic.

In primary school beatings were common, by hand, fist, strap and cane. 'The Brothers' whose own lives of harsh discipline resonated throughout their classrooms, educated the bulk of the country's Catholic youth. 'The Brothers' rose early, worked rigorously and were confined to monastic precincts. In Limerick's schools run by the Christian Brothers, educational ideology was effected by insistence on discipline, alertness to the rudiments of learning and an evangelical belief that out of chaos they would impose order. Order, which would bring to the former colony the tenets of Gaelic, Catholic Ireland, 'If ye won't learn it, by the crucified Jesus, I'll beat it into ye' was the chant of one Brother.

The innate self-confidence of the young Sean Bourke was bound to come into open conflict with that regime. Between the stocky, cocky boy of inherent good nature and the ascetic teachers lay a multiplicity of cultural differences. 'The Brothers' were mainly from rural families, carrying with them the suspicion of city children. They were dedicated to the imposition of values, which were little understood by their charges from the city's environs. Most of the teachers had been recruited to the stern religious life while adolescents and had missed out on the normal escapades of youth. Sean Bourke, by contrast had an early enjoyment of belonging to a large, rough-and-tumble family in the clannish inner city area. The family knew horses, markets, fights and the to-ing and fro-ing to fairs, shops, pubs and relations. They were a substantial people, the most notable being his father's brother 'Feathery' Bourke, scrap merchant and slum landlord. In a tradition, which was durable and enduring, talk of wars and migrations were part of Bourke's Limerick inheritance. His father had earned medals in The Dardanelles, his mother came of 'ould stock'. It was, in life terms, a pedigree not likely to accept the ritual humiliation of daily education by the Christian Brothers.

Sean mitched. He became friendly with a family, the Brophy's, who lived in a tenement in Thomas Street. The Brophy family had relations in the adjoining county of Clare. One of their sons was a classmate of Sean's and brought him to Meelick, a pastoral hinterland on the outskirts of the city. On a farm there, and while ten years old, Sean Bourke spent blissful days away from home and from school.

He became lost in the country. Enjoying the ways of farming life, adopted by the easy-going Brophys, the boy took to animals and fields with stolen time which was to exact its penalty. After repeated visits from the truancy inspector, his father arrived in Meelick to fetch him home. As remembered by Sean's twin brother, Kevin: 'Sean was hiding under a bed in the farmhouse. The man in the bed was dying, he must have been ninety. Sean thought it was a good place to hide…'

Brought back, punished at home and at school, he graduated to other escapades. Picture-going was all the rage in the 1940s and admission for children in the working-class areas was by amounts of jam-jars. Outside the Tivoli and Thomond cinemas, from four o'clock in the afternoon, queues of kids waited, clutches of glass jars strung together with string. Kevin: 'You got a penny for three jars — it cost thrupence to get in…once inside, it was another world. Gabby Hayes, Roy Rogers and his horse, Trigger. You could spend the whole evening inside, spellbound on wooden seats, looking at the screen.' The Bourke boys spent a lot of time in the cinemas. Sean especially: 'Errol Flynn, The Count of Monte Cristo — that kind of thing...Sean would get up and act out some of the scenes.'

It is easy to imagine the ten-year old fantasist acting out the adventures of swinging down the cliffs of wooden seats. An early imprinting, which was to have later adult implications. At the time though such urges were apparently satisfied in the ritual games played in disused railway wagons near the home in Bengal Terrace. Groups of kids congregated there, among the open railway wagons and enacted the scenarios of the cinema. Sean played the role of the heroic baddie. He was cheerleader and deviser of pranks.

We have his own account of the young gang on the railway bridge overlooking the road from the countryside into the city. They saw Ma Murphy approaching:

'She was sitting up on the little cart next to the tank of sour milk and the jaded donkey was pulling her towards the town at the rate of about two miles an hour.

We all saw her coming. There was a hurried conference, as there usually is when there are a few very young boys on a bridge and a likely target comes into view. But we had no missiles handy. Stones were out of the question and there was no water nearby. "I have it!" said Fonsy, Ger's brother. "I have it!" He dropped his trousers, placed one foot on either side of a wide gap in the boards and squatted down. His rectum was poised with precision over the centre of the opening. "Give me the signal, Sean" he said, looking up at me with a grin. "And you better allow a couple of yards because tis a high bridge." I took up a strategic position and raised my hand in the manner of a battery commander, like I had seen it in the films. Ma Murphy came closer, her eyes fixed permanently about halfway along the donkey's burdened back, completely oblivious to the impending danger. The rest of the boys were all down on their hands and knees peering through other

12

gaps in the boards. She was under the bridge. A couple of yards to go. "Now!" I said, dropping my hand suddenly. The first one, tapered just like a bomb, landed dead centre between the donkey's ears, exploding on impact to splash all over the animal's neck. Ma Murphy stared disbelievingly for a moment at the brown mess. She was sixty years of age and had never before seen shit falling from the sky. Hail, rain and snow, yes; but shit, never. She looked up, her eyes and her mouth wide open in an expression of shocked incredibility. But the second one was already on its way. It might have missed her, if it weren't for the donkey. Even that docile creature was so taken aback it stopped dead in its tracks. And by now Ma Murphy was staring straight up at Fonsy's bare arse. She saw it coming but couldn't believe it. She just stared at it, mesmerised. Then it landed, right on her forehead and splashed smoothly all over her face. "Jesus, Mary and Joseph" she screamed, "I'm destroyed! Holy Mother of God, what's happening at all!" A dozen pairs of eyes, like cats in the night, were staring down at her through the gaps in the boards and Fonsy's arse was still poised there menacingly. "Ye dirty blaggards!" She screamed. "Ye dirty blaggards! May God forgive ye!" And her face was brown all over.'

Most children of healthy energy get caught up in and grow out of such play-acting. In adulthood, many remember with a shudder the narrow line between the fun and fatalism of childhood. In childhood games, lurks future behaviour. Chubby, boyish Sean Bourke played those games in Limerick in 1944. Ten years earlier, six hundred miles away in an uneasy Europe, a young Dutch boy, George Behar was dressing up, to his sister's amusement, in the clothes of elders and playing the part of a severe judge. Decisive in his 'moral' views of make-believe transgressions, he rapped out sentences. Usually, it was the maid who was punished by the 12-year-old judge.

George Behar was a lonely child. His father was ailing with the ravages of mustard gas from British Army service in the First World War. Egyptian by birth, Albert Behar came from the line of Sephardim, aristocratic bankers to the Jews. Rooted in the Iberian Peninsula since the Middle Ages, the exodus from European persecution had settled the Behar's in Egypt. George's father held a commission in the British Army. Decorated with military honours from both British and French empires, Albert Behar had served on the Intelligence Staff of Field Marshall Haig.

It is relevant to criss-cross the political backgrounds of George Behar and Sean Bourke. George Behar, (who was to become Blake) was born in November 1922. Sean Bourke was born in October 1934. The fathers of the boys who were to meet as men in Wormwood Scrubs prison had served in the British Forces. Behar, like Bourke, grew-up in the folklore of wars. Each was inheritor of their father's sagas, the more potent for being little understood. Each had seen the ill-health of a father resulting from military service: Behar's from mustard gas poisoning, Bourke's from coal-dust in the lungs, inhaled while stevedoring aboard warships.

There were sharp differences, mainly of social class and temperament. George Blake was born into a cosmopolitan lineage of Cairo and Rotterdam, where his father had settled on marriage to his Dutch-born wife. The family was prosperous. George spoke English, French, Dutch and German. He regarded himself as a person who would gain distinction. Sean Bourke was born into Limerick working-class rigour, with all the early penalties and uncertainties endemic among that class in the 1930s. Temperamentally, the youths could hardly have been more different. Bourke was burly and gregarious. Blake was lean, studious and efficient to the point of being considered ambitious by his contemporaries.

They had *something* in common. Politically, they shared a culture, which was to become crucial to their meeting, many years ahead. While each grew up under the paternal aura of the British Armed Forces, they did so in countries which were intent on shaking off the Empire. Both spent their formative years in colonies whose very identity was two-headed. Bourke in Ireland, Blake in Egypt — countries where such identity with British militarism meant antagonism with elements of the native population. Seeds of questioning were sown which were to sprout when they became adults. An eventual questioning of what precisely it meant to be 'British'.

Such personal confrontation was to occur, when Blake and Bourke, in their separate circuitous ways arrived in the Mother Country of their inheritance and found it wanting. Especially in response to their individual personalities. Such confrontation and rejection lay decades ahead of the youths now growing up, unaware of each other, in the 1930s.

CHAPTER TWO

BORSTAL: END OF INNOCENCE

At nine years of age, Sean Bourke graduated from empty jam jars to full ones. Though the Irish Free State was nominally neutral during the war years, a pervasive identity with Britain filled the Bourke household. Two older brothers had gone off to the RAF in Britain. In Limerick, there was open recruiting to the war, via the city of Belfast, five hours away by train.

Wartime shortages in an economy dependent on Britain meant scarcity of foodstuffs. Jam became a delicacy, where previously it had been the staple diet of working-class families, layered thickly on bread and butter and taken with large mugs of tea.

Familiar with railway goods traffic shunting near his home, Bourke raided a wagon and stole cartons of jam, biscuits and cider. With his persistent truancy, the offence led to his removal from the school at Sexton Street. He was placed in another school run by 'The Brothers', again behind high grey limestone walls. An inmate of the time remembers that John The Baptist was 'A school for bad boys — but we mitched even more. Sean played in the school band, he was a cheerful, curly-headed boy, always up to mischief. We were troublesome street urchins. We stole from shops in town. We would organise ourselves to steal. Eventually, Sean was caught taking money from a car. He was sent to Daingean Reformatory for three years.'

Set behind high grey walls and run by the religious order of Oblate Brothers, borstal at Daingean was to become a seminal experience. More than any previous incarceration, the fortress in the Irish midlands was to mould Bourke into the 'hard man'. In adulthood, he would talk obsessively about his time at the mercy of the 'Reformers' at Daingean. 'I hated being sent there — but I didn't want to go back on the streets, either.'

Daingean was the end of innocence.

'...I was twelve and a half years of age. Absolute silence had to be maintained at all times. There was no heating in the wash house and the ice was about a quarter inch thick in the basins. I copied the other boys and broke the ice with a quick jab of the elbow before having a wash in the freezing water.'

'Brother X was supervising the wash-house. He did this by standing on a wooden box. He was nicknamed 'The Killer". I found out why on that very first morning in Daingean. Some boy was heard to whisper to another at the end of the washhouse. Brother X went red in the face. "If I catch the fella that's talking he won't be able to talk for a long time."

Then he seemed to notice something. He jumped down off the box and ran to where the whisper had come from. He caught hold of a boy about 17 and proceeded to beat him methodically with his fists. He punched the boy in the face repeatedly until his lip was split and his nose spurted blood. In his frenzy Brother X's crucifix worked its way loose from the belt of his cassock and, dangling from its neck cord, jumped about in a grotesque dance as he carried out his attack on the terrified boy.

Brother X then resumed his position on the wooden box and glared up and down the washhouse. "Ye scum of the earth", he screamed, addressing the inmates in general. "Ye dirty filthy good for nothing scum of the earth. Ye dirty pack of robbers. Ye will be no loss to anyone when ye go back to the filthy dirty hovels and the ignorant illiterate fathers and mothers that ye come from."

From the washhouse we were marched once more through the snow and the darkness to the chapel for Mass.'

The early imprinting of Daingean was to stay with him, seared into his mind with photogenic details, as this account of another beating shows. It took place when he had been two years in the penitentiary.

Brother Y had been outside the dormitory, spying on the boys: he singled out one for 'using bad language'.

'Brother Y had a ritual which he had carefully developed over the years. A boy must not be punished too quickly; he must be made to suffer the mental torture of knowing that he is going to be beaten. And so, when the five of us arrived in the kitchen to start work at nine o'clock that morning exchanging a little cheerful banter, Brother Y carried out the first move of his sadistic ritual. "Keep quiet and get on with yeer work!" He looked Mick straight in the face and scowled. "And that goes for you too...get on with your washing-up!"

And so the ritual began. It was familiar to all of us. In exactly two hours, as the clock struck eleven, Mick would be beaten. And between now and then none of us would utter one word to each other lest we be made to join our wretched comrade on the sacrificial altar of Brother Y's sadistic lust.

The soup was made. The roast was in the oven for the priests and brothers. The breakfast pots and pans and cups and saucers were washed and shined. I myself as senior boy had laid out the cutlery and the various items of delph on the crisp white linen in the priests' and brothers' refectory. Brother Y sat on a chair next to the work-table against the kitchen wall opposite the long anthracite range reading his breviary, his pale lips moving silently in an ashen face. Mick was over at the sink washing a plate for the tenth time, afraid to look up, visibly trembling. The silence was almost physical in its oppressiveness.

The kitchen clock struck eleven. Brother Y slowly closed his breviary, kissed it, and placed it on the shelf above the table. He got to his feet and walked to the small gap between the table and the dresser. He reached in and pulled out a stick about three feet long and an inch across. Nicholas from Kilkenny picked up a sweeping brush and started towards the scullery in a desperate effort to escape what was to follow. "Put that brush down and stay where you are!" Brother Y growled. It was part of the ritual that when a boy was to be beaten the others must watch. The fear in their young faces was something Brother Y seemed to get great satisfaction from.

Mick was still washing the same plate, afraid to stop, afraid to be idle and add to his guilt. "Put that plate down and turn round!" He did as he was told.

"You are the dirtiest little scut it has ever been my misfortune to meet. You are dirty and filthy and evil minded. Well, I'm going to teach you a lesson that you will never forget. Hold out your hand!"

Mick held out his right hand. He thrust it forward fully and firmly, as if to show Brother Y that whatever he had done wrong he was sorry for it and was prepared to take his punishment like a man and maybe Brother Y in his mercy would take this into account. But this bold and frightened gesture was wasted and Mick, at fourteen and a half years of age, was to receive the most vicious and sadistic beating I have ever seen inflicted on another human being.

Brother Y reduced Mick's right hand to a black and blue pulp of bleeding flesh from fingertips to the elbow, and then ordered him to hold out his left hand. He did the same to this, bringing the stick back over his head and then down with all his physical might on the boy's trembling flesh. By this time, Mick was begging for mercy. "Please, sir, oh please sir, I won't do it any more sir, I won't sir, I won't sir…" "Shut up your whimpering, you cowardly little wretch!" Brother Y's face was by now a sickly white in colour and his lips trembled visibly. He looked almost epileptic. "You are filthy and disgusting. You have a foul mouth. You have a dirty mind. You are totally obscene. You are a dirty little coward who cannot take his punishment. And you are a robber and a Daingean boy. That is the testimonial you will take out into the world with you when you go. And I hope you are proud of it, you filthy wretch!"

"Oh, please, sir, please, sir, I won't do it anymore, sir. It was a slip of the tongue, sir…" By this time Mick's knees were giving way under the sheer agony of his ordeal, and his torrential tears were forming a small pool at his feet. "Please sir, please, sir…". He looked like he was on the point of fainting. Surely Brother Y must stop now.

"Roll up your sleeves to your shoulders".

Mick looked at him in horror. "Oh, please, sir, please."

Brother Y delivered three rapid blows to the boy's upper left arm, then three more to the right causing the shirt-sleeves to sink into the sweat-soaked flesh with the force. "When I tell you to do something, you do it!"

"Yes, sir, yes, sir…" Mick's fingers were by now twice their normal size and he could not bend them at the joints. His hands and forearms looked like joints of raw meat that had been left hanging in a butcher's shop too long and had putrefied. He made a feeble gesture at forcing his sleeves up past the elbows but could not do so. His elbow joints, as well as his fingers, were beyond use. "I c-c-can't sir, I c-c-can't..." The sweat was pouring down his forehead in large beads. "I'm sorry, sir, I'm sorry, sir..."

"You filthy dirty wretch!" Brother Y leaned the stick against the wall and grabbed hold of the boy. He forced both his sleeves up to the shoulders and picked up the stick once more. The contrast between the lower half of Mick's arms and the upper was quite frightening and sickening. The broken black and blue flesh gave way at the elbows to the smooth, white skin of the upper arms and biceps so characteristic of the Daingean boy deprived of the sun. I felt myself trembling with fear and impotent rage and a deep loving compassion for my comrade in his terrible agony. The other three boys...stood transfixed at their respective places of labour, terrified to make a sound or a movement.

...Brother Y no longer told him to extend his hands. Instead he proceeded to lash him on the upper arms with all his force and continued for at least another five minutes until Mick's entire arms, from the fingers to the shoulders, were no longer recognisable as human limbs.

"Oh, God, oh, God! Please, Brother...please, sir, please..."

Mick fell to his knees at last, his young boy's strength and endurance finally spent. Sitting on his haunches, he eased his body forward and rested his forehead on the ground, his chin touching his knees. His arms hung loosely by his side, completely out of control, and the blood, trickling down his broken flesh, paused for a second at the finger-tips, and then fell to the floor to mingle with his sweat. He had finished pleading and he just moaned softly to himself.

"Dirty cowardly filthy wretch!" With all his might, Brother Y delivered three final blows to the boy's quivering back. The stick made a sickening thud as it fell and Mick eased over on his side and lay still.

Brother Y looked across at me and then at the other three boys in turn. His face was contorted almost beyond recognition and he seemed to be shaking all over. When he spoke, his breath came in short gasps.

"Let that be a lesson to all of ye. There is enough filth and dirt in this world without ye people starting. Even to think an impure thought is a mortal sin. If ye haven't got the strength to avoid temptation and sin, then by God I'll give ye that strength — with this!" He held the stick tightly in his right hand until the knuckles were white and jabbed it rhythmically at each of us in turn. "With this", he repeated, "with this!"

He looked down at Mick again with hatred in his eyes. "Get up, you devil incarnate, get up, before I give you the same again. Get up, you filthy, foul-mouthed wretch! And for the rest of the week you will wash up all the greasy plates in cold water! Do you hear me! — you filthy, cowardly little wretch!"

With what must have been a superhuman effort, Mick slowly got to his feet. He turned back to his sink and by raising the right side of his body as high as he could, and then the left, he managed to get both his dead arms into the by now cold, greasy water. Lowering his head, he pulled at the plug stopper chain with his teeth and then somehow managed to turn on the cold tap in the same manner. He let the water flow over his broken flesh as he sobbed quietly to himself.

Brother Y walked across the gap between the table and the dresser and replaced his blood-stained stick. Then he turned his attention the four of us once more.

"Let that be a lesson to all of ye, do ye hear? If I hear any of ye using dirty language, that's what ye'll get. Foul, dirty, sinful language. Evil, that's what it is. Foul and evil. An insult to God. Just one word of foul language out of any of ye and ye won't be able to walk for a month!"

...I made my way across the hall to the priests' and brothers' refectory. I took a bundle of rags from the press and went down on my knees to shine the linoleum floor. I couldn't get the thought of Mick's mutilated young arms out of my mind and the terrible agony and despair of his tortured face. I didn't realise it then, but that day was to be the turning point of my life. It was the day I lost my innocence'.

Released a month ahead of his sixteenth birthday he was now taller and noticeably sturdier — he had entered Daingean as a callow, mischievous youth. He emerged as a muscular young man, with a knowing insight into how the world worked.

Institutions of that kind, confined to all-male isolation, attract as workers, some men of sexually deviant inclination. Such men were sexually aroused by adolescent males. Young Bourke, curly-headed and handsome could easily have been a target of these attentions himself or could have witnessed the kind of events that are now known to have occurred in Daingean and that have been revealed in numerous government enquiries. Such activity was commonplace in these enclosed institutions. A later inmate of a sister reformatory, Letterfrack, described the activity in a harsh phase: 'I saw boys with their arses torn by constant buggery.'

One of Sean's friends was not surprised: 'I knew enough about Daingean, to know what Sean was talking about. I had only just escaped being sent there myself. Many of the boys sent there, I knew afterwards, as men, who told me things when they had enough drink taken...' 'What Sean told me came as no surprise'.

Underneath the good humour lay a perversity which would screw a joke to the point of pain. Something had gone hard inside him. In the classical sense, iron had entered his soul. Many of his former friends were now also returned from other penal institutions. While they compared notes about experiences, Sean easily assumed leadership. He was quicker and brighter than the others. Intellectually, he was gifted and his self-confidence, now bolstered by the notoriety of being a Daingean 'graduate', teetered into arrogance. He lorded it over his mob of followers, preening himself to the admiration of those who had not yet been 'away'. He relished tales of escapades at Daingean, topped their tales of Glin and Letterfrack, mentioned some of the tough eggs he had known — and corrected them in English grammar.

He liked to be leader and to be admired. Among the working-class youths of the North city, he was impressive. Many had physical disabilities of poor eyesight, malformed limbs, and other congenital deformities which had not been treated at birth. Among them, Sean stood out as natural leader with his impressive build, sonorous voice which could turn to a song or a colourful phrase and an acute intelligence which organised them into camp followers.

They stole from farms, slept rough and played commandos in the ditches. And if the scenario in Sean's head did not work out as he wanted it, or if one of the others departed from Sean's idea of how he should behave, then Bourke could be cruel at their expense, mimicking their efforts and casting them in ineffectual light. Apart from these lapses he was liked and admired as befitting a born leader.

Leadership for what? Where did youths of imagination and energy expand their ambitions in the post-war Ireland of the late 1940s? To what might they aspire in the Limerick of that era, beyond the menial work of the local factories, in an economy that was firmly controlled by local merchants who kept all the worthwhile jobs for their own class? Even had Bourke not had the innate anarchy of his own nature as a handicap, what routine outlet existed for him? Very little, as it turned out, beyond being pot-boy in a hotel in Lisdoonvarna.

The spa town was a favourite retreat for religious orders to take the mineral waters and for middle-aged bachelors and spinsters to engage in the matching game at the end of harvest. A town of surface Victorian gentility and black subterranean practices, its double identity suited Bourke well. By day the wide streets and hotels were a model of decorum — at nightfall by the shadows of autumnal season, furtive grapplings were commonplace.

He could not resist bringing home to Limerick some booty as a present for his mother. Kevin said: '...a stack of quality cutlery. He was done again. After that, it had to be England.'

Emigration to England had the force of fatalism, in the Ireland of 1950. Not only the unemployment pushing out thousands every month to relations already in Britain, but accounts in their letters home of the improved life and freedoms. In Bourke's case the charge of theft was an immediate incentive, as Irish courts at the time acquitted defendants on their solicitor's pleas that 'My client is going to England, your Honour.'

There was also leniency to those of whom a judge heard 'had gone to enlist in the forces.' Two older brothers were already in the Royal Air Force, each having enlisted while under age — not an uncommon practice in the post-war years in Britain (the authorities pretended to take borrowed birth certificates at face value, to get in servicemen).

Within days of his arrival at RAF Cusfort, Sean Bourke made an impression. He was well-built, quick-witted and energetic. He impressed the recruiting board in Belfast and now he was to impress further his RAF selection boards. He absorbed briefs quickly, showed expert co-ordination with his hands and had technical abilities. Most of all, he knew how to play the game and was keen to oblige superiors with willingness and suggestions.

Kevin: 'Within six months, he had shot straight past me. Sean became a Boy Sergeant, which meant he was in charge of a detail — he could order you to do anything he liked. He was always very correct when I was in his charge, showed no favouritism in the ranks. On occasion, though, he would call me out from food queue as if I had done something wrong. When I got to the canteen table, there was my meal already laid out by a junior.'

CHAPTER THREE

FLIGHT FROM FASCISM...

As with most of us, there was much in his early years that would determine the adult man who became George Blake. He was born into a Dutch merchant family that was abstemious and high-minded, that leavened religious experience with duty. But as he entered adolescence, he was to see his family scattered by war, his father die of ill-health hastened by bankruptcy and his own dreams of becoming a Minister of Religion consumed by political trauma.

By his own account, with the hindsight of an adult, his childhood was pleasant, ordered, even dreamy.[*] He was born in Rotterdam on the 11th November, 1922. That it was Armistice Day, remembered from the end of the Great War four years before or that he was at the last moment christened George instead of Jacob, might be regarded as significant by those who believe in pre-destination. He was named George because his father, Turkish by birth but a former British soldier in Mesopotamia, revered the country which had given him a battlefield commission, and a pension in the most powerful Empire after a war which had seen the ambitions of other empires diminish. That military service had also given him lethal lung cancer from gas poisoning, a common ailment among the survivors of the 'war to end all wars'.

The young George Behar did not know his father well, though he would find out about him in time. Albert Behar preferred not to talk about his war experiences. By the time his young son became more aware of him he was a near-invalid, confined with business worries as he directed, with failing health, the remnants of a glove-making business in Rotterdam. The gloves, used by ships' riveters, were manufactured in the ground floor of the family home: they lived overhead. By the time young George was seven, the

---

[*] Extensive interviews with George Blake, Moscow 2001-2002 and *No Other Choice,* Jonathan Cape, London, 1990 pp 28-46.

business was in decline, hastened by the Wall Street crash of 1929, which impacted on European ship-building. Depleted in income, the family moved to the suburbs. By 1934, there was little income as his father died, leaving George very much in the care of his mother and sisters. Upbringing by women became another influence, as did schooling in religion and history. The Behar boy identified with the ceremonies of the Lutheran Church and absorbed its tenets of pre-destination, while in history lessons he related to the House of Orange and its revolutionary role in combating the military power of the Catholic barons in medieval Holland. With youthful idealism, he was 'for the stall-holder and against the big merchant'.

It is not too much to infer that an imaginative template was set for the politics of 'right and wrong'. But it is also worth noting, as the adult Blake in Moscow was keen to point out, that he also had a very enjoyable childhood, in that he played games with boys and girls of his own age, was active in school and went for pastoral outings along the canals and fields of Holland. At the same time he was being prepared, unwittingly, for a wider world by the very nature of Rotterdam life, with its teeming port and ships from many countries. He was also given to dressing up at home as a church minister in an old black gown and administering moral judgment upon his rather awed siblings.

The death of his father, hastened by the capitalist crash of Wall Street, precipitated a move as exotically distant from Protestant Holland as was Muslim Egypt. Coming after the collapse of the family business, it was a change that made him further aware of the rulers and the ruled. Shortly before his death his father gave to his mother the address of his own sisters and brothers in Egypt, who might help provide for her welfare. They did more, offering in a swift exchange of letters to take the 13-year old George into their care, see to his education and generally bring him to adulthood. After his mother pondered the offer and discussed it with other relatives, she put it to her son to make his own future. He was torn, as any adolescent would be, between the family in which he was comfortable and loved and the prospect of unknown adventure in an exotic location. 'It was this thirst for adventure and the unknown which proved the stronger...'.

The crucial conversation with his mother, 'a great reckoning in a little room' would profoundly alter his life. The consequences of this early decision could hardly have been more full of contrasts, and as it turned out, more exhilarating.

The adolescent boy found himself transported in a cargo boat from a Rotterdam trimmed by recession to the port of Alexandria in Egypt and the sounds and smells of the East. He moved from church bells to the minaret, from a burgher democracy to Arab caste system, reinforced by British colonialism, where potentates kept the mass of the population as beggars in the streets, more lowly than any of the recently impecunious Dutch. The first meeting with his adoptive family provided a panorama of a new life. He was met at the port of Alexandria by a liveried chauffeur and taken to meet his two formidable aunts who embraced him, looked him up and down and noted, approvingly, the resemblance to their dead brother.

His new family lived in the Villa Curiel, a twelve-room mansion sheltered by palm trees on an island irrigated by the Nile, attended amply by Nubian servants and upholstered by the income of his uncle, a banker who did much Government business. It was a scenario out of Arabian Nights, intoxicating to an adolescent already imbued with curiosity. Any scruples that he had landed among the idle rich were dispersed as he became familiar with the varied members of his adoptive family. If he found they were not the lax merchants of first impressions, he found, also, that each had a defined character. His aunt, Zephirah, at sixteen had married her husband, who was blind, in an arranged marriage between merchant families and was happy. She kept an ordered household and with a maiden sister, was much given to charitable works among the poor. The young George accompanied them on formal expeditions to convents and feed-stations, at which he saw at first hand the abject plight of the population. They, however, could return by car to a house maintained by servants and money.

By contrast, both his uncles, Max and Daniel, were dismissive of such corporate works of mercy and held strong left-wing views — that only a profound change in the distribution of wealth would radically benefit the population and give them access to education and fulfilment on earth. There were many invigorating debates to stimulate an adolescent, already absorbed in history. The aunts, to his no great surprise, spoke French, English and Arabic fluently. One spoke Turkish as well, while the uncles had a wealth of languages as well as practical knowledge of how the world worked on a trade route between Europe and Asia. They read and discussed politics and literature and, as the world was being constantly re-drawn in boundaries after the war, had opted for differing nationalities while looking to France for their classical culture. Max was a playboy, rose late and had many mistresses: he opted for Egyptian nationality while the cousin, Henri Curiel was 'tall and extremely thin…already a slight stoop…immense charm and a dazzling smile made him very attractive…'. Henri Curiel's main interest was revolutionary politics, he had studied at Cairo University and taken Egyptian nationality out of sympathy with the masses of *fellah* or peasantry.

Henri, who had much time for the eager George and was nearer in age, was often out at night, locked into political debating cells which would become the Egyptian Communist Party. George had many arguments with these dashing relations. If the pull of conformist Holland, to which he returned for school holidays, still held, time would strengthen the long embrace of a merchant family of many tongues and talents. They were unmistakably Jewish in appearance and in ancestry, having been driven from Spain in persecution by the Catholic monarchs. Their ancestors had settled in Cairo, retaining the folk memory of diverse cultures and their professional capacity for banking. No prizes for realising that George Behar had a new take on the world, as he came to know that his own father was Jewish, a fact which had been suppressed in Christian Holland. (As an adult, he would look back fondly to that scholarly family, similar to many which influenced the intellectual and political movements of the 20th century).

Other contrasts between East and West would filter into the course of his later life. On a journey 'home' to Rotterdam the ship stopped in London where he alighted and walked in the East End, being struck by the low size of the natives, most of whom were of Eastern European origin. Was this the same country from whence came the tall, blonde officers he had seen playing Polo in the military clubs in Cairo? He had expected all Englishman to look like those dashing officers with swagger sticks and concluded that the caste system was endemic in England as elsewhere.

Unknown to George Behar, much was happening during the 1930s which would impinge on his later life. In the docklands of London, which he thought more shabby than Rotterdam port, a handful of upper-class students from Cambridge joined communists in defending Jews against attacks by the British fascist Moseley, going against the grain of their class background, their activity secretly noted by Comintern agents. Similarly, in Austria, Spain and Italy, there was concerted Fascist oppression against Jews, supported by the culture of the Catholic Church, but again resisted by handfuls of newly-armed communists.

While some foresaw that the de-stabilisation of Europe was at hand, few predicted the extent to which the continent would export its trauma, or how it would engulf much of the world within a few more years, inflict the Holocaust as a permanent stain upon humanity and speed the development of mass destruction by nuclear power. Neither could it be predicted that the scattered resistance of socialists and communists, motivated by humanitarian defence of the poor, would be drawn into working for Russia. Or that such devotion would be exploited in Stalinist terror. Especially when in August 1939 Hitler and Stalin signed a non-aggression pact, promising to respect the integrity of each other's territories (while already secretly plotting to annex such: by military aggression in the case of Germany, by espionage and subversion in the case of Russia). The pact was signed five weeks before they jointly engaged in invasion of Poland, on the pretext of restoring 'former' territories. A million Poles would be put into prison camps and hundreds of thousands would be exterminated as Jews by the German S.S., while Russia would exterminate the officer class of the Polish forces by mass shooting.

Russia's aggression caused expulsion from the League of Nations, the gaoling of communist deputies in France and soul-searching among cadres of the Comintern, the secret underground across Europe controlled by Moscow. Though ignorant of the detail, this wider scenario impinged upon George Behar in September as the family listened to the broadcast of Neville Chamberlain that Britain was now at war. The Behar family, in common with many Dutch, had a hope that England would save them from a repeat of the horror tales coming from countries already invaded. There was fear on the streets from the mixed loyalties in Holland. National Socialism and its proffered solutions to the ills of recession had its Nazi adherents, Dutch-style and their activities were debated in his own family and in the merchant community, with blame being put on the 'Jewish Bankers' (the young Behar by now was more aware of his hidden ancestry).

Anti-semitism in the Netherlands gained force by seeing its 'success' as a political agenda in Germany. Newspaper pictures of middle-class women laughing at Jewish shopkeepers being bludgeoned in Berlin had evoked approval in some Dutch homes. But the stronger feeling among most Dutch came from Hitler's stated intention to undo 'the humiliation' of Germany in the treaties which has ended the 1914-18 war. Even the anti-Semitic feared the invasion of Holland, as part of Hitler's promised 'recovery' of the defeated Austro-Hungarian Empire. The fear became reality in May 1940, weeks after the German forces invaded Denmark and Norway. Demoralised by what Nazi storm troopers had done in Poland, the repeat tactics of 'blitzkrieg'

— heavy bombing, followed by parachute drops, encountered but token resistance in the Scandinavian countries. Over a million troops were used in the advance on the low countries as the Nazis smashed into Belgium and Holland in early May, with a dawn attack across a 150-mile front. Death came to Dutch forces on the ground, outweighed by massively superior armour, to the air force in a brief show of resistance and to civilians by massive aerial bombing that reduced the centre of Rotterdam to rubble. A later estimate put the death toll at over 30,000. George Behar saw men, women and children crawling from the ruins of their homes.

What he witnessed became a baptism of fire for the seventeen year-old George Behar. He saw his fellow countrymen fleeing from their own city as '...from the burning hell'. Some were injured and crying, all were shocked and distressed at the scale of the destruction as water and gas mains burst, buildings toppled and panic took hold. A few had managed to save belongings which they pushed in prams and handcarts. And still the bombing continued as the German air force pulverised Rotterdam. He worked through the night in a first-aid station. When the German ground troops entered to secure the city and install a quisling administration, he saw political ideology and human frailty come into cruel conjunction. In street after street families dazed with loss were denounced by members of the Dutch Nazi Party, as were foreigners who were deemed antagonistic to the invading Germans. He saw neighbours and friends being taken away in lorries by storm-troopers.

He realised the country had paid the price of appeasement. In the months before the invasion, the Dutch government had refused British pleas to call their population to arms and strengthen their defences, for fear of provoking the Nazis to invade. Much later he would hear that as the invasion began the Dutch Royal Family had placed the fleet at the disposal of Britain, moved their gold reserves to London and, with the aid of British intelligence, had escaped ahead of the German armoured attack into the Hague which had orders to capture them. *H.M.S. Hereward* was dive-bombed by German Stuka aircraft and raked with machine-gun fire as she sloughed out into the North Sea and ran the gauntlet for England. He would hear, too, that in that flotilla had gone his mother and sisters, registered as British subjects.

That identity brought his own arrest, as the German administration went through the population records and interned 'enemy nationals'. Two Dutch detectives called to a relative's home, where he sheltered and accompanied him to prison, but within months he was released because he was under eighteen. Deciding not to wait for what might happen on his next birthday, he went on the run in the summer of 1940, after the fall of France. The British expeditionary force, which was beaten back to the beaches of Dunkirk, was saved by the armada of small boats crossing the English channel — an epic rescue which seized the imagination of those minded to resist in the low countries. The Dutch Royal Family formed a Government-in-Exile in London, to which George Behar looked for his future. Officially, he disappeared, presumed dead or fled...

On the run, with false identity papers, but young-looking enough to be overlooked by military patrols, he made another decision with long-term implications. He actively sought out contacts for the Resistance through a pastor of the Dutch Reformed Church and was asked to meet a man in the square of a provincial town. He was accompanied to a house and interviewed about his political views and family in what became another 'great reckoning in a little room.' Within weeks he engaged in many deceptions of identity as he became a courier for the Dutch Resistance. Organised on the ground by patriots, trained in military skills by soldiers of the Dutch armed forces who had evaded capture, it had a wide back-up in the countryside. Teachers, clerks, pastors, shopkeepers, housewives and students compiled intelligence on German efforts to subdue the civilian population, often aided by those who had stayed in administrative jobs, apparently acquiescent to the occupation.

The information was routed to England, to the government in exile and to SOE, Special Operations Executive, a secretive guerrilla organisation based in Baker Street in London, with a mission from Churchill to visit sabotage upon the German forces of Occupation in the recently conquered Lowlands. George Behar was gradually inducted into more important work as he travelled much of the Netherlands in various guises. Sometimes he appeared a schoolboy going to visit relatives, other times a seminarian, but always with a mission in mind, a message to deliver, or clandestine papers to carry. It was an early introduction to what would become his profession. He recalled that:

> 'Even though the Nazis had taken control of the Netherlands...life went on as normal...I was easily taken to be a schoolboy and I had completely convincing identity papers...the sympathisers to the Dutch Resistance were in every pocket of the German administration because they had to rely on the natives to make the country work and many of my countrymen thought this was the best way to hasten the time of liberation — by working from within. We confidently knew it would come...I travelled all over Holland delivering messages...and was never caught...'.

While the seven-year old Sean Bourke was mitching from school in safe Ireland, the nineteen-year old George Behar was learning the rudiments of guerrilla warfare with the Dutch Resistance and listening to the speeches of the British leader Winston Churchill, which lifted the morale of the resistance[*]. He heard on clandestine radio how the RAF

---

[*] Famously, in June 1940 — 'We shall defend our island whatever the cost may be, we shall fight them on the beaches, we shall fight them on the landing grounds, we shall fight in the fields and in the streets, we shall fight them in the hills; we shall never surrender.'

pilots had won the air battles over England, providing the first serious setback for the Nazis onslaught westward across Europe and causing them to falter over the invasion of Britain. Instead, they looked east towards Russia, opening the Eastern front which eventually proved terminally draining during two winters of attrition which incurred massive casualties on both sides.

By the spring of 1942 he was weathered as a secret agent, had become addicted to the excitement of the work and sought to get to England to train with SOE, with the intention of returning in a more operational rank with the Resistance. His grandmother, to whom he was close, died in the spring, bitter at the occupation of Holland. He wanted to be with his mother and sisters again and hoped to contact them in England. A request to SOE in London was turned down — he was not operationally important enough to be ex-filtrated. Already, too, the Dutch Resistance, in spite of its cell structure, where few knew others outside their own area, had been penetrated by the Abwehr, German military intelligence, who tracked night-time drops of sabotage agents, tortured some, executed some and with detailed planning, inserted their own agents as decoys to lure others into capture.

He mapped a route of his own, conscious that he might be arrested at any new contact or point of crossing. Everywhere, the topic was the sway of the war, as the inflamed enmities of Europe were exported to other continents, to conflagrate the antagonism between empires and colonies, all ready to settle an old score or strike a new one. So as the German panzers powered into Russia, the Italians under Mussolini sank the British naval flagship *Ark Royal* and made headway in North Africa. The Portuguese and the Spanish were seen to side with Hitler to hold onto their African and South American colonies and Japanese bombers attacked Pearl Harbour as a prelude to making lightning advances in Asia and assert their hold in the Far East. Crucially, Hitler was reported to be at the gates of Moscow.

With mangled versions of the events, not knowing how the world was turning, from early summer to the end of 1942 he went by bicycle and train and walked. Sometimes dressed as a Trappist monk, other times as a Dominican, assuming many other identities, he moved through Holland, into Belgium, to Vichy France, being helped along the way by a network of anti-Nazi resisters. He saw the better side of human nature, met people who put their lives on the line to oppose Fascism, was a guest for a few nights here or a few weeks there, often in unlikely places. All the while, as he remembered, being impressed by the risks run by people he had never met, strangers who were prepared to help him out of hatred for the German war machine.

He would learn that some of the 'civilians' were officers of British Intelligence operating under cover[*]. He learned, that contrary to their superior's official position, priests and pastors, teachers and nuns and ordinary people were part of a vast resistance to Fascism, a learning experience he would draw upon in a future that was then fathomless. Towards the end of 1942 he made his way down from a mountain on the French — Spanish frontier, surrendered at the point of a gun to waiting border guards and was interned. He still had it in mind to get to England via the colony of Gibraltar. He had turned twenty years, the last three as a secret agent of the Resistance, where he saw much that was terrible and much that left him with hope for mankind.

---

[*] MI9, which ran a network throughout Europe for escaping POWs.

CHAPTER FOUR

HOW BEHAR BECAME BLAKE

George Behar's capacity for clear thinking gave him an edge among the internees, many of whom had settled into the numbing enforcement imposed by the Spanish regime. In spite of the loss of liberty and meagre food, he kept a clear focus on his intentions — to get to England. By early 1943, the war in Europe had traduced borders as the flux and flow of victories and retreats brought chaotic fluidity to previously cast iron nation states. The territories conquered by the Nazis produced millions of displaced persons vigorously opposed to any form of Fascism. Within the camp, the Poles formed the largest, most disciplined — and therefore most potent — chance to win concessions from the Spanish.

He aligned himself to their demands. The Polish mood was inflamed by the tales of the German massacres in Warsaw. Polish Jews, fleeing underground, were chased through the sewers by specially equipped troopers who shot them on sight, killing entire families, whose bodies the Germans left in the filth of the sewers. Some of the hunted managed to acquire guns by ambushing soldiers. After they in turn were killed by German reinforcements, their former homes above them were dynamited to form mass graves in the Warsaw Ghetto. For the Poles in the Spanish camp, it was time to get up off their knees — and die standing up...

They were saved by the wider fortunes of war, as the Spanish perceived the downturn in the German war effort. By early 1943, British scientific advances in detecting U-boats and maiming them underwater, swung the naval battles in favour of the Allies in the Atlantic, while in North African territories within Spanish influence, the battles were also turning into Nazi defeats. In Spain itself, thousands of 'displaced persons' of many nationalities were held in dozens of camps — a bargaining factor to be used by General Franco as he saw the pan-Fascist dream which he shared with Hitler and Mussolini, recede under the push of Allied strengths. As

Italy was bombed by the Allies and the Russians began to push back the German advances from Stalingrad over a 200 mile front in early 1943, Franco looked to his future. Feeling the fragile sovereignty of his country and the fracturing of Spanish colonies in Africa and South America, he ordered concessions to prisoners. In Blake's camp, the Poles demanded speedy releases to join their compatriots in several theatres of war.

After a week or so of mass hunger strikes, the Spanish caved in. Intelligence emissaries visited the camp and organised the release of subjects of occupied nations useful to the Allied war effort. Behar had little trouble convincing them of his status as a British subject and accounting for his work, as among the 'negotiators' were British intelligence personnel whom he had met in the Dutch Resistance. Within days he found himself en route by land to Gibraltar, a key colony of the British Empire in its access to North Africa and the shipping lanes of the Mediterranean. On the land border with Gibraltar, he crossed from the Fascisto-helmeted Spanish military on one side to British infantry on the other. As he recalled: 'I stood on British territory'. He stood also on the brink of a new life, and for the second time — of a new identity.

Probably only in wartime could the transition so smoothly occur of Albert Behar from displaced Dutchman (British Subject) into George Blake. On the streets of Britain many nationalities wore uniforms of the Empire countries who had come to the defence of the island nation. From Occupied Europe, Free Poles, Belgian, Dutch, Spanish and Czechs were welcomed into an England under siege, into a country where middle-class women drove trucks, smoked and sported lipstick with a laxity unknown to their mothers. Professional men had become fire-fighters, drivers and foot soldiers. In the midlands, women shift-worked the munitions factories while their husbands and sons were in the theatres of war. By the spring of 1943, Britain seethed with war effort. Into this maw of change came George Behar, to join his mother and two sisters who had fled from the invasion of

Holland almost three years before and who were now part of the war effort.

The reunion was emotional. His sisters were nurses, his mother a housekeeper. Their family solidarity impressed him, reflecting the will to survive of the wider community. But though he repeatedly asked to be returned to Holland to conduct operations for the Dutch Resistance, he received no call. The refusal was fortuitous, as the German counter-intelligence had maintained its penetration of the Resistance at that time. With the aid of Dutch Nazis, the Abwehr continued to capture agents who were parachuted from Britain, expertly maintaining a radio fiction to the Dutch section of SOE, which failed to pick up warning signs embedded in the radio traffic of those previously infiltrated. Assuming their identities in radio contact with London, the Germans continued to lure further victims.

So, unknown to him, the refusal of active service in his home country may have ensured his survival, though he languished at a desk job in the economic section of the Dutch Government in exile. In the summer of 1943, one of the many applications he had filed came back with an invitation to enlist in the Royal Navy. Having changed by deed poll to a more English sounding name as had been done by his mother and sisters, he celebrated his 21st birthday as George Blake and passed out with a Commodore's certificate. Then it was Scotland and more demanding tests aboard a ship designed to replicate the 'Nelson spirit' of seafaring endurance, followed by courses to equip him with service rituals that distinguished officers from other ranks. But that potential career in special boat operations went by the board in a submarine training exercise, when he lost consciousness from compression. Whatever his undercover ambitions, they were likely to be above sea-level for the future.

Again, unknown to him, he was being marked for secret work, but with a degree of caution due to the recent failure of several Anglo-Dutch espionage efforts. Responding to further invitations in various offices near Victoria Station, he was puzzled to find himself repeating his biography to what he took to be officers of the Armed Services, but whose regiments he could never quite glean. Nor were they forthcoming about what work he would undertake. Eventually, in Broadway Buildings in Victoria, he was taken to a back part of the building distinctly different from the rudimentary partitioned offices of his previous visit.

His transition from armed service to secret service will be recognisable to students of espionage:

'The corridor where I was asked to wait, was covered with a thick red carpet and the Captain told me to sit down in one of two Chippendale armchairs, standing at each side of a narrow mahogany table covered with copies of *Tatler* and *Country Life*.

The Captain left me for a while and when he came back, invited me rather solemnly to follow him. At the end of the carpeted corridor we entered a large boardroom, the centre of which was occupied by a long polished table. At one side of this sat five men. Two were civilians, one wore the uniform of an air vice-marshall, and two that of a brigadier-general. The Captain took a seat at one end of the table and I was invited by the air vice-marshall to take the chair facing the board. He had in front of him my biography, the form I had filled in and several minute-sheets.

For the next half hour I faced a barrage of questions about myself. They were fired at me, apparently at random, by the various member of the board. I answered them as best I could, quietly and in a straightforward way. I cannot say that I was particularly nervous, I had by now come to the conclusion that it was probably more than just a question of service in fast boats, probably something in Naval intelligence, or liaison work with the Allied Navies. Certainly, the questions I was asked gave me no clue. When they had finished, the air vice-marshall, who acted as chairman, asked me to wait outside.

I had sat there for about ten minutes looking at *Tatler* when the captain came out. He put his hand on my shoulder and said that I had been accepted and would report for duty at ten o'clock on the following Monday morning. On arrival, I should ask for Major Seymour. I was pleased as I was getting bored with the dull existence of an officer of the watch at *HMS Dolphin.*

When I reported for duty at 54 Broadway Buildings, I was taken up by the ground-floor watchman to the small attic room on the eight floor where I had been before. Major Seymour turned out to be the officer who had interviewed me in Dutch. He wore his uniform jacket now and I could see that he was not a Royal Marine, as I had thought, but in the General Service Corps. This somewhat mystified me. The first thing he did was to take me along to see Colonel Cordeaux who, he said, was the head of the department to which I had been appointed and who wanted to see me before I started. Colonel Cordeaux's office was a large room at the other end of the corridor and was guarded by three secretaries, two of them young and pretty, the third a tall, extremely thin, middle-aged woman with glasses and buck-teeth. She looked like a caricature of the prim spinster, but turned out be very nice and to have a lot of life in her.

Colonel Cordeaux was a short thick-set man, with pale blue eyes and bristle moustache. He spoke in a brisk, military manner and walked with a marked limp, caused by arthritis, from which he suffered badly. He actually was a Royal Marine, so I thought this must be the Admiralty after all. The Colonel motioned me to sit down and began to address me. What he said, I must confess, made a deep impression on me.

He informed me that I was now an officer of the British Secret Service and that the building in which we were was its Headquarters.'

It was a very English exercise, redolent of the boarding school ritual of prefects, dormitories and initiation ceremonies, in the upbringing of the SIS officer class. As he would later learn, the building was divided into contrasting sections. The frontage onto St. James's underground station was a bland, Civil-Service block. Immediately at the back, however, was Queen Anne's Gate, a conservation area of 18th century town houses on an original cobbled street. It was a bit of old England preserved in the middle of London, with long windows, panelled hall doors and iron railings over servants' basements. It led onto St James's Park, in proximity to Wellington Barracks, home of elite guards regiments. Across from the barracks was Buckingham Palace in one direction, in another, the hub of political power — Downing Street and Whitehall. It was also within walking distance to the clubs of Buck's and Whites and The Garrick, where umbrella-swinging servants of the Empire both civil and secret, met in comfort and privacy.

Number 21 Queen Anne's Gate with its faded curtains and un-washed windows looked unkempt (unwitting camouflage by Army General Service Corps). The brass plate showed no insignia, the wooden shutters were closed on the basement. In fact it was the residence of 'C' the head of SIS, who slept there most nights and was at his desk before his own senior management arrived, by traversing a series of squeaky stairways to the legendary office, behind the green baize door, over which the light shone for entry for subordinates, the whole not unlike the Headmaster's study. At a nearby boardroom, senior managers met like a board of school governors — here Blake had his acceptance interview (not surprisingly this two-faced building has been much satirised in James Bond films, though the building was abandoned by SIS in the early 1970s).

The 'C' at the time of Blake's recruitment was Maj. General Sir Stewart Menzies, an old Etonian, with access to various pressure-points of the Establishment. But he was also a 'dab-hand' at intelligence, showing a talent for organising strategic deceptions which included keeping covert contact throughout the conflict with Admiral Canaris, Head of the Abwehr, almost all of whose agents in Britain would be captured

Blake was suitably impressed with the grandeur, the secrecy and the eccentricity of his new world. Recalling it all fifty years later in Moscow he smiled at his former self: 'I was excited and gratified — I had joined this legendary organisation about which much was whispered but little

43

known. I had already seen some of its work in Holland when working with the Resistance. And of course it was all so terribly English, part of the class system — back then of course, England was my new home, so therefore I felt very accepted into the war effort.'

He was assigned a code-name and a department 'P.8' i.e. Product from area 8, which took in Holland, the Scandinavian countries and the Soviet Union. Over the next few months he embarked upon courses to equip him as a spy. Having done his basic military training in the Navy, he did further small arms training near Gosport, parachute drops at Ringway and unarmed combat in Chelsea. He attended lectures on identity disguises, document fabrication, agent-handling and the cultivation of sources in foreign locations. He learned how to read the map of a city from limited information about its hinterland and transport systems and did wireless telegraphy, code-making and covert communications. He also familiarised himself with the mechanics of the Dutch Secret Service in London, which handled the input of agents into Occupied Holland.

It was second best to his heart's desire, which was to be sent back to Holland as a fully-fledged agent of SOE. Because he had already seen service on the ground there — and probably knew more of the terrain than many of the younger volunteers — SIS deemed him better used as a friend and mentor to young Dutch agents, most of whom had escaped from Occupied Holland and were keen to return in Special Operations involving sabotage of German supplies. He would be supervising batches of agents going in by parachute at night. He would be a support and confidante to these young patriotic Dutchmen who ran the real risk of torture and execution by volunteering, to hasten the demise of Nazi occupation. Most were younger than his twenty-one years and some would not survive. It was another layer of adulthood imposed by the war in Europe upon a young man who had five years before thought of taking Holy Orders in the Lutheran Church.

For the next year or so, he honed his expertise as an organiser of agents and saboteurs, working with the Dutch section of SOE, although not formally reporting to them. He was in the more covert SIS, whose influence ranged over all the European governments in exile, controlled their intelligence budgets and 'product', in order to assess for the British War Cabinet the fifth columns inside the occupied countries. SIS kept water-tight compartments between the various nationalities, for fear of penetration or national dislikes. More politically, SIS also reported on the likely shape of governments in post-war Europe, the creeping subversion of Soviet agents in the West and the feelings of governments-in-exile towards Russia. Churchill had met several times with Stalin and distrusted the Georgian's ambitions for Soviet influence after the war, while content to have Russia's immense resistance and casualties deflect Hitler as plans went ahead for the liberation of Europe.

By early 1944, the Allies were winning on many fronts — in the North Atlantic, in the Pacific, in Asia. In South American colonies, General Franco ceased 'aid and comfort' to the Germans, thereby culling their survival and ensuring his own. Not so prescient was his fellow dictator Mussolini who bellowed defiance at the Allies, even as he prepared to flee Italy.

In Sicily, gateway to North Africa, the Germans were defeated by combined American, British and Canadian forces. The Americans secretly released Mafia criminals from gaols, infiltrated them to their Sicilian homelands to 'turn' native collaborators with the Germans, thereby ensuring lower casualties on the American side of the pincer advance on the island.

In Burma, the Allies assumed air advantage by using glider planes to make surprise landings behind the Japanese lines. It was on the Russian front, however, that the greatest casualties, and greatest humiliation, was suffered by the Nazis, inflicted by a people brutalised by both home and foreign barbarity. The survival of the Russian cities on the front line and the re-grouping was, moreover, conducted by an army whose own officer class had been obliterated by Stalin in his rise to power. As the full retribution of the Russians upon the German forces became apparent, with German staff officers being overnight promoted to Field Marshals so that they might by felled by their own pistols rather than endure the Teutonic disgrace of surrender to Bolsheviks, the German dream of Arian supremacy dwindled to ugly deaths in Russia. Logistically, the German armies were depleted in men, munitions and morale by the impossible length of their supply lines to devastating battles for Kursk and Leningrad.

In early 1944, Germany came under massive pressure from the East as the Russians broke through, smashing their way out of the siege of Leningrad and inflicting over 120,000 German casualties in a few days. By April, 1944, German divisions were in retreat from Russians, who showed little mercy in the port of Sevastopol, where they dive-bombed over-laden transport ships. The Crimea, long a battleground for European domination, became yet again a soldiers' graveyard as the Russians re-took Odessa and Yalta. Meanwhile in Germany itself, a million Berliners fled the city as the Allies mass-bombed, preparing for what would become the greatest counter-invasion of modern warfare: D-Day and the Liberation of Europe.

At various locations in England, Blake was in the thick of the planning, one of many thousands of expatriates who provided detailed knowledge of the occupied countries as the Allies embarked upon protracted bombing to weaken the supply lines from Germany to its infantry and tank divisions now dug into the Normandy coast, with command and control centres ensconced further back in France. Many of these bombing targets were in factories or marshalling yards, identified by SOE saboteurs on the ground. For the agent who had been Behar and then Van Vries and now Blake it was a heady time of fulfilment, whether alone with a wireless receiver in a room in Victoria or — as became more the case — bringing decoded transcripts to various invasion planning sessions.

His information came from the agents he had infiltrated, who supplied crucial map co-ordinates, enemy numbers, regimental deployments and locations of German command staffs.

He joined about a thousand other officers in support logistics. With his linguistic abilities he found himself attached to SHAEF[*] serving General Montgomery, who would command the British expeditionary force destined for Normandy on June 6th, 1944. We need not here reprise the Normandy landings, other than to indicate the scale of the wider planning in which he was part. SIS played a key-role in the Invasion planning across a wide range of deceptions, from planting misleading information as to the timing and locations of the actual landings, to the channelling of policy decisions to the War Cabinet, from inside the German High Command, from where it had managed to nurture sources from early in the war. In addition, the top-secret breaking of the German military and naval codes, ENIGMA and ULTRA, overseen by SIS and MI5, gave the Allies advantages on troop and ship movements in the mid-way stages of the war which confounded the Germans — and did so up to D-Day. The turning of most of the Abwehr agents within Britain by the Double-Cross committee misled the Germans to believe there were ninety divisions of men about to land, instead of the actual forty-seven — not only in Normandy but on other coastal locations, requiring German resistance to be more thinly spread on a longer front.

According to historian Christopher Andrew, when the sheer military might of America and Russia became fully engaged in the war, the victory of Axis powers became impossible. 'But if the successes of Allied intelligence did not win the war, they undoubtedly shortened it — and in doing so saved millions of lives.' Andrew ascribes to Churchill the transformation of SIS from a pre-wartime domain of gifted amateurs into hardened, motivated professionals.

---

[*] Supreme HQ Allied Expeditionary Force.

In Fortress Europe, the ultimate victory was sought — to crush Germany in its seat of political and military power, in the capital where National Socialism had begat its terror upon the world. After D-Day and the advances in mainland Europe, the object of Allied planners became to humiliate Germany itself, to deliver a death-blow to its ambitions. In a decision taken by Roosevelt and Churchill, but reluctantly endorsed by their generals, Russia would be allowed bear the brunt of the advance into Berlin. It was to prove costly in Russian lives, estimated at over 200,000, and costly to the politics of post-war Europe as Stalin exacted territorial retribution for the immense Russian losses, not just in the push to Berlin but for the millions lost on the Eastern Front. Figures were of such magnitude as to be concealed from both Western public opinion and his own citizens[*]. Russian infantry fought their way from the East, literally plundering and raping along the way. The Western air forces paved the way of the Russian advances in a campaign of massive bombing of key German cities.

On 14th February 1945, to directly clear the Russian route to Berlin three key cities were reduced to rubble — Dresden, Chemnitz and Magdeburg. The combined sorties of RAF and USAF amounted to 3,600 aircraft. Dresden was annihilated by 1,600 bombers who dropped over 620,000 incendiaries in multiple waves over two days that massacred the civilian population. The same day, from Yalta in the Crimea, it was revealed that Stalin, Churchill and Roosevelt had been in conference for a week, monitoring the onslaught and negotiating the carve-up of Germany. The intention was to avert a repeat of its delusions of racist supremacy by fracturing it as a landmass. Germany's militarism and racism had twice blighted the century with immense human suffering.

That suffering was delivered back to the German population in the Spring of 1945 by the military occupation of their territories, by the flattening of their major cities, then

---

[*] Access by historians to Moscow's archives after 1990 revised upwards from about 27 million casualties.

mainly inhabited by civilians, and, insultingly, by the calculated silence of the Western powers as the Russian soldiery were let loose upon surviving civilians as they advanced into Berlin. Dozens of German women were strangled as they were anally raped, hundreds more were so brutalised as to become deranged. Civilians were machine-gunned in the streets. German military were made to cry for mercy before being executed. Officers were lined up on trucks with nooses around their necks, driven under gallows before the assembled troops who cheered as the Germans were pushed off. The stubborn, brave resistance of the Berlin garrison enraged Russian feelings, as they fought street-by-street to plant the Red Flag on The Reichstag. By early May 1945 Berlin had surrendered, Hitler and Goebbels had committed suicide, Mussolini had been shot and Franco was spared.

Over six years, public opinion had, of necessity, come to terms with the horrors of war as necessary acts of conflict survival, and revenge. There was indeed some grudging respect among the Allied scientists for the advanced technology of Germany weaponry and among commanders for the Germanic ideas of noble warfare and the cult of the warrior caste — it was, after all, endemic in their own military make-up. That respect, evaporated in the stink of human evil that emanated from the opening of the extermination camps and resulted in German civilians being force-marched into forests to confront the acts of their own government, as a report from *The Manchester Guardian* makes clear:

> 'A thousand Weimer citizens marched six miles through lovely countryside to Buchenwald Concentration Camp... In groups of 100 they were conducted on a tour of the crematorium with the blackened frames of the bodies still in the ovens and two piles of emaciated dead in the yard outside, through huts where living skeletons too ill or weak to rise lay packed in three-tier bunks, through the riding stable where

Thuelmann, the German communist leader, and thousands of others were shot, through the research block where doctors tried new serums on human beings with fatal consequences.

An American CBS reporter said some German civilians fainted or were sick and many wailed, "We did not know, we did not know..." '.

In Berlin, Marshal Zukhov (who would have a Moscow street named after him) commanded armies into the what Stalin called 'the capital of Germany, the centre of German Imperialism and the heart of German aggression'.

A week later in London George Blake put down his headphone and left his listening post by a wireless set to join the crowds surging towards Buckingham Palace as they celebrated Victory in Europe. All day, thousands snaked in dances around lampposts and monuments, hugged strangers, and set off fire-crackers that were no longer sinister. That evening, the lights came on again in Whitehall as fifty thousand marched to the Palace, demanding 'The King, The King...!' The British Royal Family came onto the balcony to receive the plaudits of the multitude outside, accompanied by Churchill who set the tone with a witticism, as the floodlights had been doused for security reasons as he appeared on the balcony '... then the lights went out' he said, reprising his historic, clarion broadcast at the beginning of the war. On this V Day, his mood was upbeat, matching the euphoria of victory: 'In the long years to come, not only the people of this island but of the world, wherever the bird of freedom chirps in human hearts, will look back to what we have done and they will say, do not despair, do not yield to violence and tyranny, march straight forward — and die — if needs be — unconquered.'

A week after the Armistice and five years after the pulverising of Rotterdam, the English-named George Blake found himself back on Dutch soil as a fully-fledged officer of the Secret Service, conducting a roll-call of prisoners-of-war. Unwittingly, he was fulfilling the thrust of his family culture, having been named 'George' after an English King but now reprising some of his father's work, who had served on the Intelligence staff of General Haig in the First World War. Now his son interviewed captured Nazis in trying to determine the fate of agents whom he had last seen as hopeful young men at a blacked-out aerodrome in Britain. Some had not survived the initial drops, others had been captured and their experiences at the hands of German military had to be recorded. He looked up relations and found an aunt frail but delighted to see him. He brought gifts of food and household goods. The military boot was on the other foot as occupation forces conducted a root-and-branch expropriation of Nazi resources, seizing country houses from German officers, requisitioning cars, wines, cigarettes and supplies which had been purloined.

To his surprise, many of his British colleagues regarded the work as an interval between enjoyments, being more interested in after-hours rewards. Some indeed thought him over-zealous, but he excused them as being recently drafted into Intelligence and lacking his professional approach. He saw how the heartfelt offerings of a liberated population were difficult to refuse though he disapproved of the way some young Dutch women flung themselves at their 'liberators'. But he was not made of stone and surrendered to the mood — it would become a heady time for his refined disposition. 'To the victors — the spoils' brought incessant parties and the wear-and-tear of carnality. As he recalled 'all the privileges normally enjoyed only by the rich were now available to every officer — parties in luxury houses, fine wines and luxury living in spas and resorts and beautiful girls avid for a good time after the gloom of the occupation years.'

He saw his interrupted career as a Minister of religion recede further in a haze of personal pleasure — but found vocational outlet in the 'social welfare' of his work, as he tracked the fate of his executed agents and recommended posthumous recognition for them and pensions for their families. With his initial reports concluded and in receipt of an award for his work on behalf of the Dutch Government in

Exile, it was with some reluctant relief that he was recalled to Broadway Buildings, to participate in a review of Secret Service operations. The war had changed SIS forever. With the rapidly expanded intake of many nationalities and backgrounds, there was no going back to the days of it being a fiefdom of gung-ho adventurers from Eton and Empire who ran it like some 'Old Boys' club, even to inter-House jostling over lineage — some so wealthy and with such connections that they paid agents out of their own landed income and tweaked British commercial companies to provide field cover for agents overseas.

After much jousting with the Foreign Office, which controlled the JIC (Joint Intelligence Committee), the reformed foreign spying apparatus was structured on similar levels to the Civil Service, paying Menzies ('C') the same as an equally powerful Permanent Under-Secretary — and so on down the line to officers at Blake's level earning sufficient to run a car and buy a house in post-war Britain. The more political reforms took longer to effect, to turn SIS from dealing with the enormous fallout from a defeated Germany towards what was perceived as the formidable new enemy — Russia. Though urged in JIC briefings from Cabinet, it would take more time and more personnel to move the new SIS, now more bureaucratic, into looking East, as it was already overloaded with the information shoal from its hundreds of officers on the ground in Europe.

Europe was a wasteland, across which six million refugees wandered through fluctuating borders that were in one sphere of military influence to-day and another to-morrow. From the Allies point of view, wheat and chaff mixed at random, making it difficult to sort the former activity of many refugees. SIS relied heavily on the likes of George Blake and personnel of SOE to interrogate captured German military, to provide identity cards for innocent civilians, while weeding out those who hoped to lose themselves in the massive diaspora of displaced persons. A priority was interrogating Abwehr, Wermacht and Luftwaffe officers, in order to extract information of use to the impending War Crimes tribunals.

Many of these were held in secure places to protect against summary execution by partisans or 'freelance' SOE units smarting with revenge as the fate of their comrades became known. Separately again, SIS had a list of scientists it sought to interview about V-1 and V-2 rockets. The 'pilot-less aeroplanes' had terrorised Londoners in the last months of the war, when England had suffered a thousand strikes. SIS found that many of those scientists had already been purloined or kidnapped by the Soviets — some were spirited away to closed ports in Northern Russia to continue their developments, under threat of death. The Americans had also been quick on the uptake, notably securing leading scientist Werner Von Braun, who in return for a pardon would lead-up their own rocket advances to the next phase of Inter-Continental Ballistic Missiles.

Consequently, SIS found itself tasked as a priority by the British cabinet, via the JIC to round-up remaining scientists, before the Russians and Americans 'cleaned out the stables'. In competition with both its former allies, a boffin chase resulted in several dozen German specialists in physics and nuclear-fission being flown to England for incarceration in elegant country houses in Cambridgeshire. Removed from the debris of war, to an illusionary rural peace, they quickly understood their situation — co-operate or be in the dock at Nuremberg.

Stalin flouted desires of the other Great Powers to sit down and negotiate for Europe to be re-built. America, Britain and France found him deaf to urgent pleas to put his name to territorial divisions that would have free elections and democratic governments...such open systems were totally alien to his own political culture and personal thinking.

Perhaps the best example of how deep and wide were the fissures of difference was the outcome of the British General Election in early July 1945. To the Prime Minister's own surprise, the Labour Party of 'dangerous socialists' won a landslide victory of 180 seats over the Tories — showing the voting power of a democracy which revered Churchill as a war leader but did not trust him to build the peace. There was, too, a feeling of profound waste by the war and Britons wanted a new start, with demobbed soldiers voting in their millions for a promised Welfare State that might, hopefully, not visit war upon their children's lifetime, but instead provide them with education and health benefits.

As negotiations resumed on the division of countries, Western powers now led by incoming British PM Atlee and American President Truman in the summer of 1945 found themselves dealing with a leader of a socialist experiment which had suffered the most loses in the war — 27 millions against the British Empire's one million and America's half million.

They were attempting to negotiate with a dictator who had mass-murdered the officer corps of his own forces during the 1930s, de-equipped his army in case it would turn against him, leaving it ill-prepared for the war and executed his rivals for power. Even as they pleaded at Potsdam with him to give some measure of autonomy to captured territories, Stalin had already copper-fastened the mechanism which would annex part of Europe: notably in Poland, whose officer corps he had murdered and secretly buried in the early days of the war and whose new rule went under the heading of 'Soviet Administration'.

Even at that stage, before the war fully ended with the atom bombing of Hiroshima and Nagasaki, Russia issued its territorial ultimatum — it would control over half of Germany, all of Poland, half of East Prussia, numerous smaller ethnic groupings in Czechoslovakia, Hungary, and The Balkans — a massive sundering of the 'old empires'. The ostensible reasoning was the 'export' of a socialist philosophy in place of the despised imperial and monarchical systems which had threatened Russia so often in the past. The reality was the sudden descent of communist power over millions of defeated peoples in no condition to resist, with former partisan leaders such as Tito weaned to Moscow.

This fait accompli, required the American forces to withdraw 150 miles westwards from their D-Day advances, which had been costly in American lives. With half of the former Germany becoming Soviet, Berlin was divided and occupied by the Allies. The Russian sector would provide a very different quality of life from West Berlin — something sensed by the surviving inhabitants who fled like lemmings, even as the lines were drawn on the maps of the secret deals in Potsdam.

Stalin was obdurate in negotiations — the theory of 'possession is nine-tenths of the law' became a fact when held by force of arms. The iron line was drawn in the wasteland of Europe, producing two very different systems of government — those living on one side would be helped by the Allies to re-build and have democratic governments. Those on the other would become prisoners in police states, their daily lives monitored by a network of neighbourhood informers. Significantly, among the earliest acts of the Soviet administrations was to solidify the system of 'social control' developed by the Nazis to ensure citizen loyalty. Now the threat of 'denunciation' — a refined State weapon used to imprison and execute millions of citizens of the USSR, brought terror into the already fearful homes of Eastern Europe.

Churchill, though out of office, continued his political prescience on a visit to America, where in the company of President Truman at Fulton, Missouri, he gave to the language a term by which the era would be known: 'From Stettin in the Baltic to Trieste in the Adriatic, an Iron Curtain has descended...the dark ages may return on the gleaming wings of science...Behind the curtain across Europe, Russia might even now be preparing for spreading communist tyranny'.

As far as SIS was concerned there was no 'might' about it. Reams of reports showed a remarkably speedy imposition of Soviet methods within their annexed territories confirming the fears of the old guard in SIS who grimly said 'I told you so'. Officials of similar views in the Foreign Office, some from old English Catholic families, pressed the 'Domino Theory' upon the incoming Labour Foreign Secretary Bevin, that the communist takeover of these countries represented as great a threat to the security of Britain — and to the Empire and Dominions, as had National Socialism. Panic planning in the British Cabinet went so far as to order a review of re-arming a defeated Germany, with a timescale of costs, logistics and manpower required. The alarm was loud in the corridors of SIS, responding to urgent Cabinet directions to increase intelligence from inside the annexed territories. In that context, Blake found himself dispatched back to Europe. He was given his first foreign command post, under cover of Naval intelligence, based in the port of Hamburg. He had two missions, the ostensible one being to de-brief captured German Naval officers, milk them of technical information and assess their war record for possible prosecution as war criminals. The second, pivotal on the first, was to identify the ones who could be 'turned' to work for British Intelligence and be infiltrated into the Russian sectors. The traditional 'carrot-and-stick' was much used. Stripped of their power and personal wealth, defeated in their own illusions of supremacy, many quickly understood the choice — long prison sentences, or new 'career opportunities' as British secret agents inside the Soviet-occupied parts of their own country.

Thus re-employed and paid from a slush-fund, sourced from German gold reserves, the onetime Nazis were infiltrated into the Soviet zones, under a variety of covers. In some cases they were dropped in full British service uniform into parts of Berlin where the insignia of all Allied armies were commonplace. There, divested of uniforms in safe houses, they drew on documentation provided by SIS to equip them with fictional German service records or identities of dead personnel or as civilian employees of a naval dockyard. Rehearsing their 'biographies', they were easily infiltrated into their homelands, speaking the language and taking advantage of the Russian effort to compile lists in the after-chaos of defeat. Anybody could reasonably claim recent displacement resulting from the massive Allied bombings Germany experienced in the months before D-Day.

They established themselves by the same skills as had made them efficient Wermacht officers, but now generously supplied with the new currency of a depleted Eastern Europe, which were caches of the black market goods of cigarettes, wines and nylon stockings. Under Blake's tutelage, though they did not know him by that name, they were also well equipped with the tradecraft of communications — drops, dead letter boxes and contact points — as to readily report on the Soviet takeover within days of being in place. Within a year, Blake had built extensive networks inside the Soviet sectors and was furnishing so much 'product' to Broadway Buildings that he was marked as a rising star of the Service.

In that context, with SIS under Cabinet pressure to increase its output on Eastern Europe, he was among a handful of officers assigned to become fluent in written and spoken Russian. Recalled from Germany, he 'went up' to Downing College, Cambridge, in the autumn of 1947, not as a standard undergraduate but as a civil servant — attending the School of Slavonic Studies. The usual lures of student life were of sublime disinterest to a man who had sated himself in the revived night-life of Hamburg and was now equipping himself for what he considered the next, challenging phase of his espionage career. Cambridge was a revelation to him, with its spires and churches, cake-shops and bicycles — more like parts of medieval Rotterdam before the Germans laid it waste. He found a revival of his theological interest at evensong in the legendary King's College Chapel, took lodgings with a vicar's widow outside the town and immersed himself in the study of Russian language and civilisation.

In the pastoral landscape of the Cambridgeshire fens, in the college halls redolent with the learning of ages, he underwent another change. He became absorbed in the history of Russia. In testing his new language skills to read the long, classical works of Russian literature, he was moved and intrigued by the characters created by Tolstoy, Dostoevsky and Chekhov out of the raw material of their own lives. 'Character is Destiny' is a mantra beloved of dramatists. Literature proved so again as he absorbed the history of a people struggling for expression through the volatile climes of geography and political evolution.

By the end of the academic year he graduated with distinction and to improve his spoken Russian, spent the early summer with a White Russian family who lived in a coastal village outside Dublin. The family lived by market gardening and fishing. Already in SIS were others of this community, engaged in translating and encrypting, holding fiercely to some Romanoff belief in the return of a Russian monarchy and the privileges that went with it, believing too that the downfall of Communism would herald their return to Russia. From the Dublin family and the aristocratic, temperamental translators in London he gained another sense of a lost Russia of imperial grandeur, a country of Orthodox, incense-filled beliefs that appealed to his religious sensibility. Though he did not know it then, he was in a word, 'hooked'.

Returning to SIS, he found that much had changed in his nine months away. The 'firm' had enlarged its Soviet listening posts, as the Iron Curtain of Churchill's prediction became firmly extended across many continents. Seizing upon the unrest brought about in Asia, South America and Africa, by the disruption of war to existing imperial or feudal systems. Moscow found ready-made populations willing to embrace Marxism as long as it promised freedom from the yoke of servitude. People of no property had gained confidence and status from serving in armed forces during the war — now they wanted control of their own internal affairs and were willing to fight under any flag that armed them. The flag usually was red. From territories all over the globe, likely candidates who displayed the same characteristics as had Stalin in his murderous and conspiratorial rise to power, were controlled and eventually placed in power by Moscow apparatchiks. The Foreign Ministry and First Chief Directorate of KGB were fully-stretched with thousands of career officers servicing world-wide revolution.

In former Czechoslovakia, Rumania, Hungary and The Balkans, local leaders were either murdered or imprisoned by Comintern cadres, backed-up by 'peoples armies' of red-banded mobs. Often driven by idealism and the welfare of their own peoples, they used housing and money shortages, as pressures to provoke unrest. America, 'home of the free' as an immigrant culture made-up of many refugees from those territories, responded in the way it knew best — with the carrot of dollars and the stick of the recently-formed CIA.

It proved potent and provoked a Soviet response in the cockpit of the undeclared war, Berlin. Judging by the numbers fleeing westwards, Capitalism and the free market appeared to be winning against Marx and barbed wire. In Europe, from January to March of 1948, the Soviet grip tightened in response to the material aid being granted by America's Foreign Secretary, George Marshall. By June it had sealed off Berlin from the outside world, starving its unwilling citizens into a hoped-for submission to Russian rule. The Allied response was to mount a daring airlift over the land blocks, flying 200 Dakota aircraft a day, delivering 2,500 tons of food in every 24 hours — an aviation and logistical feat. Britain's Clem Atlee had already condemned the worldwide Soviet activity, as 'the new imperialism', while George Marshall gave the American commitment to Berlin: 'We are here to stay'.

On another continent, another people whom America had also defended were not so fortunate. After the atomic bombing of Japan brought that imperial country to surrender, the fall-out was taken up by Chinese communists, led by a former schoolteacher, Mao Tse-tung. With Japan's colonial hold over China sundered, Mao led an army over a million strong, imbued with religious zeal, in re-conquest of their ancestral homelands. Mao had begun his campaign before the war, indoctrinating and training his cadres in mountain ranges impassable to the Japanese. America bolstered the opposition, led by Chiang Kai-shek, with arms and training. Vastly outnumbered and out-ideologued, they were shatteringly defeated at Manchuria, paving the way for a communist takeover of the enormous China landmass. Below them was Korea, divided along the 38th Parallel between America and Russia in the final days of the war. North Korea, armed and manipulated by Moscow, declared its intention to 'restore all of Korea to its people'.

George Blake, returning to Broadway Buildings, found himself assigned to Seoul, capital of South Korea. In the autumn of 1948 he was promoted within the Foreign Office to the rank of Vice-Consul, notable in itself, with chancery duties of passport regulation. He was also promoted, more meaningfully, as Head of Station, SIS, to organise a network of agents and informers who would help him assess the battle strength and political intentions of the North Korean regime — and the capacity of the South to sustain what seemed, as seen from London, another alarming advance of The Comintern. It was a formidable undertaking for a young man of twenty-six, albeit one who had seen the world tilt and then lurch, into chaos.

CHAPTER FIVE

SECRET SERVICE IN KOREA

In the early months of his appointment, Blake was cast into the cauldron of change. Korea contained ingredients of the later confrontations between East and West. A regime of unjust feudalism, propped-up by American monies and spiked with the armed intent to resist Russian expansion, its indigenous foundations were already eroding under communist infiltration. In the post-war occupation of Korea by the Allies, Russia had quickly established control over the northern part of the peninsula above the defining 38th parallel, refusing to co-operate with America in having elections. Instead, a Stalinist state had been enforced, with one-party rule, that of the Communist Party. It was called 'The Peoples Republic of North Korea' and rapidly set about eroding the fragile system in the southern part of the peninsula, below the 38th parallel. With his interest in social systems honed by his reading of Russian history at Cambridge, Blake rapidly came to the view that the nature of the ruling class in South Korea could not sustain itself against Communism and would in fact, provoke its eventual disintegration.

'Man is born free, but is everywhere in chains' was a guiding mantra of the revolutionary catechism. For Blake in Korea, the chains rattled in his face every day. Propaganda versions suited to Asian history were in circulation in Seoul, at great risk to the communist believers who distributed leaflets from underground printing presses.

The Consular work brought him into contact with businessmen and speculators, many of whom were purloining American economic aid, so that little of the powdered milk and canned meat intended to feed the poor was actually delivered to them. These products could be bought expensively on the black market in Seoul — but inland the peasantry toiled long and hard in the farms and rice fields in order to exist. Blake would recollect that 'never before had I encountered such a contrast between rich and poor.' Many of the officials controlling Western Aid were Korean émigrés, whose immigrant adulthood had been spent in Hawaii and had returned to positions of influence because of their knowledge of the language and customs, as part of the 'guns and grants' policy of the American effort to stem Communism. To get a full picture of American influence, imagine a well-fed 'fixer' in a Hawaiian shirt, peddling power and privileges.

Wearing his own inscrutable diplomat's face, Blake perceived the widespread corruption, registered the loud-mouthed boasting of profits from American Aid, in a patois of American slang and mangled grammar that offended both his moral and aesthetic sensibilities. The ancient ways of an old, albeit feudal, civilisation were everywhere corrupted by the dollar.

> 'Often at dusk I would go out into the streets, savouring the smells from the eating houses, looking at the coppersmiths patiently hammering out their vessels, watching the beautiful Kisang girls, the professional entertainers, in their brightly coloured silks...Flashy American cars would pull up in front of the large Chinese restaurants. Out of them emerged well-dressed businessmen and politicians who would spend the evening there carousing with their favourite entertainers. A little further on I would have to push my way through a clamouring crowd of beggars, clad in filthy rags and displaying their festering sores and maimed limbs...Many of them were children who slept out at night under bridges...'

The reality of Western Aid had black humour. A consignment of bibles, intended to convert the natives, was delivered to the British Legation. As nobody among the staff had the wish to distribute them and Blake could not bring himself to burn them, they gathered dust in storage, a bulky reminder of the sentimental liberal Western view of the East.

In his diplomatic work, Blake perceived that the threat to stability came more from the shorter version of Karl Marx than from The Bible. Facing the manifest injustices, he compared the communist underground with the Dutch Resistance which had faced the Nazi tyranny in WW2. He came to see the communist functionaries as motivated by noble intent, with the welfare of the people as their ultimate objective. But on the surface, he was mindful of his role as a diplomat, attending functions, cultivating contacts across a wide range of South Korean Society, including a young police captain who boasted to Blake of the methods he used in extracting information from the purveyors of communist propaganda.

In pursuit of 'confessions' suspects were suspended head down, boiling coffee was poured into their mouths, burning cigarettes were applied to the feet, along with the traditional secret police refinements of electric current to the testicles. Blake later wrote that he found the man's company 'disgusting' but rationalised as an SIS operative that '…one cannot always be choosy as regards the people with whom one has to collaborate.'

To Blake's way of thinking, there was much that was rotten in the body politic of his host country. The more he perceived the working of the political system, the more he disliked it. A country of sharp social contrasts, whose provocative gap between rich and poor was presided over with dynastic disdain by Syngman Rhee, Blake found that the 'Old Dictator' brooked no opposition. Compared to the totalitarian regime in North Korea, the South was 'democratic', but critics of Syngam Rhee in the rigged Parliament were regularly arrested on fabricated charges. The security police brutalised people in the streets and did not even bother to conceal their torture of victims inside the wooden police posts, which were open on one side. The population could readily see what lay in store for them if their voiced protest. This situation was encouraged by American 'advisors' to the Syngman Rhee regime.

63

Blake sought respite in personal contemplation, in picnics to the countryside, which enchanted him and significantly, in visiting the shrines of the ancient religions. Somewhere between versions of Buddha and God, his soul was undergoing radical change. Korea would become a forcing-house of personal determinism. He felt himself loving the peasantry, admiring their ancient endurance and fatalism, while finding the system that governed them loathsome. Wearing his role as a diplomat, he cultivated contacts across the spectrum. As a spy in His Majesty's service, he began to read the likely outcome, should the official enemy, the communists, invade from the North. South Korea was ripe for plucking by any group which could organise internal dissension and at the same time promise reforms of land and wealth distribution. In essence, South Korea was ready for communist take-over and fitted into the 'domino theory' of Comintern expansion. Thus did George Blake, formerly Behar, function in a state of controlled schizophrenia, evolving his professional lives along increasingly divergent paths.

Within months of his arrival in Seoul, George Blake, Vice Consul at His Most Britannic Majesty's Legation in Seoul filed to the Foreign Office in London in a series of coded telegrams his own political projection that South Korea could not withstand the ideological attack from the North. It simply lacked the moral fibre, out of which came sustained material resistance. The American influence in South Korea was a bad one, corrosive of native values, hectoring and bad-mannered in its personal expression. American behaviour was resented by the people they intended to protect from communist aggression.

Apart from his rota of contacts, which was necessarily part of the job, George Blake naturally gravitated towards the company of missionaries. His personal preference was for the company of thoughtful, philosophical men. When they were also 'men of the cloth', Blake's enthusiasm for them was clear. Two with whom he became close were the Anglican Bishop of Korea, Cecil Cooper and Commissioner of the

Salvation Army in Korea, Herbert Lord. That priestly part of Blake which had been blocked by the war in Europe now received some expression, at a remove, by these friendships.

Blake also imbibed native Korean culture and its association with that of the Chinese. He had intellectual curiosity about civilisation. We do know that he formed an opinion, from what he saw around him, that Communism was a morally superior force which would benefit mankind better than Capitalism or Feudalism or Imperialism, systems which meshed in the chaos of South Korean life, but which were unable to make humane the living conditions of the majority of the inhabitants. It is clear, from all who knew him, that he took a very 'moral' view of the world. It powered his views and his activities. He had in common with other ideological spies of his time, ambition to get things done. Not in the overt way of being seen to actively bring about change, but in being the manipulator behind the scenes and controlling the 'doing of others', the classic function of the spy.

For all his impending turmoil of loyalties, he had, in essence, absorbed the tenets of Secret Service training, of being, in the words of the Deputy Director of SIS in London, George Young, 'the stoker in the hold who would influence the Captain on the bridge'. As an employee of the British Foreign Office he was making political projections that warned of impending unrest, while also routing secret reports to SIS of the underground contacts who were actively bringing about that unrest. Quite how those reports influenced British foreign policy must remain conjectural as the speed of the escalation took the Western powers by surprise.

In a concerted invasion, breaking accepted rules by which territories respect other's sovereignty, North Korean forces attacked airfields, towns and cities of Southern Korea. Russian fighter planes strafed and bombed airfields, rendering many of them inoperative and inflicting high casualties. Most frighteningly for the ill-trained Southern forces, an apparently endless stream of communist infantry filled the swathes cut by the awesome T-34 tanks which rolled through defences of the South. The joint failure of the American and South Korean armed command became manifest when the communists pushed south on the 25th of June 1950.

Overnight, 600,000 armed communists poured across the 38th Parallel and careered South, receiving only token resistance from a demoralised army and from a peasantry well inured to the shifting fortunes of warlords. Cadres of jargon-spouting officers urged on mobs of peasant soldiers, to loot and burn buildings pointed out by sympathisers among the population. Supporters of the Syngman Ree administration, many no doubt corrupt, were taken out, abused and randomly shot. Houses and shops owned by foreigners, identified in the same manner, were looted.

Blake was in church when he noticed American personnel leaving from the Baptist service. Hastily, he tried to absorb the details of the invasion, tried to make sense of confusing accounts, made up of second-hand fact and first-hand rumour. American service personnel had standing instructions to leave the territory in the event of invasion. British civilians who wished to leave would be facilitated with an Airlift to Tokyo, thence to board an American war-ship. As he saw the hurried departures and witnessed the fear and confusion of flight, it seemed an unhappy re-run of the invasion of Rotterdam. Troops on the rampage, helped by local sympathisers — now communist cadres where ten years previously it had been Nazi collaborators. The effects on the native population were the same — fear, flight and death.

Whatever his own ideological uncertainties, his first actions were to protect the vulnerable clerics. He spoke with Herbert Lord of the Salvation Army and native helpers of church missions. Their instinct was to stay with their congregations. He arranged for shelter of Catholic priests and nuns. The aptly named Mr Faithful, Secretary to The Consul accompanied the British civilian evacuees out of Korea. Blake was left with Vyvyan Holt and Vice-Consul

Owen, the full complement of His Majesty's Legation. Holt took the view that as he was accredited to the Government of South Korea, he would remain. He might as easily have taken the opposite view, given that regime's speedy flight. In characteristic British fashion, they made tea and settled down to await approaches by the Chinese communists.

They could hear the shooting, watch the palls of fire rise over the city, smell the smoke, as official buildings in Seoul were set to the revolutionary torch, pointed out by the underground printers whose treatment at the pleasure of police captains had left them with little sympathy for the architecture of Seoul.

On the street outside the diplomatic compound, a platoon of the South Korean Army made a brief show of defending the Legation before abandoning the body of a comrade, which Blake led a party outside to retrieve. The soldier was buried in a corner of the Legation garden, an experience which left the diplomats depressed and fearful. Having taken their lead from the Head of Legation, Vyvyan Holt, who continued to regard himself as His Majesty's Representative to a government 'temporarily absent', the diplomats settled down to observe the scouting parties of North Korean militia. Many were marked only by a red arm-band to show their guerrilla status, some were manic with battle fever and gathered outside the diplomatic compound, awaiting orders. For a man of privately nurtured faith in Communism, Blake was about to have it put to a severe test.

CHAPTER SIX

CAPTIVE OF THE COMMUNISTS

For all their vaunted investment in Intelligence activities, the American and British governments were taken off-guard by the momentum of the North Korean advance. Even the primary demands of Military Intelligence, to ascertain the Order of Battle of the other side, seems to have been lacking. In the weeks before the invasion, when routinely swapping information of communist scouting inside the 38th parallel, Blake had been specifically assured by his opposite number in G2 (American Military Intelligence) that the United States would not intervene. America would keep the bulk of Pacific armed forces on the other side of the two Japanese seas, south and west of Korea, as part of the post-war agreement imposed by the victorious Allies after the defeat of Japan.

That victory had been signalled to the world by the explosion of two atomic bombs and a destruction of life and buildings not experienced in human history. Another major war might spell the end of mankind. Senior officers in American Intelligence in Washington were unsure of the extent to which Russia had developed its atomic capabilities. In America, the Rosenbergs were under investigation for passing to KGB secrets of the Atomic Energy Commission. Meanwhile, President Truman was mindful that intervention in Korea might draw the two great communist powers, the Soviet Union and China, into conflict with the West. Already, plans were underway to form NATO, an alliance of European armies whose express purpose was to counter the build-up of Soviet Bloc arms in Eastern Europe countries and act as a deterrent to Russian expansion.

As Blake understood it, America would not respond with armed intervention over Korea, but would wait and watch. The ferocity of the invasion, however, alarmed American public opinion and the Congress of the United States forced Truman's hand. He moved ships and troops to the defence of South Korea. America and Britain, the two great imperial powers of the West, denounced the invasion as an 'Act of Aggression' which threatened world peace. The American armed forces were placed under the command of the formidable General Douglas MacArthur, who had led the war victory in the Pacific. The mandate was the resolution of the United Nations which decreed that 'all members furnish such assistance to the Republic of Korea as may be necessary to meet armed attack.'

In effect, it was left to America to immediately supply 'such assistance' by hastily scrambling air supplies from Formosa to augment the ill-prepared local forces. As Russia had pointedly absented itself from the UN debate, it was in no position to counter the Resolution or criticise President Truman's initiative. Private overtures to Stalin from President Truman to use his demonstrable influence to halt the North Korean advance were rejected. In an early exercise of what would become reflexive American foreign policy, 'the yanks would go it alone'.

Elsewhere the response was laggerdly. Though Britain placed its fleet of 22 ships and two aircraft carriers in the Far East under MacArthur's command, it had yet to commit ground troops. Other Western powers whose interests were deemed threatened by the invasion, agonised over armed retaliation. Over many governments hung the spectre of Hiroshima and Nagasaki and uncertainty over Russian atomic capability. France, whose remnants of Empire were under attack in Indo-China, was already heavily bogged down in a war of attrition that would signal its demise as a power in Asia.

Australia, a burgeoning power within the British Commonwealth, looked to Britain for a lead, though its own territorial interests were more immediately threatened by the invasion of South Korea. While these events were in train in Western capitals, the cutting of cable communications between Seoul and the outside world left the British diplomats in ignorance. Five days after North Korean troops surged across the 38th Parallel, George Blake made contact with the advance party of communist militia which had surrounded the British Legation. Blake went out to hear their views, to parlay with officers who pointedly told him the British flag might be regarded as a target for North Korean bombing. Above the compound, the Union Flag fluttered like some outpost of Empire.

Next day an English-speaking Korean officer, Major Choe, negotiated the lowering of the Union Jack and informed Blake that although they were diplomats, they should go with him for their own safety. The flag was folded and handed back with a courtesy that contrasted with the earlier threatening behaviour of the communist guerrillas. But the occupants of the British Legation, whose numbers had increased in the days since the invasion, were not consoled to be told they would be driven north to Pyongyang, capital of North Korea and well inside the 38th parallel. Blake had earlier burned the copies of his secret documents which listed local contacts and agents whom he had recruited through SIS work and whose assessments featured in weekly reports to 'Head Office' in London, in effect, Broadway Buildings in Victoria. He also took the precaution of pouring the Legation's supply of hard drink down the drain. Some of it was highly prized bourbon, which had been donated by the departed Americans.

A week after the invasion, on July 2nd the staff and the clerics left the Legation as prisoners of the communists. They were herded into an army truck and driven out of Seoul, now a city ravaged by the revenge of a peasant army. They drove past the relics of American presence, past burned-out Hawaii-style bars, empty hotels and thousands of pages of notepaper, headed with the American eagle, blowing in the wind — flimsy evidence of the once-mighty hold of the dollar. Now a ghost city, Seoul seemed a reminder of the false security supplied by the 'occupying power' of the United States and the failure of The West, victorious in the recent war against Fascism, to guarantee against encroaching Communism. The diplomats linked up with another convoy of prisoners and headed across the 38th Parallel for Pyongyang, 140 miles into North Korea.

Without explanation, along the way, they stopped in a valley. Some of the troops conferred at a distance, while others kept the group at bay with rifles. It seemed to Blake then that his last moments had come: they were about to be executed. The tension was heightened when an American engineer, who had been on a drinking batter over the weekend of the invasion and consequently had been abandoned by his Embassy, came around to find himself a prisoner of the communists and wondered if he was 'in the rats'.

Assured by the diplomats that he was indeed sober but a prisoner, he had to be restrained as the troops stood off, guns at the ready. North Korean officers took control of the convoy with jeeps front and rear. It was, as Blake recalled '…a nightmare journey…the smell of rotting corpses hardly ever leaving our nostrils...'. They were driven steadily North past burned-out remains of villages and farms, over dirt roads pitted with bomb craters, by the rotting corpses of humans and animals. The Peoples Republic had exacted a scorched-earth penalty on the South as a punishment for its 'bourgeois' system of land ownership and feudal corruption.

After many hours of constant driving, with only minimum stops to relieve natural functions, they reached Pyongyang. Here, herded into a disused school, they realised they were beyond reach of rescue. In effect, the school was an internment camp. They were given subsistence rations of rice and cabbage and allotted sleeping quarters. Had they but known it, the Americans were fighting a lone-stand, having retreated with heavy casualties into a southeast corner of the peninsula by the Pusan air base. Here supply planes from the American bases in Japan aided them, from where repeated sorties to bomb the communist supply lines were launched. The North Korean supply lines became stretched as their invasion penetrated deep into the South.

They resorted to increased air-cover, covertly flown by Russian pilots, and the punching power of Russian T-34 tanks, to maintain the momentum of the advance south.

The spearhead T-34's cut a swathe through American infantry, exposing not only a clear run southwards but a planning failure by American command staffs.

By the end of July, detachments of marines in troopships were steaming out of San Diego in Southern California bound for Japan as a re-grouping point from which to plan an assault on Korean coastal defences. However, hundreds of American GIs were already prisoners of the first wave of the invasion and were being humiliated in long marches north, showing themselves to be remarkably unfit for the trek. Many went down with exhaustion and dysentery. Those not carried by their comrades were shot by their captors.

The diplomats fared better. By end of July they were joined by the French consular staff and a group of Catholic and Protestant clergy, priests and nuns. Among them, French and Irish clerics of the Roman Catholic persuasion, English and American women Presbyterian missionaries, The Mother Superior of the Carmelite Order of Nuns, Bishop Patrick Burns who was both a Catholic priest and a diplomat, being the accredited Papal Legate to Korea, the elderly Fr. Paul Villemot and Fr. Francis Canavan. Though products of differing religious persuasions, they had in common a desire to do good in Asia. Now their differences evaporated under shared common privations and the indignity of being packed tightly into trucks. The nuns and women missionaries in particular, had fed and clothed the poor of Korea for a generation. To the communists all the church members were part of 'Western Imperialism' and its exploitation of Asia.

Philip Deane, a journalist with *The Observer* and by all accounts a role model of the hard-bitten correspondent, was brought in, having been wounded and captured with an American tank platoon. He was able to update them on the state of the war, which was going badly at that stage against the Americans, then suffering severe casualties. The front line had moved even further into the south. Deane recorded that George Blake was a tower of consolation, doing heavy chores and taking it on himself to negotiate reasonable behaviour from their captors. This required diplomatic nerve when they heard on a covert radio a news bulletin from the BBC that Britain had formally entered the war with ground troops en route and reserves called up at home.

The captors' attitude hardened; clearly they were aware of the escalation. The hostages were not to know it, but the Korean conflict now threatened world stability. General MacArthur had galvanised the American war machine, with the backing of a public opinion that had become belligerently anti-communist. Winston Churchill the most respected statesman of the post-war era, was forecasting a third world war, unless communist aggression in Korea was stopped, his warning helping expand a climate in Britain which saw munitions factories go into night shift and budgets increased for arms spending. Britain and America were on a wartime footing and prepared to defend the Free World. Under the Anglo-American leadership, infantry were promised from Belgium, Columbia, Philippines, and countries within the British Commonwealth.

Australia was committing troops, while France was sliding further into the mire of what would become the humiliating defeat of Dien Bien Phu and the end of French power in Indo-China. Nationalist China threatened the crucial Western Base in Formosa. In many of Britain's Asian colonies, the same symptoms of unrest which had provoked the Korean situation were up-surging into revolutionary agitation and were meeting with further repression.

At the crux of what seemed like a contagion of anti-Imperial wars, Korea was where a stand would have to be made. When Blake heard that Britain was committed to join with American defence of South Korea, he was bitterly disappointed. For all the brutalities of the communists, he had hoped Britain would not side with America. He seems not to have considered how Britain could behave otherwise, given its role in defeating Fascism and — crucially — its foresight in seeing post-war Communism as *the* threat to the Free World.

Against that ripening Western opinion, American troops were encountering high casualties in the wet fields and

73

impassable mountains. It was foreign territory to most of the young GIs who, enlisting post-war, were used to the easy living in the subject nations of Japan and the Philippines. Short of anti-tank guns and artillery, the infantry suffered heavily at the firepower of the T-34 tanks on the wet plains and were mown down in the gulches and valleys by an enemy who knew the countryside since childhood. Demoralised by ambushes, by guerrillas disguised as passive peasants in the fields, American soldiers were jumpy and nervy. Inexperienced platoons panicked and massacred innocent villagers in retaliation. At the village of No Gun Ri, over 200 villagers in flight from the marauding North Koreans were mistakenly taken to be camouflaged guerrillas and were mercilessly mown down by American troops. According to a US soldier who was nineteen at the time, his unit in the 1st Cavalry surrounded several hundred civilians and pinned them under a railway bridge. Sustained machine-gun fire was directed at the Koreans for about thirty minutes, because 'sporadic fire had come from under the arch'.

About a month later, on August 26th, Britain landed its first troops, among them battle-hardened regiments, who had been shipped via Hong Kong. By then, as the hostages settled into captivity in Pyongyang, it seemed as if the North Koreans would win the war. All but a corner of the southeast was under their control and they continued to inflict heavy casualties on the American troops. Still, in captivity, life had to go on — forcing habit changes. Blake gave up smoking in favour of local apples. They had some books which were re-read and translated to keep them intellectually alert.

The British expertise in sending commando parties behind the enemy lines to reconnoitre positions gave strategic intelligence to American artillery, which inflicted heavy losses from a safe distance. There was a high rate of civilian casualties as the heavy guns pulverised communist strongholds and supply lines. By September, the combined UN forces were riding on a high tide into Inchon harbour, hundreds of miles up the western coast and well behind the enemy front line.

The harbour defences had previously been knocked out by British marine commandoes. It was MacArthur's intention to deliver a powerful 'left hook' up the coast, in a daring sea-based advance. From a troop landing fleet of 260 vessels, supported by massive firepower from fleet heavy guns, the American marines rode in on the 30-foot high tide to take the strategic port of Inchon. The assault, reminiscent of the D-Day landings, which regained Europe from the Nazis, took seven hours to effect. It was achieved by expertise in the use of amphibious craft and securing landing bases by pulverising defensive bunkers before the main troops arrived.

Such was the softening-up bombardment, that little resistance was encountered, beyond a few stubborn machine-gun posts. The North Koreans fell back beyond Seoul, providing the UN forces with the first meaningful change of fortunes. Taking advantage, Americans and British meshed their fighting force along the east and west coasts, south of Seoul. A separate American army under General Walker advanced out of the Pusan perimeter from their 'last stand' corner, gradually gaining ground, northwards.

While this war of attrition continued, of GIs' digging into foxholes within sight of enemy lines, of massive disruption and suffering of the civilian population, the hostages were trucked further north, to the border between Korea and Manchuria. They had left Pyongyang because of American bombing. They had to leave trucks and run into the fields as American fighters strafed the convoy. In a camp near Mampo, they detected a changed attitude in their captors. Seven hundred American soldiers had joined them as prisoners, captured in the first wave of the invasion. With the reversing fortunes of war running on the wind ahead of the actual action, the guards appeared willing to discuss defection to the American side if the hostages would intercede for them.

George Blake was among the French and British diplomats who persuaded two Korean guards to desert and guide them towards the advancing Allied lines. Finding pathways that skirted the roads, they walked a full day, rested up at night and walked again until noon, when they observed a Korean detachment heading north. Assuming them to be retreating, the diplomats urged their guards to make themselves known, but were disconcerted to find them returning with changed demeanour.

Apparently news had come through that a massive army of Chinese had crossed the Manchurian border to aid their fellow communists and had reversed the Allied advances of a few days before. The battle to re-take Seoul had been renewed. The Korean guards reversed their position in the face of this intelligence and said all would have to return to the camp. Surprisingly, the hostages found they were not punished when they arrived back at Mampo. They were shortly moved to another camp, run by a different Commander, one of less kindly temperament.

He wore knee-breeches and a tight-fitting jacket and revelled in his authority as 'a Major of the Peoples' Army'. They christened him 'The Tiger' and he was remembered by Fr. Philip Crosbie, an Australian as…

'…tall for a Korean, slim, quick and nervous in his movements. When he walked he leaned forward a little… protruding teeth gave him a perpetual grimace. His bright eyes were keen and restless'.

This new man was to prove a harsh over-seer, as they set out again, for what threatened to become an interminable forced march. He subjected the weary captives to military discipline, unsuitable, to say the least, for the elderly missionaries. For the American POWs he reserved an undisguised contempt.

Crosbie noted the Americans' exhaustion:

'…my gaze went sometimes to their faces, sometimes to their feet. Some of which were bare, and some were already bleeding. Some feet paced steadily, if wearily, on; but weaker men, dragging on the shoulders of their comrades, put ghastly, shuffling syncopation in the rhythm of the march'. The civilians fell in at the end of the march, trying to make a line of support for each other as the guards ran back and forth, urging Bali! … Bali! — Korean for Quickly! Quickly!

'The Tiger' brooked no concessions to the civilians and missionaries and insisted on sixteen miles a day over rough mountain tracks. Herbert Lord, the agreed interpreter for the group pleaded leniency for the elderly civilians. 'But they will die if they have to march' he told 'The Tiger' who responded, 'Then let them march till they die!'

In their movement to the new camp they registered the massive damage which American bombing had inflicted on villages and countryside.

Blake resolved another attempt at escape. The journalist Philip Deane agreed they should attempt to slip out of the camp at night, trek south, hoping to link up with American troops. Perhaps their guards had deceived them on the state of the war, maintained Blake. That night, when it came to going, Deane demurred. So did another prisoner, who said they would be shot as spies if captured by communists. Blake set off on his own and managed to make his way for about three hours before being spotted by a Korean scouting party who were about to shoot him when he exclaimed in Russian that he was a diplomat.

Not only a diplomat but also a white man, as it turned out. Brought at gunpoint to an officer who interrogated him, Blake revealed his identity, which the captain found of great interest while his squaddies listened to Blake's replies, finding him an object of great amusement in his speech and appearance. The Captain escorted him back to prison camp, discussing the rights and wrongs of the war along the way, a dialogue which Blake found intriguing.

Before leaving him, the captain gave him friendly advice. 'Don't try to escape again — with your appearance, with your pink skin and big nose, you will be seen straight away as a foreigner...my soldiers may not be so patient next time...'. Blake was handed over to the camp commander who assembled the inmates, put Blake standing in the middle and lectured him for twenty minutes, telling him he was abusing Korean hospitality and serving as a bad example to other 'guests'. This open-air harangue was translated by Commissioner Lord of the Salvation Army to the assembled

Western prisoners on the Manchurian border in September 1950.

With but a day's recovery, he was on the march again, one of a long column of prisoners which set out along the Yalu river, again heading north. Seven hundred American POWs had joined, most demoralised, many suffering. Unknown to them, on the wider battlefield, the ebb and flow of war, of victory and defeat, was now the intense focus of the world community. In the previous weeks, the Americans shot down a Russian bomber which they claimed 'threatened' their offshore fleet, while thousands of North Korean troops, thrown against the UN entrenched forces on a 50-mile front, were routed with huge casualties.

As the UN troops reached Seoul, in the talking shop of the UN, America and Russia exchanged bitter words. In Europe the NATO alliance was hastened into becoming an integrated army, to resist Russian-inspired expansion from Eastern Europe. In Indo-China the Viet Minh made huge advances against the French military. In Korea, as the UN Forces, spearheaded by the Americans, headed towards the 38th parallel, the Chinese communist leader, Chou En-lai warned that China would intervene if the Americans crossed the 39th parallel.

Oblivious of these events, but knowing that another tilt had taken place in the war, George Blake was roused at dawn, given a ball of maize as food for the day and set off to walk. With him were priests, nuns, lay missionaries and diplomats. They could have hardly realised it, but many would not survive. Those that did were changed forever.

CHAPTER SEVEN

THE CONVERSION OF GEORGE BLAKE

They could not know that they would be captives of the North Korean communists for almost three years, or that many would die during that time. Even the pessimism induced by capture could not have prepared them for the long march northwards or for the suffering, the sacrifice and the occasional heroism which the march invoked.

Lacking the gift of prophecy, they could not foretell the profound personal changes they would undergo, or of how the world would change, or even of their own small but significant part in the evolving political mosaic of Asia and Europe. All they knew in October 1950 was that they were prisoners and the American POWs were likely to be shown scant mercy as they headed north. They were heading away from the tide of battle and possible rescue. By about the middle of November 1950, they reached a Prisoner of War camp at Hadjang. It was 15 degrees below freezing. Most wore only the summer clothes they had when captured, augmented by a thin blanket for sleeping. Some wore it during the day, which left them more vulnerable at nights when the temperature dropped sharply. The cold took its toll — Sister Mary Clare of the Barefoot-Carmelites died, as did Fr Hunt. Blake assisted in their burial in shallow graves, because the ground was frozen hard.

Minister Holt and his deputy Norman Owen were taken seriously ill. Neither would recover their health. The attrition rate among the Americans was high — as they dropped behind, they were shot. The Tiger had given orders that no one was to be allowed to fall out. Sometimes he fell behind himself and during this time, officers asked the guards for instruction on collapsing comrades. The guards told them leave them, but when The Tiger caught up with the fallen men he halted the column and asked the officers to explain. When told to identify the guards who gave permission and no guards came forward, he decided to make an example.

Herbert Lord translated and interceded, as Crosbie starkly recorded:

' "Then I will shoot the man from whose section most men were allowed to fall out. Who is he?" Lt. Thornton of Texas stepped forward. He was calm, master of himself. He merely whispered to Commissioner Lord: "Save me if you can, sir". The Commissioner tried, but The Tiger turned on him in fury. "You shut up" he snarled, "or I'll shoot you, too. You're only the translator". As he stood there muttering to himself as if in doubt, a band of soldiers passed along the road. He called to them: "What should be done to man who disobeys the People's Army?" "Shoot him" they shouted back. ...The Tiger's hesitation ended; but the need to justify himself still held him. Stripping off his overcoat, he pointed to the star on two bars, the insignia of a major... "I have the power," he said "to do this". A guard blindfolded Lieutenant Thornton. The Tiger drew his pistol, cocked it, and stepped behind his victim. Then he flicked up the back of the lieutenant's cap and shot him through the head'.

Blake later defended their 'extermination' as being more humane than leaving them to die slowly. If the stragglers had been left behind, they would have been doomed to a slow but certain death from hunger and cold. He was struck by how ill-prepared were the American soldiers for the demands of captivity in a cold climate[*].

In the village, which had some kind of covered shelter, the American GIs continued to die at the rate of two or three a night. A group had gone to sleep, arms around each other, hugging their body warmth and in the morning the weakest would be dead. Some died standing up, crowded against the thin walls by the press of others and so exposed to the biting air from outside. Others, with no will to survive, gave up and crawled to the edge of the crowd to die alone, whimpering for their mothers. Many had dysentery and died in their own excrement. The civilians and the surviving missionaries bore up well, though most were at least twice the age of the

---

[*] Author's interview with George Blake, Moscow, February 2001.

American soldiers. Blake put the contrast down to the difference in backgrounds. The Americans were '...used to the hygienically prepared food in the army canteens, to their doughnuts and Coca-Cola'. They had been serving in the Army of Occupation in Japan, 'Many had owned their own cars and lived with Japanese girls. Overnight they were transported from this paradise to the wild mountains of Korea where they had to fight against overwhelming forces and to suffer the bitter experience of defeat and capture...They were so miserable they just didn't want to live any more and gave up the struggle for survival.'

The tough missionaries, some in their seventies and in their eighties had lived much of their adult lives in simple Korean villages which the West called 'primitive'. Blake adduced, as was his wont, a moral lesson. The missionaries' bodies and minds were better able to adjust to the conditions of captivity. '...though it is natural in man to do so, we should not aspire too much to the good life and, if it is good, we should deliberately impose restrictions on ourselves. A certain amount of deprivation is not necessarily a bad thing. It makes it easier to cope with evil times when they come...'

In that winter of 1950, in Northern Korea, the evil times came aplenty. By mid-November, by dint of fierce fighting and high casualties, the UN forces had fought their way to Pyongyang, capital of North Korea. The final assault into the city, from where the captives had been taken further north, was led by South Korean forces, their morale and equipment renewed by the Americans. The Western media, in particular *Life* magazine in the US and *Picture Post* in the UK reported graphically on the war, with pictures of GIs and British troops enduring the punishing advances over a huge amount of territory. In the two months since the Inchon landings, the war seemed to be going the way of the Allies, though the American public was puzzled by the conflict between their President Truman and their legendary commander MacArthur. The two men differed over their respective responsibilities for the progress of the war.

Imbued with the sweeping gain of territory, MacArthur was heedless of Chinese warnings not to cross into North Korea and, having flouted one warning and taken Pyongyang, he pushed even further towards the Chinese border, a move fraught with enormous implications for world peace. Truman and his advisors wanted a limited war to resist aggression in Korea, not a MacArthur-led crusade against world Communism. Moscow's agents had exploited and infiltrated so many anti-colonial movements in so many territories as to provoke America into countering movements which were of national or ethnic independence. As seen by Truman, it was crucial that MacArthur's militarism be made amenable to political control — otherwise America would find itself immersed in a nuclear World War Three.

The American president was in receipt of assessments, which showed the old imperial powers, and in particular his closest allies, the British, to be under serious threat of insurgency in many outposts. The French, leader of 'The old dominions' and the old certainties, in colonial Asia, had weeks before surrendered 250 miles of front line to China-backed Vietnamese. Russia was proving belligerent at the UN.

Pertinently, in the secret intelligence world previously inhabited by George Blake but to which he was now an outsider, foreign intelligence activity was directed towards atomic capability. That Russia was making advances in that area would become startlingly clear within months, with the defection of major British diplomats, Burgess and Maclean. But all that — and the wider events — were unknown to the captives as the see-saw of war drastically changed again in December 1950.

Enraged at the capture of Pyongyang, thousands of Chinese volunteers swept across the border. The Chinese had meant their warning, and now UN forces tumbled back in disarray as the seemingly endless numbers of Chinese crossed the Yalu river and overran the Allied lines. As they crossed the Taedong river they were machine-gunned and napalmed by American fighter pilots in a turkey-shoot which bloodied the yellow river. Yet they kept coming, to the surprise of the gung-ho pilots, some of whom were traumatised by the slaughter they felt forced to inflict. One pilot recalled them coming over 'like a crowd at a football match' while the US army described a bottomless well of Chinese manpower. As the Americans withdrew from Pyongyang, they torched their supplies of motor fuel, leaving the city under a pall of fire. The battle-hardened British 29th Brigade provided rearguard cover for the American departure. As they fled south, the Americans were harried by guerrillas firing from rice fields and villages, leading to more retaliatory massacres by disorganised American troops upon innocent Koreans, whose political loyalties they were unable to read in the panic of retreat. The American public were largely unaware of these atrocities: some pictures of captioned 'captured communist guerrillas' were of innocent villagers.

In the wake of this further retreat of UN forces and the high casualties, the Allies confronted serious questions. Would it be better in the long run, as had been decided in bombing Japan, to shorten the war and save an unknown number of lives, communist and allied, by dropping a nuclear bomb on North Korea? Would that provoke Russia and China into retaliatory action of similar magnitude? MacArthur lobbied to have the war escalated, not ruling out atomic explosions along the Manchurian border from where the mass of Chinese troops entered the conflict. Alarmed at this prospect, Britain's Labour Prime Minister Clem Atlee sought assurances from Truman that the atomic bombing of Korea would be ruled out — his Cabinet and voters would not tolerate it. Secretly, Atlee permitted his own Atomic research to go ahead, keeping developments from his own ministers; some of whom he felt had left-wing sympathies with Russia.

In Congress, MacArthur's comments found favour among Republicans. Truman's advisors urged the General to cease making 'political statements'. Secretly, the American defence establishment prepared to explode nuclear devices in

Nevada. Some strategists took the view that such an expression of American power would intimidate Russia and China into peace talks. Abroad, on several fronts America strengthened its military presence. General Eisenhower, hero of the liberation of Europe, became head of the NATO armed forces while at home an increased budget was passed for 'selective enlistment' of more troops for Korea.

Within the FBI, charged with countering communist subversion in America, resources were directed to 'red sympathisers'. It was not an easy time for thousands of intellectuals, writers and artists who had ideologically supported Communism as a political system to alleviate the evils of poverty and exploitation, but who were opposed to violent means to achieve those ends. As with the previous escalation of the war, the details were unknown to the captives. As the weeks went by and the year turned, they became known to the captors as individuals rather than as symbols of 'western oppression'. Living conditions improved. In spite of meagre diet and restricted mobility, the diplomats and surviving missionaries drew on their intellectual resources to make the time bearable. Elaborate word games were devised, meals recorded in salivating detail, books remembered and imaginatively retold as an antidote to boredom.

The French and British diplomats spoke many languages between them. Holt and Blake knew Russian, Owen knew Arabic, many of the French were fluent in English and Japanese. They translated imaginary texts to pass the time, drew on each other's knowledge of history and world affairs. A consensus evolved that Communism, as a creed, might become a system of world order, given the demonstrable failure of the old imperial systems to avoid wars and make good the majority condition.

The POW commander clearly heard of these discussions. The Soviet Embassy in Pyongyang returned to North Korean control by early spring of 1951, sent books by Marx and Lenin to the prisoners. As they were in Russian, only Holt and Blake could take advantage of them. Though not the lightest of bedtime reading, being heavy tracts of political sermonising, they were devoured by the two Britons who used them to continue the philosophical discussions, which had filled in leisure time at the Legation. Now, trying to make sense of their captivity, the texts assumed a more meaningful relevance, helping them understand the motivation of the Korean communists.

It is worth considering here the political climate of the 1950s, as it pertained to those who gave thought and concern to the State of the World. While that grand-sounding concept may appear pretentious or illusionary to many, the fact is that the scale of destruction wrought by the recent war provoked serious thought about political systems. The most far-reaching reaction became the Schuman Declaration, later expanded into the European Union. Initially devised as an economic bloc of coal and steel producers, it took on Schuman's intent that economic self-interest would prevent any member from waging war on another. The relevance of the effects of the war upon Blake and other spies was that since the Middle Ages, thinking men and women have been in thrall to an ideology that promised 'truth, justice and equality'.

From the French Revolution in the 18th century to the spread of Christianity in the 19th and Colonialism in the 20th century, systems which seemed to advance human progress were widely adopted by thinkers and activists. By the 1950s, Communism seemed 'the coming thing', with Russia's carefully orchestrated social engineering apparently offering alternatives to the enslavement of millions, which had been the effect of Imperialism. That it was dishonest and brutal in practice was camouflaged from those who needed some alternative to the patent failures of existing systems.

George Blake, a man of philosophic bent now found himself immersed in empirical thought. Theory and practice meshed before him in the war for both minds and territory, which characterised the Korean situation. By the beginning of 1951, the war had cost hundreds of thousands of lives.

Ancient communities had been destroyed on both sides of the 38th Parallel.

He would recollect: 'After what I had seen of the South Korean regime, I found it impossible to feel that keeping it in power was a worthwhile cause'. '...although I was their prisoner, my sympathies lay with the North Koreans...' '...the destruction and the suffering of the civilian population and indeed of the young American POWs, with whom we had been thrown together, seemed utterly pointless to me. Nor could I feel that my own imprisonment and that of my fellow British inmates was for the good of our own country. Then it would have made sense and I would have borne it gladly'.

'I remembered how in Holland, during the war, when I heard at night the heavy drone of hundreds of RAF planes overhead on their way to bomb Germany, the sound had been like a song to me. Now, when I saw the enormous grey hulks of the American bombers sweeping low to drop their deadly load over the small, defenceless Korean villages huddled against the mountainside; when I saw the villagers, mostly women and children and old people — for the men were all at the front — being machine-gunned as they fled to seek shelter in the fields, I felt shame and anger. What right had they to come to this far-away country, which had done them no harm and only wanted to settle its own affairs, to lay waste its towns and villages, to kill and destroy indiscriminately?'

He had plenty of time to engage in this questioning of his own loyalties during the months of enforced captivity. Minister Holt, while overtly maintaining his official position with their captors, in personal conversation with Blake, which because of their circumstances was prolonged, revealed a disillusion with Western politics, which influenced his junior. Having witnessed in his career 'the splendour and decline of the British Empire' Holt's extensive time as a colonist had led him to conclude that the next stage in the development of the human race was — Communism.

In such deep conversations did George Blake undergo a profound change of heart. Choosing to overlook the *means* by which Communism had improved the living standards of millions in Asia and taking Holt's encouragement, between them they concluded that the British Empire — and its imposed Christianity — had failed to benefit India as Communism had for other parts of Asia. For professional diplomats, it was a serious conclusion. For Blake, it posed another serious, private question. What to do about it?

While engaged in this dialogue, they were only partially aware of how the war outside exacted its attrition. The suffering of the natives they could glean at first-hand, but they only heard long after the event of the sacking by President Truman of General MacArthur, which happened in April 1951. Harry Truman said Douglas MacArthur was relieved of his command because he did not agree with the American policy in Korea, which was limited containment of the war.

MacArthur was immensely popular in America, in spite of the high casualties. American families, receiving the bodies of their dead sons and husbands, saw themselves enshrined in the fight against Communism.

A Congressional enquiry into the dismissal heard General Omar Bradley, Chairman of the Joint Chiefs of Staff, allege that MacArthur's move towards China '...would have involved us in the wrong war, in the wrong place at the wrong time, against the wrong enemy.' MacArthur was replaced by General Ridgway, no less a warrior but observant of American Policy. To assuage domestic feeling, Ridgway was pictured with a grenade strapped to his shoulder and in full battle dress. As often in wars, a change of commander was also a subtle signal to the enemy that a more placatory approach was being taken.

The nuclear escalation in Korea was modified, though America continued to make public its nuclear development, culminating in a test explosion in the Pacific on May 12th which was reported as 'being hundreds of times more powerful' than the atomic bombs which destroyed Nagasaki and Hiroshima. The message to the Soviets was clear: America wants to contain communist expansion with conventional warfare, but if provoked beyond stated limits, has the capability to inflict enormous first-strike damage on enemies.

It was a message received in Moscow with a clarity not usually characteristic of Soviet foreign policy. Russia had invested dedicated resources to developing atomic weapons but felt it was behind American capability. As far as is known, the Russian manufacture of atomic weapons, from about 1945 was modelled on plans given to KGB by British and American agents who believed, in the interests of peace, that the West should not have a monopoly of nuclear destruction. Russia's test explosion of a nuclear bomb in 1949 had been received with alarm in Washington.

The Western powers, notably Britain, France and America, concentrated on maintaining their superiority in the nuclear balance of power. In America, Julius and Ethel Rosenberg were sentenced to death for betraying 'atomic research information' to Russia, even though the offences had taken place in 1944, when Russia was an ally of America in the fight against the Nazis. The Rosenbergs were Jewish and protested their death sentence was the result of anti-Soviet hysteria prevalent in America because of the Korean War.

In Britain's Foreign Office a review of security about atomic secrets closed the net on Donald McLean and Anthony Burgess, two diplomats with access to secret information who were working with American defence research. They absconded to Moscow, evading questioning about their private political loyalties. Though unknown to the public on both sides of the Atlantic, their flight was merely the inkling of a deeply embedded caucus of Soviet agents within Western Establishments — agents whose loyalty to Communism had begun before the Second World War, when communists on the streets of Germany seemed the only party willing to violently confront the growing Nazi terror. That dedication had been honed by the enormous losses and suffering endured by Russian peoples during that conflict.

Reading the potential for worldwide destruction, Russia made overtures for a cease-fire in June of 1951, when the

Korean War was a year old. Though sceptical, The White House responded by instructing General Ridgway to lay down an order of negotiations. Within a month, a line-up of senior generals from both sides had agreed a formula, which could lead to a cease-fire. In the POW village near Mampo, more concessions were made to the captives. By then, George Blake had made-up his mind to change sides. 'It was a grave decision, taken in grave and exceptional circumstances. Around me raged a cruel and bitter war. Violent times beget violent and extreme actions'.

He speculated that had he been living comfortably in London he probably would not have arrived at the same decision, irritated though he was by the British class system. But being in Korea, seeing the effects of the American bombardment, hearing of the casualties among the troops of his adopted country, he felt it was all a terrible waste of life. And for what — for the corrupt regime of South Korea?

Through the summer of 1951, as the respective delegations of East and West tried to nail down a permanent ceasefire, their political masters were still shaping up to each other on a global scale. America exploded its second Hydrogen Bomb, followed by a Russian test of an Atomic Bomb. America signed defence treaties with Australia and New Zealand, strengthening its power in the Pacific. Japan was returned to a measure of sovereignty, conditional upon accepting American military bases and two divisions of troops on a war footing.

Communist China forcibly expanded into Tibet. Russia armed colonial states in Africa who were agitating for independence from the British, French and Portuguese empires. In Egypt, strong anti-British feeling, nurtured by communist thinking, escalated into confrontation over control of the Suez Canal. In Europe, NATO invited both Turkey and Greece to join its standing army. In Nuremberg, the last batch of Nazi generals were hanged and a restored German parliament voted for compensation for 'the unspeakable crimes' of the German people against the Jews.

These last measures unwittingly cleared the way — and created the psychological vacuum — for the next flash point of global confrontation. East and West, under two opposed systems of government, prepared to vie for the 'hearts and minds' of the world. The communist system promised '*From each according to his ability, to each according to his needs*'. The West promised democracy, elections and the unlimited right to better oneself. The battered city of Berlin would be where the secret battle would turn. The wall dividing it would represent the wider global division between East and West.

While these elements in the wider political world were coalescing, George Blake was nearing the end of his introspective dialogue. It was a debate reminiscent of old style theology. Seeking proofs for the existence of God was meaningless, since Faith was a matter of belief. The fact that he had been ill-treated by soldiers of the communist NKPD did not diminish the moral superiority of North Korea over the 'corrupt' South. The sermons heard at his Calvinist Church resounded — to build the Kingdom of God on Earth. If Christianity had demonstrably failed to bring an end to wars and injustice it did not mean the Christian ideal should die. The ideal could be achievable by other means. Where The Church had failed, could not Communism succeed? It had the will, the means and the ruthlessness.

Although the captives had been subjected to lectures and indoctrination, titled 'brainwashing' by the Western media, the attempts to 'convert' them to Communism had, by-and-large, failed. The diplomats in particular were skilled in language usage. Most were university graduates for whom the recitation by rote of versions of Marx and Lenin were offensive to their intelligence. So the dogma spouting officers contented themselves with haranguing the peasant squaddies. After one such evening session in Autumn 1951 a major was surprised to see George Blake at the door, with a note in his hand.

Putting his finger to his lips to indicate confidentiality, Blake handed the major the note, who took it without comment. Blake had written in Russian that he wished to be interviewed by an official of the Soviet Embassy in Pyongyang, as he had something of importance to communicate. In the seesaw of battle, the communists had retaken Pyongyang for the second time. He also wrote that all the diplomats should also be interviewed individually, to avoid drawing suspicion on himself. He had taken another step in what was to prove an epic journey through the inside politics of the second half of the century.

CHAPTER EIGHT

HOW GB BECAME KGB

It took almost two months to receive the response he wanted. During that time his request shuffled along the cumbersome administration, which characterised the Soviet system. For all Stalin's vaunted 'modernising' of the vast territory that was Russia, the post-war rulers had made a self-perpetuating bureaucracy out of government. It took weeks to administer tasks, which in the West were done in days.

KGB was no different. In spite of its fearsome reputation, based partly on the tortures and executions which were conducted in its basement floors, it was, administratively, as much a lumbering bureaucracy as any of the government departments which ineptly administered the enormous expanse of Russia.

Even before the October Revolution of 1917, and in tandem with the subsequent swings and balances of power, Russia had been a Police State. Ruling caucus relied heavily on brutality, betrayal and murder to keep control of the Kremlin, the vast fortress that dominated Moscow. From within that odd amalgam of churches, civil service offices and apartments, successive waves of 'revolutionary governments' had tried to control a territory which covered a sixth of the world's inhabited surface across ten time zones.

The USSR was made-up of so many cultures, religions and races that it required a vast apparatus of civil servants to administer. When local populations were resistant to Kremlin wishes, apparatchiks used whatever means were required, hence the growth of secret police as an enforcing instrument of state policy. In turn, the state security services trawled for dissent and expanded its influence by informing upon, or concocting, conspiracies against the prevailing junta. Those who 'resisted' were dealt systematic torture and murder.

The subsequent ritual bloodletting was so severe that paranoia constantly reigned among leaders. By the end of the Second World War, KGB had been involved in the mass murder of its own citizens on a scale reckoned by modern historians not to have been exceeded by any domestic intelligence service[*]. Most of the post-war butchery was ordered by Joseph Stalin, under whose aegis in 1950, the foreign espionage activities had been expanded. Since mediaeval times, it had been a feature of Russian policy to look for enemies both abroad and within, such that a subversive connection existed between the two — thereby allowing the frequent usurpers of power to put the name of 'foreign collaborator' upon any group that opposed it. Although claiming to be a 'moderniser', Stalin institutionalised the suspicion of 'foreigners', 'Jews', 'international Zionists' and 'bourgeois capitalists'. It was into this culture that Blake was, unwittingly, consigning himself.

By the time his note had been passed from the KGB's Chief of Maritime Province, to the service's KI division in Moscow[**], which controlled foreign agents, it had been decided that Blake was potentially so useful that only a handful of senior officers would know about him.

Accordingly, as a holding operation, the first phase of Blake's request was responded to while more long-term measures were being put in place. KGB Chief of Maritime Province conducted initial interviews. Blake recalled Dozhdalev as being '...a big, burly man of about forty or forty five with a pale complexion...for reasons best known to himself, he wore no socks.' Another KGB officer, posing as a lecturer in Political Education, made dialogue with the rest of Blake's diplomatic group as a cover. Moscow-trained indoctrinators had been at work in the POW camps, 'converting' captured GIs from 'the error of bourgeois ways', an exercise considerably helped by the traditional system of

---

[*] It seems obscene to quibble about a million here or there, but that figure of over 40 millions, would mean that Stalin murdered about a quarter of the population for whose 'welfare' he was responsible.

[**] Komitet Informazione (Committee of Information), from 1947-52, it reported to Stalin, via Head of KGB, who would have told Stalin only what he wanted to hear.

punishment and reward, i.e. better rations for pliant young converts.

The Political Education officer was fair-haired, affable and spoke excellent, if formal English. He interviewed individual members of the group, beginning with Minister Holt whom he invited to condemn the Western 'interference' in the war. Holt refused, saying he had no instructions to that effect from his Government — and complained about being imprisoned while a diplomat. When it came to Blake's turn to be interviewed, although he met '...a young, fair Russian, with pleasant, open features...', the real dialogue was with Chief of Maritime Province, with whom he discussed his possible future work for KGB.

On returning to the group, Blake told them that the same young Russian had interviewed him, whom the newspaperman Philip Deane christened 'Blondie'. This subterfuge by Blake against his fellow captives continued during the early months of 1952. 'Blondie' interviewed all of the men in the group about once a month[*], but Blake's secret sessions were spent with Dozhdalev with whom he negotiated his 'first position'. He would supply information on SIS operations directed against the Soviet Union and its allies but would not reveal SIS activity directed against other (democratic) countries. He would accept no reward for this information and he wanted identical treatment to other prisoners, '...on whose utterances and actions I was not prepared to give any information'.

These conditions were necessary to Blake, in order that he would retain his own moral view of himself and to justify the betrayals he was about to undertake. Although he did not know it, his new political masters at Moscow Centre had since the 1930s been in receipt of similarly motivated agents in Britain, Canada, France, Germany and America. The ideological recruit to the interests of the USSR was not new

---

[*] Although a highly skilled Political Education officer, 'Blondie' did not make much headway in 'brainwashing' the other captives. In fact, the opposite happened: he later defected to America.

to them, a reflection on the culture of the 1950s in which a minority of thoughtful activists in many Western countries sincerely believed that the Soviet Union was the harbinger of a new utopia, a new world order that would eradicate inequality and therefore war.

While these conditions were being assessed at KGB Moscow Centre, Blake continued to meet with Chief of Maritime Province — who required him to write details of his SIS service and activities, including the structure of the organisation, names and rank of its officers, as well as technical expertise. Again, while Blake had the impression he was being helpful, he was later to realise it was merely a routine exercise in testing his authenticity. The files in Moscow contained more voluminous information on the structure of SIS than would have been known by Blake, a comparatively recent recruit to the service. As the meetings progressed, Blake felt himself liking Dozhdalev, to the extent they engaged in wider-ranging discussions on world politics and history.

When Blake expressed puzzlement at the cult of personality, which surrounded Stalin, saying that his understanding of Marx was that the masses and not the individual drove history, he got the impression '...that somehow he agreed with me'. All in all, KGB's Chief of Maritime Province seems to have been a skilled operator of the profession in which they were both practitioners. Handling defectors and potential agents was part of Intelligence work. Appearing to agree with their doubts and conflicts, as an exercise in 'controlled schizophrenia' was part of the job.

While thus engaged in changing sides in what was to become The Cold War, other events were taking place at Moscow Centre, which would have profound bearing on Blake's future. The coded communications from Head of Maritime Province to KI were treated with due seriousness. Blake would clearly be a major asset when he returned to Britain and progressed through the ranks of SIS. His recruitment fitted perfectly into the long-term strategy practised by Comintern, to recruit 'ideologues' whose progress in their host countries would eventually benefit the communist cause.

This had been the reasoning behind the calculated handling of the most powerful coup of modern espionage, when KGB's foreign intelligence arm, not only controlled 'the Magnificent Five' of British spies, but also co-ordinated their respective advancements within the British Intelligence establishment.

What Blake was not in a position to know, and had he known, it might have given him long pause, was that the Magnificent Five were about to be unravelled. In May of the previous year, Burgess and Maclean had fled behind the Iron Curtain, their safety from long prison sentences ensured by a combination of British laxity and KGB organisation[*]. Kim Philby, though he attempted to bluster that he was the victim of McCarthy-ite hysteria because of his 'youthful indiscretions' was no longer trusted by SIS and would shortly leave the service.

KGB Residency operating out of the Soviet Embassy in Kensington Gardens, London, had handled those spies. The London Residency operated a highly skilled team of drivers, radio operatives and decoy specialists, conducted themselves independently of other Embassy staff and made life difficult for their MI5 watchers. Because of the location of their operations base, they put personnel onto London streets via several exit points from Kensington Gardens. Radio technicians at the London Residency also managed to 'jam' MI5 radio surveillance.

A key member of KGB London was Nikolai Borisovich Rodin, who used various names, the most common of his

---

[*] British laxity may be gauged from how the Foreign Office reacted when Maclean returned from 'diplomatic sick leave' after he went on the rampage in the US, destroying a woman's bedroom in a drunken rage. After a doctor's report which indicated him to be unstable, Maclean was promoted to Head of the American Desk at the Foreign Office, from where he continued to file voluminous reports to Moscow, via KGB, London.

aliases being 'Korovin'. He was well known to the Cambridge Five. Probably on account of his success with them and the likelihood that Blake would eventually return to enhanced work in SIS at Broadway Buildings, Rodin was assigned by Moscow Centre to travel to Korea and meet with Blake. The means by which he did so reveal how structured was KGB in its organisation and the influence on the conduct of the war in Korea.

By the spring of 1952, Winston Churchill was six months back in power as Prime Minister, having been returned by an electorate tired of Labour's internal bickering and who were keen to make reparation for having voted him out after the war. Churchill, more cognisant than most of the Soviet territorial threat to the West, improved political relations with America and had given the US its first military air bases in Britain, from which nuclear strikes would be launched against the Soviet Union, if the Korean peace negotiations 'irretrievably broke down'. In response, the US gave Britain massive defence aid. KGB London had helped warn Stalin of these developments via Donald Maclean and Burgess, whose ostensible liaison work on behalf of the British Foreign Office in Washington and New York masked a stream of significant secret information to KGB.

As viewed from Moscow, it made sense that, in spite of the 'blowing' of Burgess and Maclean, the newest 'replacement' should be assessed by a KI officer already familiar with the structure of SIS and its function in British foreign policy. Nikolai Borisovich Rodin set about researching Blake and prepared to meet him in Korea, even as that prospect seemed to get a set-back in the summer of 1952. The peace talks had become bogged down over the issue of POWs and the conditions of their release on both sides. By August, hostilities had resumed with greater ferocity. Allied forces attacked Pyongyang again and American strike planes flew close to the Russian border with Korea, setting oil refineries on fire and keeping Russian planes at bay along a corridor christened 'MiG Alley'.

As the war seemed to get worse and world peace seemed fragile, George Blake heard from the Chief of Maritime Province that his offer had been accepted. On their last meeting Dozhdalev explained Blake should be patient, they would get in touch with him in time. Dozhdalev kissed him on both cheeks as they said goodbye, signifying that Blake had crossed over. We have his own account of his feelings, told like a religious conversion:

'My inward struggle was over. I had been accepted and was fully committed. There was no way back. I, too, could look upon myself as one of the many millions the world over who were actively engaged in building a new, more just society. My life would never be the same again, whatever happened. I had a purpose. Everything fell into its place'.

As the months went by and Blake did not hear from KGB, he ruminated on the deception he had embarked upon. Deception had begun in his teens with the Dutch Resistance, when he was ostensibly a schoolboy, in whose satchel were details of German troop movements. That deception was justified, so why not now for an equally good cause? After all, when an employee of the British Foreign Office, he had deceived even his mother and sister by not telling them he was also an SIS officer in which capacity he would open other people's mail, compromise or blackmail them or, '...in exceptional circumstances, organise their assassination...' (SIS in which Blake served, conducted murder of political activists who threatened Britain's overseas interests).

'One would never dream of doing any of these things as a private individual...but one is quite capable of doing them in one's official capacity when one is acting in what one believes to be the interest of one's country or one's cause'. Writing forty years after the events described, and possibly affected by a guilt he may not have felt at the time, he added: 'I do not consider there is anything clever in deceiving people who trust one and I never enjoyed doing it or exulted in it'. He thought spying '...an unfortunate necessity...As long as there will be confrontation and rivalry, as long as armed forces continue to exist and the danger of war remains...' *

War was very much on the captives' minds as they entered their third year of captivity. With peace negotiations at a stalemate, both sides became bogged down in a war of attrition and cruelty. American infantry continued to be ambushed and civilians suffered in retaliation. In November 1952, Chinese POWs in an American camp flouted an order preventing them having their own celebration of a communist anniversary. In response, American troops turned their guns on the unarmed prisoners, killing 52 and wounding 140, Further North, in communist China, preparations were made for the first 'five year plan' which would see mass murder of civilians by communist cadres. Americans elected the former head of NATO, Dwight Eisenhower as their President, with the office of Vice President for Richard Nixon. Outgoing President Harry Truman approved plans for the US to publicly explode another Hydrogen bomb, in the interests of 'weapons research.' In a signal clearly read in Moscow, the Atomic Energy Commission chose an island in the Pacific in which to explode a weapon so powerful that the island disappeared without trace.

By December, President-elect Eisenhower had visited the front line in Korea. The former Commander in Europe had been shocked by the devastation of the landscape and the casualties now running into hundreds of thousands, creating a veritable wasteland. Altogether a prospect daunting to an incoming President.

---

* Why did so many idealists become Communists, in the face of the facts? According to historian Michael Scammel, in a seminal essay, the reasons were not only political, such as Communism opposing Fascism in the 1930s, but also 'because it expressed our deepest hopes and fears...Marx promised the leap from the kingdom of the necessity to the kingdom of freedom...there is something in all of us that hopes for justice in this world and an end to inequality. Communism was successful when it made hope look less like a dream and more like a plan'. (*New Republic*, December 20, 1999).

In Mampo, meanwhile, the hostages settled down to a routine that produced spurious rows with their guards over rations or the length of their daily walks. Blake taught a French diplomat Russian by using *Das Kapital* as a textbook and did camp chores as he waited to hear from his new political masters. He maintained good relations with the missionaries, in particular Monsignor Quinlan. Quinlan's capacity to be strong under pressure and to help others, in Blake's view, bordered on the saintly.

Joseph Stalin's determination to bolster communist China meant another half a million Chinese 'volunteers' as dispensable fodder during that winter. But on March 5, 1953 Stalin died, ostensibly of a brain haemorrhage, thereby letting lose an internal carnage of bloodletting within the Politburo. Out of the apparent chaos emerged Nikita Khrushchev, a chubby ex-peasant given to fatuous smiles that belied his history as a brutal apparatchik[*]. Khrushchev organised Stalin's funeral and beat off the competition of Malenkov by having a dual power base, as Secretary of the Communist Party and also being on the Politburo (which in theory was subservient to the Party). Malenkov was given the job of Prime Minister but the power lay with Khrushchev who within weeks had encouraged the Head of KGB, Lavrenti Beria to liquidate some of Stalin's closest aides whom he deemed dangerous to his position.[**]

Nikita Khrushchev also drastically reduced the Politburo membership, thereby making it more amenable to his own control. In the classic style of a 'revolutionary' he set about reviewing the Stalinist legacy, including the prosecution of the Korean War. By April of 1953, there was an exchange of POWs, though the war continued less than a mile from the hand-over point. About a hundred GIs in padded Chinese

---

[*] Khrushchev was one of the few Politburo members whose politics did not date back to 1917. A product of the Soviets, he became a Stalin henchman, responsible for the slaughter of 2M inhabitants of the Ukraine, in efforts to increase grain production.

[**] Beria would not last long. He would be charged with being a 'Western agent' and executed.

jackets were repatriated. Some were 'zombie-like' and brainwashed. The American Army duplicated the Russian-style indoctrination by 're-educating' the suspect soldiers.

Among the hostage diplomats and missionaries, the death of Stalin produced a quick lesson in the Russian-style transition of power. As Blake recorded, the day after Stalin died, his picture disappeared from the walls of the guardroom. 'This must have been the first and most rapid de-Stalinization measure in the whole of the socialist commonwealth'. It augured well for the hostages: within a fortnight the British group, which included the surviving Irish missionaries, were on their way to Pyongyang. The North Korean use of diplomats as a 'human shield' against bombing had long been a bugbear of peace negotiations. For the first time in thirty-four months they had the pleasure of a hotel room, bathroom and clean linen. In Peking they boarded the fabled Trans-Siberian Express, bound for Moscow.

At the Otpor frontier station, the train stopped and the 'British Delegation' as they were now officially called were invited to fill out individual forms at the custom house. When it came to Blake's turn, unknown to the others, he was met by a Russian who introduced himself as Blake's future 'opposite number', with whom he would be working in London. He was about to enter upon another 'great reckoning in a little room'.

Although not named in Blake's memoir, the man at the frontier post was Nikolai Borisovich Rodin, who had travelled from London via a circuitous route to Otpor to complete the recruitment of the British SIS officer. In the back room of the custom house, the two trained spies established a working practice and a system of signals for a future meeting in Holland. Then Blake got back aboard the Peking-Moscow Express. His future controller also went aboard and settled into the journey, occupying a compartment on his own, three carriages away from Blake.

Thus separated and at the same time intimate, Blake and Rodin travelled for five days across Siberia, neither making conversation or showing any signs of recognition as they alighted at regular stations for a break, where they passed each other on walks along platforms. Blake was now an agent of the Russian Security Service, whose activities on behalf of 'state security' had killed more of its subjects than any foreign enemy and whose scale of murder would exceed that of the Nazis. A file would be opened for him in the Lubyanka archives under the code-name of DIOMID and access to it 'severely restricted'.

Arriving in Moscow, the former hostages were taken to the British Embassy where they dined in the splendour of the 19th century building overlooking the Moscva river and with the lights of the Kremlin glowing across the river. The Head of Moscow SIS station observed his arrival from a vantage point in the Embassy but did not make himself known, even though both had been close colleagues back in London.

Then the group was bound for Britain via an RAF ambulance plane, which landed at Abingdon airfield, Oxfordshire on a Sunday afternoon in April. Although the war in Korea would not end for another four months, the arrival of the British diplomats was seen as a hopeful gesture. The safe arrival home of Commissioner Lord was celebrated by the Salvation Army band rendering *'Now Thank We All Our God'*, as the group stood on the steps of the aircraft. During the melee of greetings, Blake made straight for his mother. It was the second time war had forced separation and re-union.

There were press and TV interviews and questions about conditions in captivity. A tall, elegant man in a black coat and brolly took Blake aside, welcomed him back on behalf of SIS and asked that he present himself at room 070 of the War Office the following week. Then Blake said meaningful goodbyes to the other hostages with whom he had spent almost three years in captivity, whose strengths and weaknesses he knew so well, as they knew his, with one crucial exception. They did not know he had become a Soviet agent.

From now on, he would attempt to weaken the defences of their way of life, out of belief in a wider cause and 'greater good'. Had the kind of Communism from whose clutches he had been released made inroads into Western Europe, through the effort of sufficient like him, he would have had some hard choices to make. But in the euphoria of being back in England, he probably did not see it that way...

CHAPTER NINE

BOURKE — THE MISSING YEARS

Although Sean Bourke distinguished himself in the RAF old habits threatened his new stability. While the rank of Boy Sergeant satisfied his desire to excel, the role became more than his deviant nature could control. Thefts from stores and rumours of misconduct led to interviews with his superiors. With compelling plausibility he denied the allegations. He enjoyed defending himself against his accusers.

His stance was that systems were there to be overcome. As it was, in the hiatus of 1951, anyone in service uniform functioned in the after-glow of victory, carrying a kudos, which the nation felt for its servicemen. British troops were again active — in Africa against the Mau Mau and in Korea against communists. Being in the armed forces earned respect.

He exploited that goodwill. With his handsome looks, facile charm and smart turnout, he found easy access to all he wanted. But surface satisfactions were not sufficient. The log of complaints built up at RAF depots.

Bourke went missing. After a series of allegations in late '53, he went away and turned up at the London 'digs' of an older brother. Irish labour was in inexhaustible demand in the post-war building boom. Real names were rarely used. Contractors, sub-contractors and gangers engaged in mutual conspiracy to withhold tax, falsify figures and maximise profits. It was easy for a fit young man to move in and out of work...

He found a niche in that subterranean culture, working as a labourer and bricklayer. For some months he lived in the Acton area of London, home to colonies of Limerick immigrants. His accent also implied a higher lifestyle than that of a labourer. In the evening, divested of builder's muck, he dressed well and kept different company. He bought *The Times* and liked to discuss politics and world news with educated habitués of his local. Oddly enough, as someone who knew him then recalled, Bourke had pretensions to 'being an Englishman' (an uncle had made his wealth from dealing in feathers and scrap. 'Feathery' Bourke fled Limerick every summer to take a world cruise, where he donned the dress of an old Anglo-Irish merchant).

In his nephew, old tendencies asserted after an evening's drinking. If there was mischief about or a practical joke that ran out of hand, Bourke was given to much self-dramatisation afterwards. Ordinary life bored him. He yearned for high drama and the adrenalin of danger.

Following an after-pub incident, which involved the police, Bourke left Acton and moved South of the river to Camberwell. Although his means of livelihood were unclear, he made a hit with the local amateur Shakespeare Society, performing roles in a rich mellifluous voice. He entertained ideas of becoming a professional actor, influenced by the success in London of Richard Harris, also an émigré from Limerick. But he had no secure means of earning and drifted off again, this time to Crawley New Town which was one of the early 'new towns' of mid-fifties Britain, vaunted as an experiment in social living. Building Crawley required much labour to fulfil the dream of post-war change; Bourke was possibly attracted by reports of high earnings and a new 'scene' where he might make a new life for himself.

He picked up many skills of the building trade. He built brick walls, which his colleagues admired, taking pride in the plumb-line register of height and scale. His time in the RAF had made him an expert telegrapher. Repairs to radios, electrical circuitry and on-site machinery made him popular with 'subbies', the sub-contractors who made profits from the piecework of the labour they employed.

He was now officially listed as a deserter from the RAF but as he had enlisted in his real name and was now working in Crawley under an alias, he could stay free of gaol and uniform. Even that freedom bored him. There were more break-ins and caught on one, at an RAF station, he appeared before Shrewsbury magistrates on the 11th June 1954 and was sentenced to Borstal Training, being one year below the age of legal adulthood. The theft was of a radio transmission set.

He served one year and four months in what was a third level institute for criminal education. Inside, he perfected his expertise in electronics and made underworld contacts. While in Crawley he had made friends from among the incoming population of a new town. On his release in October 1955 he decided to 'settle' in Crawley and with the confidential help of the parole board, Bourke moved a step back into ordinary living with a job as a factory hand in Manor Royal.

Once again, he was trying to 'go straight.' He said as much to himself as he left the gates of the Borstal. Wits and demeanour sharpened, he was finished with law breaking as a mug's game. He despised most of the villains he had met inside. He thought them ill educated and crass. England of the mid-fifties was a vibrant place for a young man, if he could only stay on the right side of the law.

So it seemed to him, as he got 'digs' in Ifield Road, Crawley. He was neat and tidy and an early riser. He engaged in the factory's social club and was a popular singer at functions. From that time, he is remembered as extremely handsome, with a smile and charm and a ready line in chat. He played to the English idea of the 'charming, witty Irishman.'

Irishmen of his kind were never taken quite at face value, though the extent of his private practices would have surprised even those who suspected some darker side to his nature. Most knew him as an agreeable, well-read and highly intelligent companion who liked to discourse on many subjects. But Bourke bored easily with routine minds and needed the lift of his own 'other world', to maintain his own fascination with himself. In that, he was similar to George Blake.

During 1955, however, he subsumed those instincts in a determined effort to rehabilitate himself and took pride in his changeover. The RAF training did not go amiss: his ability with electrical repairs, his erudite command of language, his capacity to motivate others — all combined to push him into the forefront of social activities that a new town valued.

Life for Bourke was golden in those years. He was in the bloom of his early twenties, mixed easily and was socially popular. He founded a jazz club and was featured in the 'Teens and Twenties' pages of the *Crawley Observer.*

The club prospered with two hundred members. A few months later, he joined the ATC as a civilian instructor in Wireless Telegraphy. It was both a rash and daring move, expressing in perfect swing the lure of his nature. He had been convicted of the theft of a radio transmission set while AWOL. Now discharged and returned to civilian life, after a decent interval he took his chances and re-joined the Air Training Corps — as a wireless telegrapher!

He was in part-time service for four months when he was promoted Squadron Warrant Officer, responsible for discipline throughout the unit, supervising cadets at RAF camp each summer and setting standards in telegraphy. He spent ten hours a week outside his factory work in the ATC, which is a cadet corps for youngsters who make a subsequent career in the Air Force. His enigmatic identity of an assembly line worker by day and social host by evening attracted goodwill from local managers who thought Bourke was destined for higher things.

Efforts were made to get him office work, to put him into the white-collar social grade, which marked the pecking order of new towns in the Conservative Britain of the 1950s. In October 1959, four years after he had arrived in Crawley from Borstal, the Metal Box Company took him on as an accounts clerk in the wages section. October held a private significance for him, marking major transitions in his life. He had been released from two periods of Borstal in that month and had made seminal decisions about his life. In October 1959, had his make-up been different, he might have set out a new life as a middle-class upholder of suburban values. Might have...

In that month he resigned from the Air Training Corps, saying the pressure of two jobs was too much. In fact, as he reasoned with himself, the real pressure was to accept a commission. The repeated recommendations from his superiors to accept officer rank were becoming embarrassing. He had a foreboding his record would turn up in the vetting conducted by the Air Ministry before commissions were confirmed. His whole new life in Crawley would come tumbling down. So he resigned from the ATC, not without private bitterness.

Such was his reputation for youth work, however, that a Captain R.J. Bannister, C.O. of the Army Cadet Force in Crawley asked him to join them. Bannister knew Bourke's work and, in the competitive spirit of the services, thought he could use Bourke's abilities. Bourke made it a condition that it be non-commissioned in a part-time role. So a few months after resigning from the Air Army, he was in demand again, with the Army cadets.

He took on making an electronic Quiz Panel, of the type popular in television games. To help him, two army cadets called to his house during holiday time. On 26th July 1960, one of the cadets, was stopped by a plain-clothes police officer, asked to turn out his pockets and account for his movements. It was no different from the kind of questioning an innocent might undergo in the course of, say, local burglary enquiries. There had been a spate of break-ins in that vicinity. The young Cadet was also asked about Bourke and he told of the Quiz Panel. As the questioning continued, the youngster grew mystified. The police officer said he could go, adding: 'I hope there is no funny business going on at that house between you people.'

When the young Cadet told Bourke, he went berserk.

CHAPTER TEN

BLAKE — MAKING OF A DOUBLE AGENT

Earlier, while Sean Bourke worked as a labourer in the building of Crawley New town, the Korean War was over and Blake was on prolonged leave back in England. He was thirty-one years of age, an unmarried and 'un-established' Foreign Office employee. Underneath the sober dark suit, the uniform of his attendance at offices in Victoria and Whitehall, he was a more experienced hand at espionage than many of his contemporaries.

In recognition of his ordeal in Korea, C — Head of SIS, welcomed him back personally. The meeting had taken place behind the legendary green door so beloved of James Bond moviemakers. The Office of C was on the fourth floor of Broadway Buildings, which backed onto elegant Queen Anne's Gate, close to St. James's Park. Hence the obligatory park scene, replete with ducks in British espionage thrillers. When Blake reported to Broadway Buildings and made his way along twisty 18th-century stairs to the office of C, he met Major-General Sir John Sinclair. According to Kim Philby's memoirs, Sinclair was 'not overburdened with mental gifts' — but the Major-General was also 'humane and energetic', qualities which made him want to hear from Blake at first-hand how he had coped with captivity.

Blake found him kindly but embarrassed when the issue came up of how the British diplomats had been captured. Sinclair said it was a pity they had not left before the takeover. Blake reminded him that his own instructions had been to stay in the event of war. Moreover these orders had come from Sinclair himself when briefing Blake on the mission more than three years before...

Sinclair changed the subject, wished him well and suggested he take a few months leave to recuperate, while the Service discussed a future assignment. Blake had already been 'debriefed' by two colleagues, who had spent a morning testing him for some unspecified effects of 'brainwashing'. In the best British tradition, the discussion had been polite and languorous, in room 070 of the War Office, behind Horse Guards Parade, a room that was traditionally used by SIS to interview potential recruits. Blake was clearly a more seasoned campaigner than his two interviewers, who appeared mainly interested in the communists' techniques of interrogation. He was able to tell them that he had not been tortured or ill treated, though the conditions of captivity had been onerous.

Later questioning had focussed on what he might have gleaned about Russian nuclear capability. They thought it a pity he had not brought back a sample of earth form Siberia, which they could have their boffins test for traces of atomic explosion. Hiding his amusement, Blake offered his shoes, which he had worn since his journey on the Peking-Moscow express. Sensing the absurdity, the offer was declined. The de-briefing lasted two days, ended amicably — and Blake took up C's offer of prolonged leave by spending his accumulated salary on a new Ford Anglia car, with which he journeyed to Holland with his mother and sister. He revived the arrangement, which he had memorised at Otpor in Siberia, about meeting Nikolai Borisovich Rodin.

He strolled down a main avenue in The Hague and into another film cliché. In the square, waiting on a park-bench was his contact, carrying, as agreed months before, a local newspaper. Blake has conducted a practiced anti-surveillance run beforehand, as had 'the man from Otpor', alias Nikloi Rodin. Though neither were to know it at the time, their precautions were sensible. Later documents revealed that Rodin had evaded routine security surveillance on his visit to Holland. One can only speculate how short would have been Blake's career for the Soviets, had Rodin not managed to evade the Dutch Security Service, from whom MI5 had requested a routine monitor on Rodin's visit.

During that meeting on the park bench, Blake and Rodin set up the tradecraft for subsequent meetings back in London. They agreed signals, dead letter drops, 'brush' contacts and emergency telephone numbers. Locations were chosen near

Underground railway stations, for ease of arrival and departure and to evade Rodin's stable of MI5 'watchers'. For Blake, this first meeting was uneasy; he did not take to Rodin, the way he had taken to his first KGB contact in Korea, '...too much of the iron fist in the velvet glove...' he felt, a situation not helped by the headlines in the paper they were both carrying, which blazoned the arrest of Lavrenti Beria, the head of the Soviet Secret Police, on charges of being a 'Western Agent'. Clearly, Khrushchev intended to have his own intelligence service, reporting to himself. The new Chairman of the Politburo had not forgotten Beria's bloody record in eliminating 'enemies' of Stalin — the new head of the USSR had an all too personal knowledge of those murders, in which he was complicit, in his own route to the top.

Rodin called upon his experience with other British agents, consoling Blake by telling him that his own case was watertight. Only a few at the very top of the Soviet Foreign Secret Service would know of agent DIOMID. For their part, the Russians had already valued DIOMID as a prize possession. He spoke five languages, was war-weathered, and had no vices, which had been the downfall of others — no addiction to gambling, drink or sexual deviancy. Moreover Blake was in a position to form judgements on the political world.

He was in many respects a cut apart from his colleagues in both the Foreign Office and the Secret Intelligence Service. More to the point, from the Soviet interest, Blake was about to be appointed to Y Section of SIS, specialising in 'wiring and miking' embassies of the Eastern Bloc. The British were regarded as leaders in 'tech ops'. Whatever advance information Blake could deliver on likely targets for electronic surveillance would be highly valuable to KGB who would alert sister services in the satellite states. Even more than Russia itself, the stability of the satellite states annexed after the war depended on subduing the native populations with secret service methods.

Even as the two spies conferred on the park bench in The Hague, measures were already in place in Moscow to handle Blake circumspectly. Maclean and Burgess were in sanitised safekeeping; Philby was neutered and awaiting only further revelations. Other double agents in SIS must have been developing nervous twitches[*]. Moscow Centre decided an entirely different 'cell' would be created for Blake. Rodin would be moved from KGB Resident, London. As he had been instrumental in organising the defections of Maclean and Burgess, Moscow felt he would be heavily targeted by MI5 in revenge.

Accordingly, a career KGB officer, then serving in a Scandinavian state, was recalled to Moscow and underwent training to specifically become Blake's case officer in London. Though Blake fails to identity him, the chosen one was Sergei Aleksandrovich Kondrashev who prepared for his assignment by studying maps of the London transport system, especially its bus and underground routes. By the time he had memorised the DIOMID file, he felt he knew Blake already. In October of 1953 he arrived to the Embassy in Kensington Gardens, London as a First Secretary (Cultural Affairs) by which title his arrival was notified to the Russian Desk of the British Foreign Office. SIS identified him as KGB and posted his details as routine to MI5, for the 'watch' list.

As it happened, Kondrashev was an able evader of surveillance. He had been told in Moscow the British 'watchers', sticklers for punctuality, began their surveillance of suspect KGB officers promptly at nine — usually not before. In the murk of a London autumn, it only required being out of the house earlier for Kondrashev to have a head start on his pursuers. It is worth defining here the operational differences between various foreign services. The British Foreign Office ran two distinct services in tandem. Not all Foreign Office officials were automatically in the Intelligence Service. The majority were straight-forward Civil Servants,

---

[*] Among the nervous were Blunt, Cairncross, Long, Melita Norwood and others yet to be publicly 'outed'.

nurtured in the concept of service to their country. Chosen for their abilities, fluency in languages and 'presentability', most were career diplomats who in time could expect to become Ambassador or Permanent Secretary, ascending the heights of the diplomatic ladder.

Those who were in SIS, on the other hand, could expect a more adventurous life with a guaranteed amount of danger. An eventual Ambassadorship was not barred to them, but in practice only a minority of SIS activists achieved that rank. Most had so dirtied their hands in covert operations it was deemed unwise to expose them to the scrutiny of representing Britain as Ambassadors in territories where their past records might be publicised. To cite from an SIS training lecture, diplomats and politicians were captains on the bridge — spies were stokers below deck. Or as it was put 'diplomats were swans — spies were geese'. A swan could swan-it over a goose any day.

By contrast KGB dominated the Soviet Foreign Service. In a Russian embassy, the nominal Ambassador had the trappings of power — the car with the national flags, the secretaries, and the invitations to functions in the host country. But the real power in an eastern European embassy lay with the *Residentura* — KGB's Resident who could pull rank on matters which affected 'State Security'. As the Russians saw it, conditioned by their insular and bloody history, full-scale, determined espionage made them equipped to conduct traditional diplomacy better. The major spies in the West believed in the Communist Manifesto and thought they were maintaining the 'balance of power' by giving to 'inferior Russia' the secrets of Western technology.

This was the world Blake returned to, after the bout of convalescence. Welcomed back to SIS and with spurs earned in Korea, he was appointed Deputy Director of Technical Operations. He led several operations abroad, targeting embassies and hotels in European capitals used by diplomats of the USSR and its satellite states. Entry was made with the co-operation, of the local authorities who provided cover while the wiring was installed. Blake supervised the installations, liased with the local security agencies and wrote a report for his Head of Y section, Peter Lunn, who had made his name in SIS by running intercepts from the Vienna Tunnel. An international competitive skier, Lunn was at home in Austria, where he had conducted a phone-tapping operation against Soviet communications which had excavated material of prime value in determining the strength and disposition of Eastern Block forces after the war.

By October, Blake was also doubling for KGB and reporting regularly to Kondrashev on the operations of Y Section. Blake's memoirs do not identify Kondrashev, but we can take it that his KGB case officer was fully informed of SIS monitoring of an international conference in Geneva in May 1954. Meeting to resolve outstanding matters from the war in Korea were foreign ministers of America, Soviet Union, Britain and China. With the aid of the Swiss security service, taps were put on telephone lines into the main bedrooms of the communist delegations. Blake led the team, holed-up in the suburbs that analysed the tapes. As he rather blandly recalled: '...the communist delegations observed strict telephone security. They never discussed anything with even a remote bearing on their position and tactics...or gave an inkling as to what concessions they might be prepared to make...'. A hardly surprising observation, since agent DIOMID, via London and Moscow, had alerted them that efficient telephone taps were in place on their hotels. For Blake, reading the conversations, there must have been the divided feelings of seeing the Soviet and Chinese ministers being security conscious, while at the same time having little to offer his superiors from the resources of Y section of SIS.

In understanding that time, two perceptions may be kept in mind. The first is the bitterness with which the 'Cold War' raged along the frontier of a divided Europe. It was a solid stalemate of confrontation — the magazines of the 'free West' showed pictures of Russian soldiery as ignorant, threatening and murderous, a species as foreign as it was possible to imagine, whose high-stepping rituals confirmed the reports of mass torture in Russian territories. Everywhere the Russian bear put his claws, misery, deprivation and mass executions followed. So opined *Life*, *Paris Match* and *Picture Post*, magazines then dominant in how opinion was moulded.

The second perception is that same Russian Bear had ten years before laid down in the winter wastes of the Russian snow to halt the Fascist advance on Eastern Europe — which had it succeeded, would have brought into Nazi domination the largest continent, stretching from Europe through Asia. The cost in Russian lives and suffering had been so immense that only those with a comprehension of Russian optimism since the Revolution could appreciate the depth of sacrifice. That was how the idealistic agents felt under their masks. Of all the countries, which affected political thought in Europe and America, Russia was the dominant power of the 1950s, the country about which most information was sought and whose State excesses under Stalin horrified public opinion in the West. In an exercise of 'controlled schizophrenia', the secret agents of the USSR remained embedded in the secret Etablishments of The West.

It was not easy. Maclean's drinking, the odd behaviour of Burgess and Philby's philandering were sometimes put down to the pressures of serving simultaneously two masters. Although the pressures were great — Philby has written of feeling abandoned by his Russian mentors — alcoholism, homosexuality and compulsive fornication are already in the system of individuals, though the pressures of the double life may sharpen the appetites. Blake displayed none of these 'character defects'. He was sober to the point of being regarded as dull by his colleagues — an impression that suited his double life.

Once a week, by devious routes, he met Kondrashev and passed over to him almost every document of any importance that crossed his desk. It was a formidable task of betrayal, over two years, using a variety of methods. Blake used a miniature Minox camera, but sometimes when time did not allow for photographs or his own 'eyes only' carbon copy was the only one available, he took those — an undeveloped strip of film and carbon copies and passed them to Kondrashev in a variety of locations. A cinema near Baker Street was one hand-over point; a railway platform on his way home was another. The top deck of a London bus going south over Waterloo Bridge was the place where one key briefing paper was handed to KGB — a document whose subsequent transmission to Moscow laid the ground for what would become one of the great coups — and failures — of Cold War espionage.

Because of the importance of intelligence being generated from Peter Lunn's tunnel in Vienna, it was resolved between CIA and SIS to mount a more ambitious operation along the same lines in Berlin. The British were the prime movers, providing their exemplary expertise in technical matters — recording, monitoring, transcribing and indexing. Because access to the cables would have to be engineered from the American sector, the nearest Allied Territory, the Americans would build the tunnel under the cover of an existing army warehouse close to the border and would also carry much of the cost. The tunnel would be about a quarter of a mile, would go under the border in Berlin into Eastern Europe and access the landline cables of Soviet Group Forces.

Although Western spy agencies had a multiplicity of sources in Eastern Germany, on the ground as it were, there were ponderous gaps in its knowledge of the size, deployment and disposition of Russian army, air force and rocket units, from whence would likely come 'second strike' retaliatory attacks in the event of 'global hostilities'.

As devised over many meetings in Berlin, Frankfurt, Vienna, London and Washington, the tunnel would rectify that 'information deficit'. The monitoring would build up a fuller picture of The Order of Battle — the key information about the adversary which every army needs before conflict. Because of the detailed work compiled by CIA Berlin, the key cables were already identified. What remained was to develop equipment to separate the voice and telegraphy channels, translate the traffic from German and Russian and ship it to skilled analysts to make mosaic of the disparate discussions. In the tense climate of the time, both sides were sure the other would strike first.

It was a highly ambitious, well thought-out project, the results of two years concerted research. It would involve considerable resources from US and British Army engineers, from teams of tappers, translators and transcribers to monitor, on shifts, 81 speech circuits. It was approved by Allen Dulles, Director of CIA and by his opposite number in SIS. It would cost millions of dollars. In the week before Christmas, a group of CIA officers met with nine SIS counterparts in London to agree the blueprint, code-named 'stopwatch / gold'. A month later on top of a red double-decker bus, agent DIOMID handed the over the minutes of the meeting to his KGB case officer. The material was deemed so sensitive that according to one report, it was carried in a steel case to Moscow. The case had an explosive device indented in the locking mechanism, which would have blown the fingers off any MI5 agent intent on opening it by hand. The Russians would know all about the tunnel before the digging had even begun.

CHAPTER ELEVEN

BERLIN — SWAMP OF ESPIONAGE

During the 1950s in Berlin, the secret services of East and West became an industry unto themselves. The failure by Russia to honour the treaties, which marked the end of the war, meant that a new war was declared, albeit without the formal declaration of hostilities. Russia believed that the Allies were conspiring against it. The Allies, on the other hand, were made fearful by the militaristic expansion of the Soviet Empire. Russia refused to leave territories it had occupied in the drive westward to conquer Berlin — in effect laying down what Churchill christened 'the Iron Curtain' that divided a Europe reduced to wasteland by war. Underneath the stalemate of suspicion, this war was prosecuted by the respective secret services.

In particular, America and Russia beefed up their intelligence gathering. Both ideologies were growing in post-war energy, in critical mass, in forging identities completely opposed to each other. Crucial to their difference was the way life was lived within their respective territories. The Union of Soviet Socialist Republics functioned as an enforcement of diverse nationalities whose innate desire to break free of Centralism and govern their own affairs was thwarted by a massive secret police force. The USSR it may be fairly said, was held together by internal terror, based on external threat. In a neat trick of psychological conjuring, the antagonism of The West, caused by Soviet illegal annexation of territories, was held by Russia's rulers to justify mass terror upon its own population.

In extreme contrast, America functioned as a voluntary federation of states, whose common interest focussed on individual prosperity and fulfilment. Americans held a genuine belief in the virtues of democracy, just as most Soviet citizens sincerely believed in the collective credo: 'from each according to his abilities, to each according to his needs...' But individual Americans had more control over their own lives than Soviet citizens had over theirs, though communist governments persisted in the illusion of equality. As in all wars, each side exaggerated their own virtues and emphasised the vices of the enemy.

Berlin, flattened city and symbol of a defeated Germany, was divided by the Allies into self-governing sectors, administered by French, British, American and Russian control commissions. The allied commissions, generously intent on rebuilding Germany, sprouted ancillary functions, which were used for spying activities towards the Russian sector. By the time George Blake arrived in the spring of 1955, the profession of espionage in Berlin had assumed a day-to-day reality; he joined a group of about thirty SIS officers who operated out of the Olympic Stadium, where Hitler's Third Reich had conducted massive propaganda exercises during the rise of National Socialism.

Blake had been married the previous summer, to his secretary Gillian Allen, with whom he had worked in Broadway Buildings. Her father was a Russian specialist within SIS. Such service marriages were not unusual and were regarded by the management as easing the domestic pressures incurred in the nature of the work. Gillian was typical of the well-spoken, well-educated 'young gel' from the Home Counties who worked in the secretariat of SIS. Most had been educated at the same fee-paying schools, spoke with upper-class accents and in office lore, were marked as 'off games' during menstrual leave.

Between the Dutch-born colleague of thirty-three and the very English Gillian Allen, ten years his junior, there was genuine love and affection. Blake had the aura of a war-proved hero, having been in the Resistance in Holland and later a captive of the communists in North Korea. His affectionate concern for his mother, now adjusting to English life and heavily dependent on George for support, had also impressed Gillian. The wedding, in the Marylebone district of London, within walking distance of many SIS safe houses, was attended by colleagues from 'the office'.

What none of them knew and a matter of which Gillian could not have an inkling, was that she was also marrying agent DIOMID of KGB. Blake discussed his misgivings about the marriage with his Russian controller before embarking upon another layer of deception. As he rationalised: 'if I told her that I was a Soviet agent, she would be absolutely horrified. What is more, I would confront her with a choice with which nobody should be confronted, let alone a young and inexperienced girl...' '...if I broke off the relationship, without giving a very convincing reason, she would never understand and be terribly hurt'.

Recommended by Kondrashev to proceed as part of his acquired Britishness, Blake resolved his misgivings by comparing himself to a soldier who might go the front a day after being married. In his line of business, life held no guarantees. He did, however, believe strongly in predestination. He had met Gillian, they had fallen in love. He would follow the logic of that and hope the 'for worse' part of the bargain would not turn out to be too terrible. He arrived in Berlin, as a recently married officer of SIS, with a devoted, compatible wife and a series of professional assignments.

Among the spying professionals, Berlin was known as 'the swamp of espionage'. Every second person, it was said, was an agent for at least one of the occupying powers and in many cases were double agents. While the professional intelligence officers of the French, British, American and Russian powers were trained in the tradecraft of their profession; they relied on native Germans for the bulk of 'product' — the day-to-day gossip of the other side's personnel and movements.

A sub-industry was spawned among the German population, that of earning a black market salary by supplying duplicated detail to the Allied intelligence services and then crossing the sectors to reveal the activities of their Allied handlers to the East German and Soviet intelligence services. It was truly a quagmire in which many a spying career seemed at first to flourish, only later to flounder in a

Germany sundered with sharply divided loyalties. Early on, in his ostensible work as an SIS operative, Blake found some of his calculated efforts running into the sand. Because West Berlin was out of bounds to senior personnel in the Russian sector, he devised a scheme to lure male officers of the Soviet Group into the West and compromise them. Many of the senior Soviet military were under pressure to bring back nylons, silk underwear and jewellery to their wives. Where the married officers also had girlfriends, the pressure was more immediate and they relied upon German workers who had free access to the shops in the Western Sector to purchase these goods.

It was a scenario for the 'honey-trap' operations of which all the intelligence services had experience.

As the SIS station built up a file of Russian commanders and their foibles, George Blake devised a scheme to set up an 'exclusive shop' in an apartment, to which German 'leg-men' would entice their Soviet bosses. Using various aliases, such as Herr Stephen (German) or de Vries (Dutch), Blake, masquerading as a black market businessman, would hope to meet Russian military personnel and try to turn them as agents of SIS. The ruse appeared to work and Russian targets were being cultivated when the entire operation had to be wound down as SIS entered into a deniable mode.

One morning, months after 'the shop' was operational, the German manager, with the stage-name of Trautmann, did a runner — and emerged on the front-pages of East German newspapers as a double-agent who had been working for the Russians, thereby 'trumping' the SIS operation. Gone with him was the expensive stock of Western luxury goods; doubtless they had to be written off in some creative accounting at Olympic Stadium.

George and Gillian Blake settled down to make a home among the espionage community. It was the early years of their marriage and they had a spacious five-roomed apartment in a residential suburb, enhanced as a family unit by the birth of their first child, a son christened Anthony.

Gillian well understood the work which engaged her husband, though not his real double role.

Max Calling...

Blake, would deny involvement in the case of Major Pyotr Popov, one of the success stories of American intelligence activity, though the outcome for Popov was fatal. The importance of the Popov case is not only how it characterised espionage activity during the cold war but also how it gave insight into the deeper fissures of ideology between Russia and the West.

The handling of Major Pyotr Popov of GRU (Military Intelligence) involved keeping him in place for six years while he provided information which was costed by CIA analysts as being worth half-a-billion dollars, priced at then rates of electronic surveillance. Code-named BIGOT, the operation demanded the concentration of a handful of senior CIA officers. Information from Popov enabled the United States to have a copy of Khrushchev's six-hour denunciation of Stalin to the Soviet Praesidium and deployments of Soviet forces in Eastern Europe. That such a massive army of half a million soldiers could have been engaged in hostilities was a likely prospect at the time. The Berlin Blockade of 1948, followed by communist expansion during the 1950s and the brinkmanship of Korea, had concentrated the minds of Western Intelligence agencies on the urgent need to know the Soviet Order of Battle. Popov provided it in detail, during years of regular meetings.

A thirty-year old major in GRU, when his contact with CIA began in early 1953, Popov was well placed to supply a stream of information from his work in the Soviet military police force. Popov's gains were financial and personal but driven mainly by profound disenchantment with the Soviet system. Although attaining the military rank, which Communism promised bright and hard-working careerists, Popov was a country boy at heart. On visits home to the agricultural heartland, which fed the cities, Popov could not reconcile the bright hope of Communism with the drudgery, which he saw his brother and sister endure. As a peasant family they had grown up among a community of serfs on a large farm. Showing academic promise, Popov had been taken on the fast-track selection process, which the system marked out for the special. But Stalin's destruction of private farms had dumped the other Popov siblings into a collective where they had less status than as serfs.

Although hailed by propaganda as the promised equaliser of peasants with their landlords, the 'collectevi' farms were a disaster. The old system had tied landlord and serf to mutual obligations and it had worked. Each knew their place; the dignity that went with it, and importantly, the peasant received a share of the farm produce. Now, as Popov found on visits home, his brother and sister were worse off — as labourers sharing a one-roomed unsanitary hut in respite from gruelling hours on the farm.

Was it for this he had studied all his teenage years, become a graduate of the Russian Military Academy, had been willingly recruited into the elite GRU and posted to Vienna — watching and reporting on armed forces' loyalty, fulfilling the great mission of peace — while his family declined below the status of serf? This was the complaint, which his CIA handlers gleaned, in their initial cautious response to his overtures. As part of their testing that he was not a potential double agent, they left American farm magazines as reading material in the safe house for Popov to read. He in turn was sceptical that such magazines, with their detailed articles and photographs of vast holdings represented the truth of American agriculture. It seemed a vista beyond the imagining of anyone growing up under Communism.

Not very deep in the peasant folk memory lay the experience of getting the short end of the stick, from whichever prevailing power. Popov had money and marriage problems, compounding his alienation from his own country. He illustrated one of CIA's working slogans: 'The peasant is the Achilles heel of Soviet Communism.' He was also a 'walk-in'. The Russian had approached a known American

Intelligence officer in Vienna in 1952, offering information. Once he was accepted as genuine, CIA flew in a fluent Russian speaker whose parents had fled the Revolution[*]. During the next five years, he was adroitly milked of substantive knowledge by a small team of CIA whose reports ran to thousands of pages. He became the 'jewel in the crown' of American espionage efforts in Europe, supplying crucial information across the range of Russian military forces — to the extent that for a further twenty years the Americans held a classified clamp on his existence.

Within the group of CIA handlers, Popov was known as 'Max'. He was often late for meetings, sometimes taking chances of discovery in journeys to West Berlin which surprised them for an officer of the fabled GRU division. Popov's information during the mid-50s was routed to Washington, where Richard Helms, in charge of CIA operations against the Soviets, personally appraised The President. In return, much of what Popov revealed was used to justify the growing budget of CIA, then being converted from the wartime OSS into a giant intelligence-gathering agency.

Already one of the Agency's influential figures, James Angleton harboured doubts about Kim Philby, due to the failure of two key operations of which Philby, as head of the anti-Soviet section of SIS, had knowledge. An obsessive and introvert, Angleton spent much time pondering and, correctly, ascribed the failure to Philby's other role, as a high-level Soviet agent. But Philby had been personally cleared in Parliament by P.M. Macmillan. Though time was to prove Angleton correct, in the early stages of the Popov case all Angleton could do was instruct the case officers to exclude SIS from the Popov operation. According to the subsequent American post-mortem, however, even that stricture did not insure against a casual comment, which, in one American view, betrayed Operation BIGOT.

---

[*] CIA officer George Kisevalter, born in St. Petersburg, known to Popov as 'Col Grossman', US Army.

By 1955 Popov had been promoted to a full Lieutenant Colonel in GRU and due for another promotional posting, which was usually preceded by a period in Moscow, to 'de-contaminate' officers who had served in proximity to the West. In Pyotr Popov's case, as we know, the damage had already been done through the unlikely aegis of American farm magazines. The routine return to Moscow put CIA in a quandary. Popov's worth to them was such the Agency decided not to risk contact in the Russian capital where their officers, under diplomatic cover, were likely to be under such surveillance as would put at risk their source. Reluctantly, CIA decided to wait under Popov resumed a posting near the West. In the meantime, teams of analysts trawled through his material, which among other gems supplied the full manual of Soviet Group Forces for 1951, at a time when CIA had yet to find the 1947 manual.

Encouraged field officers painstakingly made contact with Popov and instructed that his resumed de-briefing should initially be arranged by telephone through a series of coded calls in Moscow. He would introduce himself to the switchboard as 'Max Calling'. In the event, he was posted to Berlin. Through a quirk in his personality, Popov ignored the arrangement and approached two British SIS officers whose identities he knew from his own GRU reports. Popov followed one into a toilet, handed him a letter and left. The officer handed the letter to the SIS station. There, in the kind of casual comment upon which life-and-death turns, the colleague translating the letter from Russian said 'Looks like Harvey's got a GRU case in the Zone'. The reference was to William Harvey, Head of CIA station, Berlin. According to former CIA officer, William Hood[*], the listener was George Blake. Blake has consistently denied he was the source of Popov's unmasking. In the 'wilderness of mirrors', such conflicts are impossible to resolve on empirical evidence. Perhaps, as often, the truth lies obscured, with each side extracting their version for public consumption.

---

[*] *Mole,* William Hood, Weidenfeld and Nicolson, London, 1982.

According to Sergei Kondrashev, who was Blake's senior KGB case officer, Blake had no involvement in revealing the Popov role in operation BIGOT. This denial is confirmed by the General of KGB, who oversaw the Popov investigation, who also says Blake (DIOMID) had no role in the unmasking. As seen by Maj. General Valentin Zvezdenkov, suspicion fell upon Popov because of failed operations and his volatile love life, in which the mistress whose welfare had first incurred him to sell secrets, later defected from Communism because of the invasion of Hungary. When the relationship with her married lover finished, she approached the Russian authorities with her allegations about his 'loyalties'.

From the same KGB perspective, however, an enquiry, which may have originated with DIOMID, may have unwittingly brought Popov into the frame. Among the many prized pieces of intelligence which Popov sold to the Americans was the text of a speech by the Soviet Defence Minister, Marshall Georgi Zhukov, to a closed session of military commanders of Soviet Group Forces, Germany. Zhukov was regarded as formidable by the American State Department, being among the handful of Russian commanders who were instrumental in beating back the German advance in Russia. He was known to influence Soviet foreign policy. What he had to say in closed session in Karlshorst in March 1957 set the alarm bells ringing in Washington and more than justified CIA investment in Popov.

In preparing his commanders for readiness for war with the West, Marshall Zhukov revealed new combat weapons, including infantry and tank up-gradings, fighter-jet range, and armaments and the payload and reaches of ICBMs[*]. He promised that Britain would be reached within two days of hostilities and claimed that secret Russian threats had forced America to opt out of helping the ill-fated Anglo-French-Israeli invasion of Egypt, provoked by the seizure of the

---

[*] Inter-Continental Ballistic Missiles.

canal by Nasser. It was an upbeat address, designed to put his troops on a best morale footing, at a time when World War Three seemed likely.

So important did CIA rate that address that the copies were put under tight, restricted circulation, which included the Berlin Station of SIS. In confronting Blake's subsequent denial of betraying Popov, one former CIA Chief speculates that once Marshall Zhukov's address became circulated to SIS in Berlin, it would be known to Blake though the source was muddied. Without knowing who the source was, Blake would have passed it on as part of his regular delivery to KGB. Whatever the true reasons for being alerted to Popov, KGB put the GRU officer under heavy surveillance, compiled the evidence and had him recalled to Moscow on a pretext. There, because of their superior ability to penetrate CIA wireless traffic within the American Embassy, KGB monitors were able to record 'Max Calling'. As an incidental example of how espionage has its hierarchy of values, and how both sides observed the tradecraft of doctoring sources, the Russian team investigating Popov was not told how he was revealed.

Instead a series of failed cases in which Popov had been involved were reviewed. He was arrested in the course of making a 'brush contact' with a CIA officer on a Moscow metrobus. Pleading immunity because of his cover as an Embassy official, the CIA officer was released. Popov was subjected to prolonged, enforced, interrogation, in which a senior General took part.

Among the evidence put to him was the case of an 'illegal' he routed to New York. Popov had informed CIA of a long-term penetration agent, a woman who would take up residence as a 'sleeper' until activated, many years in the future. Acting on this information, the FBI set up surveillance. She became aware and the mission was aborted. From that and other failed cases came the evidence that broke the GRU double agent in December 1958.

After he confessed, KGB tried to run him against CIA, now desperate for his welfare. Through other penetration sources, including the Berlin Tunnel, the Americans heard of Popov's unmasking. As is standard when an influential agent is compromised, Operation BIGOT was wound down, safe houses and communications systems were aborted and, as one of the disappointed CIA officers put it, 'all dangling ends were cauterised'.

Not to be deprived of some compensation on home territory, KGB made a last throw to run Popov against CIA. After eight months of intense interrogation, which involved extreme sensory deprivation, Pyotr Semarovitch Popov had been reconstructed sufficiently to make contact with CIA, in Moscow. The meeting was in the toilet of a restaurant frequented by Westerners and KGB monitored it. Popov, wired for recording, looked haggard and demoralised. In an effort to outwit the 'wiring', he scribbled a note to the contact, asking that President Kennedy appeal directly to Comrade Khrushchev for his survival. The note said: 'They have stopped beating me now — please try to do something for my family. If my plan works, they will let me go abroad again as a double-agent. If not, my only hope is that your President will intercede for me...relations are good now...whatever happens do not break contact...'

CIA did precisely that — break contact. Popov had been burned and threatened other operations by revealing American espionage agents. Popov's naive hope that because 'relations are good now' (there was a mild thaw in the Cold War) did not stand the test of real-politik. CIA distrusted him, due to his prolonged interrogation. With much heart-searching, as CIA told George Kisevalter, who had become emotionally close to his fellow Russian, Popov would be abandoned. In Russia, that meant disgrace for his family and extermination for himself. One story put about afterwards by CIA was that their former agent was thrown live into a furnace, watched by fellow officers. Later documents from KGB said he had been shot by firing squad after a hearing by the Supreme Court which heard the State outline his treachery, including numbers of Soviet agents arrested abroad and the damage he had done to 'The Great work for Peace'.

Church and State.... The Church keeps a watchful eye as De Valera sets out on his political odyssey, Ennis 1917. Twenty years afterwards, his new Constitution for an independent Ireland granted a special status to the Catholic Church and protected its clerics from some State laws (courtesy of the National Library of Ireland, Keogh Collection, KE132).

The Limerick of Bourke's childhood.... O' Connell Street, circa 1940. Repeated stealing from motor cars led to the 12-year old Sean Bourke being sent to Daingean Reformatory (courtesy of the National Library of Ireland, Valentine Collection, VAL 3053).

The gang were on the railway bridge over-looking the road, where the unfortunate milkwoman encountered missiles.... The bridge today (author archive).

Uncertain ground.... Sean Bourke pictured in Moscow outside The Metropole Hotel, on a long-range lens, 1968 (author archive).

Home is the Hero.... Sean Bourke, shortly after his return to Ireland, 1968, with RTE interviewer David Thornly (L) and RTE producer, Seamus Smith (author archive).

Between two Bishops.... Bourke moved into his late uncle's villa, seeking squatters rights in advance of a court judgement on the will (courtesy of the *Limerick Leader*).

November 1973 - less than a month after moving in, the villa was destroyed by intruders using a bulldozer (courtesy of the *Limerick Leader*).

A temporary peace.... Bourke fishing and enjoying rural peace sometime in the 70s (above and next page) (courtesy of the *Limerick Leader*).

Man of Words.... The skilled writer at work in the political office of Jim Kemmy, 1977 (courtesy of the *Limerick Leader*).

Lost for words.... By 1981, he was bloated from alcohol and in deteriorating health (John Murphy).

Stone Walls were part of his boyhood.... Daingean Reformatory in the Irish Midlands. Officially known as St. Conleth's Industrial School, its regime of brutality included widespread beatings and buggery of the boys (author archive).

City of Spires and lowly Desires.... Limerick's Cathedral spire, the lunatic asylum and the cemetery where Sean Bourke lies buried (author archive).

Interestingly, there was a plea for clemency from his former colleagues in Military Intelligence, aware of the intense pressures of their work. His hapless wife was exonerated from punishment. CIA switchboards would no more hear 'Max calling...'.

Whatever the truth of Blake's role in the Popov case, it was his crucial involvement in betraying the Berlin Tunnel that has earned him a permanent place in the history of Cold War espionage. As we have seen in an earlier chapter, he was Secretary to the Anglo-American team, which planned the ambitious operation to tap into the communications network of the Soviet Group Forces in Germany. By the time he was assigned to Berlin, he was no longer functioning in OPERATION GOLD. To show the extent of Cold War espionage, it is necessary to summarise the Tunnel experience.

A Tunnel into Espionage Folklore

The Berlin Tunnel was among the most ambitious of Western efforts to gather information about the deployment of Soviet armed forces in Europe. Because armies require extensive communications, espionage organisations devote effort to monitoring those systems. In Europe after the war, it became a priority of the Allied intelligence services to access the (repaired) postal, telegraph and wireless systems. As we have seen, SIS had success with tapping operations in Vienna, while KGB had scored a notable return by monitoring American lines in Potsdam. Over and above the physical monitoring of lines, much effort was spent by both sides in cultivating human sources among officials who operated the phone and telegraph systems.

Out of that awareness, OPERATION GOLD was probably the ultimate communications monitoring for the time. From the joint meetings of SIS/CIA in London in December of 1953 came the expertise to target the Soviet HQ at Karlshorst, by digging underground from the American Sector, crossing under the frontier by tunnel and constructing on the far side a 'tap chamber' which would record all the communications from Soviet Group Forces. It involved the civilian, military and intelligence establishments of Britain and America; it was demanding of budgets and security. It delivered information on such a scale that it was being processed for years afterwards.

The statistics are impressive. An ostensible radar station was built, which the Soviets could expect to see close to their border as both radar and jet planes were in rapid development by armed forces of East and West. Using the 'radar' building as cover, a vertical shaft was dug, which encountered water at the rate of 400 gallons an hour (in spite of test borings in Britain and America on similar soil which the geologists had assured would be water free). With pumping and air-conditioning installed, a tunnel was dug under the supervision of US military engineers. Taking the example of their native Ford car manufacturer, who used the wood from component packing cases as chassis floorboards, the Americans used the slats from packing cases in which the steel tunnel liners were delivered to make a track for trucks to carry back the excavated muck. That earth in turn was taken away at night in large army trucks and dispersed.

Heavy steel doors were installed at intervals, the one on the Russian side warning "no entry" in Russian, and the one on the American side warning that entrants were about to enter the American Sector. The tunnel was sandbagged and mined, with explosives concealed along the walls. Once the Americans had completed the tunnel to the point where it was under the target cables, the British completed the upward 'tap chamber' and took on the actual monitoring and recording. In the American view — and in spite of Philby — British technical ability was paramount for the dogged attention to detail and the quality of monitoring, which required banks of reliable reel-to-reel tape recorders.

British Post Office technicians designed and built the actual chamber up into the cables and installed the metallic clips onto the cables, which had then to be amplified and routed so that loss of energy would not hasten fault searches.

Again, the statistics are worth mentioning. Three main cables were tapped, in which 1,200 separate channels produced about 500 active traffic circuits at any one time. One hundred Ampex recorders were continuously in use, delivering over a year about 50,000 reels of magnetic tape, which were flown to Langley and GCHQ for analysis. As each reel contained over 2 hours of material, a figure well in excess of 100,000 hours was transcribed. The teams had been trained in Britain from the previous year.

To keep up with immense flow of information, much of it apparently prosaic but crucial in compiling the changing mosaic of Soviet military build-up in Eastern Europe, the teams reported on 3x8 hour shifts to the 'Radar Station'. These teams were made-up of multi-lingual listeners, transcribers and typists. The transcribers did not function underground (like miners!) but within the less claustrophobic space of the radar station, to which the monitoring circuits were routed along the tunnel from the tap chamber.

Secrecy was paramount and cover stories were devised to account for the tunnelling activity. Observation posts were manned over 24-hours to monitor Soviet activity on the frontier, across in Karlshorst, which was the HQ of Warsaw Pact. Microphones were placed on the perimeter face, to pick up any alerts from enemy patrols. All this against the irony, unknown at the time, that the Russians were aware of the plans, 'before a spit was dug'. We now know from KGB archives, and reflective also of the bureaucracy of an organisation with 23,000 employees, the decision was taken not to reveal the tunnel in case it would also reveal agent DIOMID.

In what may seem an extraordinary turn of events, the Russians took no counter action for almost a year, allowing a steady flow of high-grade intelligence to the Western agencies. According to one history[*], drawing on CIA and

---

[*] *Battleground Berlin, CIA vs KGB in the Cold War.* David E. Murphy, Sergei A. Kondrashev and George Bailey. Yale University Press, New Haven and London, 1997. Murphy was former CIA Chief in Berlin and was intimately involved.

KGB archives, the primary reason was the security of George Blake. Secondly, was the fact that KGB already had its own secure overhead network, which CIA had failed to monitor. Thirdly, once the information from Blake made its way to Khrushchev at the top, it was decided to 'discover' the tunnel at a time which would provide the diplomatic advantage. It was another example of espionage as diplomacy by other means.

Two of the (three) authors of *Battleground Berlin* namely David Murphy and Sergei Kondrashev faced up to each other in Berlin during the crucial period of the 1950s, serving on 'opposite ends of the tunnel'. Kondrashev, was Blake's Controller in London to whom he handed the original plans. It is worth citing their view of an enterprise which has gone into espionage folklore.

Among the myths which they counter was that because the Soviets knew of it in advance, they dropped 'chicken feed' (disinformation) into the system. Not so, say the authors: because DIOMID was such a prime source who might be unmasked if the Soviets completely revised their communications systems, they allowed the tunnel to function for almost a year, though senior personnel received additional warnings to be security conscious in their conversations.

The tunnel enabled the Americans to complete a picture of Soviet forces in Eastern Europe, which was vital in preserving the balance of power at the time. This judgment was confirmed by George Blake in Moscow who told me that at the time each intelligence service was convinced the other side's forces were about to strike first in armed hostilities.

'...the tunnel was seen as a unique, timely, and reliable source of intelligence information on USSR, East Germany and Poland. The tunnel's taps offered hard data on Soviet political actions and intentions in Berlin and on its relations with the Western occupying powers, as well as indications of differences of opinion between the Soviets and East Germans on the problems of West Berlin's status'. '...the tunnel provided detailed information on the nature and limitations of

Soviet military and economic control over East Germany and other Soviet-occupied territories'.

Far from being a failure, as has been the view of most historians of the Berlin Tunnel, it is reasonable to assert now, in the light of recently released CIA and KGB files, that in fact it was a success. That indeed is how it was viewed in the West; long before the propaganda writers of either side addressed the stage-managed discovery in April 1956, at the height of the Cold War.

To Nikita Khrushchev is ascribed the delay in the exposure of the tunnel until the maximum political use could be made of it to 'embarrass' the Americans. As heir to Stalin, and denouncer of his regime, Khrushchev was attempting to forge a policy of 'peaceful co-existence' with the West, without at the same time losing the support of the Politburo. Russia could not be seen to weaken in the face of Imperialist aggression, as evinced by such a calculated piece of espionage as the tunnel. But neither should it provoke a reaction, which threatened the new policies of détente. Russia had agreed to withdraw from Austria and give recognition of sorts to West Germany.

Over-reaction to the 'discovery' of the Berlin Tunnel would defeat Khrushchev's need to be recognised on the world stage as a reformer. Whereas a reaction of more in grief than in anger would point the finger at the bullyboy Americaniski, while providing extra coverage of Khrushchev's visit to Britain, scheduled for that week. Accordingly, instructions were given to a special KGB signals group to unearth the tunnel, followed by a formal protest and an invitation to selected media correspondents to present themselves to the Soviet HQ at Karlshorst. Broadly, that scenario was followed in an undoubted propaganda coup for Russia.

Behind the Iron Curtain, the less-free media reported the tunnel in terms desired by Moscow. In the West, the discovery was reported with tinges of admiration for the expertise involved. As instructed by Khrushchev, the British involvement was down-played, though undoubtedly the

Russians were aware from the original blueprint provided by Blake that British technical expertise was crucial to monitoring. As to the conclusion of the whole enterprise, the final days of the tunnel were worthy of a thriller writer's imagination.

In order to fulfil the political exploitation of the tunnel's discovery, while maintaining tight source protection, the advent of heavy rains in early April 1956 provided the special signals unit of KGB with a credible reason to begin digging above the tunnel. The rains were causing frazzle on the underground cables out of Karlshorst, including the heavy trucking cables being tapped. From their own constant monitoring of the cables and from a 24-hour manned observation post of the Karlshorst target area, CIA were aware of this activity. As soon as Soviet units were seen to be digging along the line of the tunnel, the Allied duty personnel sought higher instruction.

Two sets of opposing administrations came into play. By dawn on the 22nd April, the lines on both sides of the Berlin divide were literally buzzing with activity. The Russians were seeking instructions from Moscow, the Americans from Washington. The wider political scenario was being jointly, if not mutually, orchestrated.

Local CIA Chief, William Harvey, asked if he should detonate the tunnel, once the Russians passed underground into the American sector. He was told, 'no!' He compromised by setting up a heavy calibre machine gun behind the door, which notified intruders they were entering the American Sector. The gun was unloaded, but Harvey, true to his gun-totin' image, pulled back the bolt so that the audible sound reverberated down the tunnel and deterred further Russian advance[*]. The Russians called in the senior Soviet commanders of the region, alerted them to review their communications, put airfields on alert and switched communications to the secure overhead KGB channel, which

---

[*] Called 'Wild Bill' Harvey because of his truculent demeanour which sometimes included wearing pistols, cowboy style.

was used to carry the diplomatic instructions from the Foreign Ministry in Moscow.

As planned, a formal protest was sent to the Americans, the tunnel further excavated on the Russian side and the media invited to inspect it. The British involvement was obscured. In New York and Washington, the Russian consulates went into prepared overdrive, with formal protests. In London, Nikita Khrushchev and his Foreign Minister were being received at Buckingham Palace. It was all smiles and grace and favour.

Behind the scenes SIS were encountering other obstacles apart from the tunnel curtailment. Monitoring of the telephone lines in the hotel accommodation of the Russian delegation at Claridges, sub-contracted to MI5, showed the Russians to be extremely careful, while wireless traffic from their Embassy in Kensington was proving impenetrable.

In the world of 'espionage as diplomacy by other means' the British were taking a private beating, compounded by the disappearance of an SIS frogman who had been dispatched to examine the hull of the ship, which had brought the Russian premier to Britain. The cruiser *Ordzhonikidze* was regarded as being heavily primed with electronic systems and had long been a target of Western agencies curious about its defences. Having brought the Russian delegation to Britain, it was docked at Portsmouth where SIS and Naval Intelligence set up an extensive, joint surveillance operation.

After some inter-service bickering, SIS tasked one of their frogmen to inspect the hull and propeller.

Commander Crabbe was an adventurer with a good war-record and a favourite of Nicholas Elliott, Head at London Station. But Crabbe was also an out-of-condition, chain-smoking and hard-drinking frogman whose best days were behind him. When the Russians became aware he was under the cruiser, they started up the propeller, which decapitated Crabbe. Although the Russians were prepared to provide photographic evidence of the covert inspection in protest to the Foreign Office, they would not release the sonar record, which SIS wanted to see. Sonar would reveal the thickness of the hull.

Crabbe's role was officially denied, provoking one Moscow paper to accuse Britain of 'shameful underwater espionage'. Britain continued to stonewall, until the sadly named Crabbe's headless body was washed ashore. The official explanation that he was 'conducting equipment trials' rang hollow even to the British public[*].

Anthony Eden, the Prime Minister, a vacillating and easily embarrassed politician who took his own weaknesses out on others, was already embroiled in lunatic SIS schemes to assassinate the nationalist Egyptian leader Colonel Nasser, about whom he had a fatal foreboding. Fatal, as it turned out, not for Nasser but for Eden's own political career. Although he had opposed the Crabbe operation, he was viewed by the spy services as a notorious prevaricator, so they went ahead. After the debacle became public, Eden punished SIS by forcing early retirement on John Sinclair the 'C' of Blake's recruitment and installing Dick White of MI5 as the incoming Director. SIS was top-heavy with privileged public school products who did little to conceal their class snobbishness towards the 'PC Plods' at MI5. White's appointment was seen as insulting and demoralising to SIS.

These failures, Portsmouth and the Tunnel, were symptomatic of the wider fatigue showing in Britain's facade of Empire. The war had changed more than the Establishment understood, inflicting a seismic shock to the imperial system of King, Lords and Commonwealth. No longer were diverse territories in India, Asia, Africa and Arabia, with millions of poor peoples, prepared to accept Britain's overlordship of their destinies and trade routes. Their soldiers and populations had been sacrificed, as they saw it, in a battle between British and German empires, leaving them with little economic compensation but a strongly whetted appetite to control their own fortunes.

---

[*] Crabbe had been tasked by Nicholas Elliott, whose other spectacular failure was to accept Kim Philby's 'gentleman's word' that he would return from Beirut to Britain after admitting to being a Soviet agent.

Cyprus, Kenya, Malaya, the Middle East were all in the process of disengaging from an Empire not only unwilling to let them go but employing brutal methods to hold onto them. In the weeks before the Khrushchev visit, the newspapers carried pictures of bloody clashes between British troops and local protesters in many territories. Before the year was out, those reports were replicated from other outposts of Empire. In Cyprus, there was a price of £10,000 on the head of General Grivas, who had led resistance against the Germans but was now hunted by the British for his EOKA guerrilla activities. In Egypt, Col Nasser would provide the watershed for imperial Britain with his seizure of the Canal and the subsequent humiliation of British withdrawal in the face of American displeasure, which was unwilling to allow the British invasion to be turned into another confrontation with Russia, as had happened in Korea.

The USSR, while making gains in Asia and Africa, was under siege nearer home. In the summer, the Poles rioted, killed KGB teams and demanded the withdrawal of Russian troops. They failed. By November, Hungarian independence fighters had forced the Russians to sit down and parlay — a ruse used by Soviet Forces to regroup and invade Budapest with full frontal assault of 1,000 tanks, supported by infantry and air units. Budapest was flattened with such ferocity and loss of civilian lives as to provoke a worldwide protest and warnings from America — but no armed action. Communist parties in the West suffered a haemorrhage of members and profound disillusion at the brutality of the Russian retaliation to the Hungarian uprising.

No such heart searching appears to have affected agent DIOMID. While the world was thus changing, George Blake was coming to the end of his Berlin assignment. One of the few SIS officers who was aware of OPERATION GOLD, he had watched with trepidation the Russian 'discovery' of the tunnel, about which his KGB handlers had forewarned him, with the assurance it would be done in such a way as to protect him. 'So skilfully had the 'discovery' of the tunnel been stage-managed...' (he later wrote) '...that a subsequent

SIS/CIA enquiry into the circumstances surrounding the collapse of the operation produced the verdict that the cause had been purely technical and that there was no question of a leak.' '...I passed some anxious weeks until the results of enquiry became known...'

CHAPTER TWELVE

TWO LIVES CONVERGE

When George Blake concluded his Berlin assignment, he returned to London to await another posting. The dominance of the Americans in European espionage, the closing of the Berlin Tunnel and, crucially, the morale blow to Britain's imperial confidence by the Suez debacle brought a review of SIS field assignments. Although the incumbent Dick White as 'C' had approved various attempts to murder the Egyptian leader Col. Nasser, he realised that SIS had been badly served by the old-style gung-ho adventurers, who in everyday speech referred to the adversary as 'Gypos' and 'Wogs'[*]. The Egyptians, adding to Prime Minister Eden's sour view of SIS, had rumbled most of the madcap schemes.

What the service needed to regain a measure of control over Arabian affairs were professional intelligence officers who had a degree of sympathy with, and genuine curiosity about, Arab culture. George Blake, returned with commendation for his work in running agents in Berlin, was among those nominated to replace the old style 'Palestinians' who were being put out to grass. Since his childhood he had magic memories of his time with his grandfather's family in Cairo, had rusty Arabic and a love of the region. What SIS could not know, anymore than Blake himself could gauge, was the continuing influence from that formative age of his cousin Henry Curiel, who had been a founder of the Egyptian Communist Party. The influence of Curiel had been crucial in the evolution of Behar, to Blake, to DIOMID. Now, in his adulthood, he was completing some kind of life circle and keeping faith with the beliefs of his cousin.

---

[*] The schemes ranged from injecting poison into chocolates intended for Nasser, to organising dissident Egyptian army officers to assassinate their former colleague. Both KGB and CIA warned Nasser of the British plot. *Spy Catcher,* Peter Wright, William Heinemann, Australia, 1987, pp 160-163 and, *MI6 - 50 Years of Special Operations*, Stephen Dorrill, Fourth Estate, London 2000, pp 601-651.

What SIS saw was a keen officer who was willing to uproot again after Berlin and move to Lebanon and bring his wife and family to the village of Shemlan, where the Foreign Office conducted MECAS, the Middle East Centre for Arab Studies. After Suez there was less tolerance in many Arab states for several British multi-national companies which were believed to have conspired with SIS to provide cover for operations against Arab host countries. Men like Blake were needed.

Within SIS, the posting was regarded as a promotion as well as a money-earner, as the allowances were generous and officers who completed the 18-month course could be expected to be appointed as a Head of Station in an Arab territory. Apart from delighting his family with news of an exotic location, Blake discussed the posting with Rodin, also known as 'Korovin' his London KGB controller who was all in favour — it would mean deeper penetration for their prime source in SIS, at a time when Kim Philby was effectively neutered. Philby was at that time also in the Middle East, but his days as an effective agent were numbered[*]. It must have been some satisfaction to Nikolai Borisovich Rodin to see DIOMID, whose recruitment he had organised in Korea seven years before, ascend the ladder of the enemy secret service.

In September 1960, Blake set out for Lebanon, driving overland between seas and arrived to the village of Shemlan on the coastal mountain range above Beirut. He was installed in a house with servants; Gillian followed in a fortnight and they settled into a family routine, which was among the happiest of times. Blake studied intensely by day and stayed home with Gillian and their two small boys in the evening, where they often had dinner on the veranda of their whitewashed house, overlooking the Bay of Beirut. He and

---

[*] SIS deceived CIA by telling them that Philby had been dismissed. Although ostensibly reporting for *The Observer* newspaper, Philby continued to work for SIS and would defect from Beirut to the Soviet Union.

Gillian were self-contained in their family, only rarely venturing out on social occasions, which were often picnics in the countryside and walks in the mountains. She was expecting their third child and would probably travel back to England for the birth.

As he had arranged, DIOMID was also contacted by KGB's regional head, who agreed with him that being operationally non-active, they need meet but every two months, unless an emergency arose. Blake did have a sixth sense about an 'emergency' but suppressed his fatalism in his studies of Arabic, which he found entirely absorbing: 'I got a deep satisfaction from the beautiful, logical, almost mathematical construction of the language'.

Far away in bleak Crawley, by contrast to exotic Lebanon, another individual was engaged in a different kind of perusal which would impact upon both their lives, though in the Spring of 1961 neither was aware of the other's existence. Sean Bourke was busy studying law books, in order to prosecute a case for defamation against the local Chief Constable, whose 'servants and agents', he claimed had defamed him by questions to his neighbours, including to the two boys visiting his house to make an electronic quiz board.

Bourke had engaged a solicitor to take his case but was not making much progress. Replies from the legal department of the Sussex Constabulary took months and invariably asked for further documents to support the 'alleged defamation'. Frustrated and angry, Bourke pored over law books from the library and began to assemble his own case. Again, he found himself stonewalled, in his attempt to issue formal legal proceedings. In spite of detailed preparation, he appeared unable to serve proper papers, which would be backed by the local court as a valid document requiring a police response.

While Sean Bourke, petty criminal with fantasies of grandeur, was thus engaged in potential litigation against the Sussex Constabulary, far removed from his world, the files at CIA in Washington were growing thick with voluminous extracts from the Berlin Tunnel tapes. The espionage industry, one has to repeat, is just that — an industry.

Although extensive extraction had been done in the years since the closure in 1956, much remained to be collated. Among the many leads on enemy penetration, a persistent series referred to a KGB agent within SIS Berlin Station. The issue came up in one of the many regular CIA briefings of SIS and was logged for action by an overworked and undermanned team of analysts.

Around the same time the Gehlen Organisation[*], which was the West German Intelligence service, also sourced a list of KGB 'doubles' in its own service. As previously noted in post war Germany, the occupying powers relied on natives for the day-to-day work. Many native Germans were routinely rumbled as being double agents. Sometimes they were fired, other times imprisoned or exchanged or occasionally 'turned' to becoming triple-agents. Blake, using one of his SIS cover names of Van Vries had regularly used such a runner, one Horst Eitner, to lure Soviet personnel into buying black-market goods in the West.

KGB, using exactly the same mechanism, had persuaded Eitner to work for them. Known by the nick-name 'Mickey' because of his resemblance to the cartoon character Mickey Mouse, Eitner's oversize head and tilting gait had made him a familiar — and deceptively comic-figure among the swarm of agent-runners in Berlin. He was popular with women, had money to spend and could use espionage work as cover for romantic assignations away from his wife, Brigitte, who was also a 'runner' for CIA. She had paid dearly in that role, having served five years in a Siberian prison when rumbled by KGB counter-espionage in East Germany. She was more than a little irked when during an evening on the town, Horst made advances to one of her friends, also released from Siberia (anyone reading of conditions in Siberia's 'corrective institutions' might readily appreciate the bonding that grew up between prisoners). When Horst, flush with money and alcohol, did not desist, Brigitte reported him as being a Soviet

---

[*] Officially the Bundesnachrichtendienst but known as The Gehlen Organisation after its Chief, General Reinhard Gehlen.

spy and led investigators to their flat where she revealed the buried microphones installed by KGB.

Enquiries started back up the line from Olympic Stadium and were being processed in London when another set of revelations caused certain files in Broadway Buildings to be urgently exhumed. This time the information came from CIA, who sent an officer to London to brief SIS on two spies, whom the Americans believed were operating in England, one within SIS itself. Because of the tainted atmosphere left behind by Philby, the Americans were circumspect as to the source. Eventually SIS established that leads had come from within the Polish Intelligence Service, where the deputy head of a section, Lt. Col. Michal Goleniewski had received much KGB material. When Goleniewski decided to defect with his mistress, it was done with all the field-craft of the trained intelligence officer. He wanted a new life. Having written to CIA, via dead-letter boxes and cut-outs, he announced a date for his physical defection.

So adroitly was this done, that the CIA reception team thought at first they were dealing with an intermediary, only to realise it was Goleniewski himself who had taken great care to survey his method of exfiltration beforehand. Code-named SNIPER because of the long-range accuracy of his letters, the defector refused to meet any officer from SIS, as he believed the British service was so penetrated by the Soviets as to put his life in danger. Accordingly, his debriefing was done in America, where among weighty revelations was his claim that an important agent of KGB was connected to SIS in Berlin and had also passed onto his Soviet controller material relating to the Polish communist government[*].

Once the detail from the Americans became apparent, the top floor in Broadway Buildings creaked with the weight of internal enquiries. When asked before by CIA about a

---

[*] 'LAMBDA One' was the name which Goleniewski gave reports from KGB agent DIOMID. 'LAMBDA Two' turned out to be Harry Houghton, the KGB spy in Royal Navy underwater weapons research.

possible penetration, SIS had accounted for the SNIPER material, which had clearly emanated from them, as having been taken in a burglary from a Brussels safe. Now, at the repeated request of CIA and this time collating the SNIPER allegations with that of Horst Eitner, the investigators saw patterns, which pointed towards George Blake, as he had personally sourced some of the SNIPER material in his work miking and wiring Soviet Bloc embassies for SIS.

Though passed onto his KGB controller, it had not been sufficiently 'doctored' when making its way to the Polish Intelligence Service as part of the shared 'product' from Moscow. In a sense, Blake's fingerprints were on the material. He had been foolhardy and dedicated enough to supply KGB with carbon copies of reports. As the internal enquiry progressed, personal animosity towards Blake emerged from some senior officers, one of whom said he had found him 'Always too willing to smile at anybody who came in the door', recalling his impression of Blake in Berlin (not the least reason for that, in hindsight, was Blake's alertness to photograph sensitive material when on his own in a shared office, liable to be discovered on a colleague entering).

The enquiry team trawled through SNIPER's information, assembling the case against Blake. SNIPER had copies of four separate batches of SIS product relating to Poland, including a 'watch list' of potential recruits. When other suspects in possession of the same material were eliminated and it became clear that Blake had originated some of this material, the focus shifted to a means of having him return for questioning without arousing his suspicions.

Nicholas Elliott (in spite of the Crabbe fiasco) was Head of Station in Beirut. His secretary, who had worked with Gillian, was dispatched to sound out the likely family movements over the next while. As it happened, one of the young Blake boys was in hospital with pneumonia, having been caught in a freak rainstorm during a family outing in the mountains. Gillian was staying overnight with him. When the secretary visited the family there, she invited Blake to attend a performance of *'Charley's Aunt'*, being played that evening by the local British amateur drama group. She had one spare ticket. Gillian Blake urged George to take a break from his books, as exams were pending and he had been burning the midnight oil.

During the interval they happened to run into Nicholas Elliott who mentioned he was glad he had met George, as it would save him a trip up the mountains to the language school. A letter had come from Head Office, inviting Blake to attend for interview in relation to a possible promotion. Elliott indicated an exciting assignment was in the offing. Could Blake travel over Easter, after the exams, and present himself on the Tuesday morning at Broadway Buildings? He would need to call at the embassy for travel documentation and expenses. Blake agreed and with Elliott's good wishes left for home after the performance. But he was uneasy. The more he thought about it, the less he liked it. The course would finish in July; the Easter exams were crucial. Why bring him all the way back to London before then, unless some urgent operational need had come up?

He did not sleep much that night, pondering the possibilities. Had there been a defector from KGB who knew of DIOMID? Why was the secretary keen for him to attend the play? Was it a holiday weekend when Burgess and McLean defected — were his superiors making sure another defection of a traitor would not happen on a holiday weekend? Was Elliott at *'Charley's Aunt'* by design? With Gillian at the hospital, he tossed and turned and by morning had taken a more positive view. He had been recalled before, in order to deliver some expertise on Soviet Bloc targets. It could be the same again — Russia was making belligerent noises in the Middle East and had effectively annexed Syria while arming anti-imperialist forces in the region. He should view it all positively. 'If I fled on no more evidence than a hunch, would I not be haunted for the rest of my life by the uncertainty that I had abandoned my post for no good reason...'. Instinct and reason competed for a decision.

Then there was the difficulty of Gillian and the children. He would have to confess to her, and leave her to make the agonising choice of staying behind to face the disgrace while he fled to Syria — or accompany him to an uncertain future behind the Iron Curtain. It was one thing to spy for Russia because one believed in helping the noble experiment of the first Socialist State in human history — but another matter to live in the harsh conditions of that 'noble state'. As he later wrote, 'Was I not about to cut myself off from all that was most dear to me for a mere shadow? Was this not a case of *"The coward fleeth when no one pursueth" ?'*.

Thus consoled with a Calvinist mantra, he decided he would go to London, but not before seeking advice from his KGB controller. The 'emergency' they provided for, had now arisen. Taking paranoid care to avoid surveillance, he made contact and explained his unease, asking for an urgent direction from Moscow Centre. Was there anything the First Chief Directorate knew which would pose a danger to DIOMID going home to Head Office?[*] Within twenty-four hours the reply came that as far as Moscow was concerned, it was safe to go. Duly emboldened, he called into the embassy, where Nicholas Elliott confirmed his travel arrangements, asking in passing if he would like to put up at the St. Ermine Hotel, across from Broadway Buildings. Blake declined, as he had already cabled his mother who had a flat in Radlett, Surrey, where she worked as a housekeeper to a wealthy family. On the flight, he mulled over two omens. One was that on his last night with his colleagues at the school, where Blake's name had been posted on the exam results as passing with distinction, they had afterwards gone to a nightclub. Blake's winning streak had ended with a last throw, which lost all his considerable winnings. The other was Elliott's mention of the St. Ermine Hotel, which had permanent wiring in certain rooms for SIS casework.

---

[*] The First Chief Directorate handled KGB personnel abroad and agents under their control. Blake assumed the FCD to have sources in '5' or '6' who might know if he were to be interrogated.

Once he was airborne, Elliott cabled London with mission accomplished. In Broadway Buildings, two senior officers, the urbane classicist Terence Lecky and the hard-nosed Soviet specialist Harry Shergold set about preparing their questions for Blake's arrival. They had spent long days exhuming evidence from the bulky files, had made many visits in the capital and briefed a Supt. of the Special Branch in Scotland Yard. SIS had repeatedly assured William Harvey that this one would not get away — there would be no repeat of the Burgess-MacClean disaster.

Special Branch, acting for MI5, monitored his arrival at London Airport and was on call on the Tuesday morning when Blake, be-suited as any office commuter, emerged from St. James' Underground station and turned left for the personnel department of SIS at Petty France. That stretch of street was almost entirely occupied by various sections of the service, including the personnel department, to which he reported when returning from a foreign assignment. Blake's unease refused to go away and was sharpened when Harry Shergold suggested they go across the park to Carlton Gardens, rather than to nearby Broadway Buildings. They went 'over the duckpond' to the elegant house on other side of the park which housed 'Y' section which conducted interviews — and interrogations.

'I knew the game was up as we walked across the park' he would later recall. 'But I was determined not to make it easy for them — after all I had been trained in intelligence techniques. I wanted to see what evidence they had...'. Lecky and Shergold began as interviewers and evolved into interrogators, taking him in detail through his recent professional history, trumping his explanations with material supplied by the defector Goleniewski. As was standard practice, they began by inviting him to discuss some aspects of casework, which had puzzled them. Why, for instance, in Berlin had KGB installed microphones in Horst Eitner's flat when Blake had left Berlin and handed the agent over to a successor? Blake replied that he had no idea, though the implication was clear — the Soviets had no need to mike

Eitner when Blake was his British case officer because they would hear everything from Blake in time. Similarly with other cases Blake's successor had found he himself was being highly surveilled. Why?

In what he would remember as an essentially polite English exercise, his colleagues persisted with questioning. Could he not see that something grave was amiss in his casework? Equally persistent, Blake conceded nothing, pointing out that the very nature of deception led to suspicion, sometimes engineered by hostile services. From time to time, other officers joined Lecky and Shergold in the questioning. At the end of the first day, he was told he was free to go, but should present himself again the following morning. He was too depressed to object to the surveillance that was placed upon him as he went home by suburban train to his mother's flat in Radlett. He knew the game was up but had to pretend to his mother that all was well as she asked about Gillian, heard his account of son Anthony's pneumonia and recommended Gamages store in London as the place he would buy mosquito nets for his return.

The first week of April 1961, saw him again in Carlton Gardens. He was more alert and resigned, knowing the tape recorders were spooling relentlessly next door, that the liveried servants who manned the exterior of the Nash building were trained marksmen, that somewhere along the line since 1954 what he most feared had occurred — a defector had somehow fingered him. What he would later learn was that his interrogators were in possession of extensive material, that the investigation was being driven by CIA and that both British security services, SIS and MI5 were heavily demoralised by consequent internal suspicion.

A recent success also based on Goleniewski material emboldened Lecky and Shergold to persist. A month before, the most successful KGB spy ring in Britain, outside of 'The Apostles', had been broken up. Headed by 'Gordon Londsdale'[*] a deeply penetrative sleeper, the naval spies

---

[*] Real name Konon Trofimovich Molody. Selected from the age of ten to become a sleeper in the West, Molody was sent to Canada, given a new

Harry Houghton and Ethel Gee and their Soviet controller Lonsdale had been shipped off to Wormwood Scrubs prison by Lord Chief Justice Parker. Discovered in a suburban house and a London book shop was a complete technical support system for Londsdale's network, which had transmitted the secrets of submarine research and weaponry over years. Although Goleniewski was able only to provide slim leads to 'a spy in the navy', the British security services had isolated the spies, placed them under protracted surveillance and amassed sufficient evidence for conviction. Goleniewski had proved to be accurate.

Lecky and Shergold were confident the Polish defector was also right about LAMBDA 1 — the problem was to get him to confess or supply evidence for conviction. Although SIS was not above killing its enemies by poison or staged ill-health, it preferred to keep them alive for information purposes. A dead double agent was useless in the furtherance of adversarial knowledge. In spite of some who disliked him, Blake was generally well regarded by many of his colleagues, for his conscientious approach to his work. Furthermore, after Suez, Dick White had ordered there be no more assassination plots. It would have to be the courts for Blake; the problem was how to get him there...?

During that first week in April 1961, the questioning was intense. John Quine, who had been Head of Station in Warsaw, joined the group who briefed the interrogators. Although Blake knew they knew more than they showed, he continued to stonewall. With essential English manners, the mood was courteous and polite. But as patience frayed, it became a contest of nerves. He was left on his own at times, which he interpreted as a ploy to see whom he might contact. His own recollection is that his world had caved in: 'I was in

---

identity and tutored in espionage. Arriving in Britain in 1955, he set about recruiting a string of agents whom he controlled until 1961. See *Spycatcher*, Peter Wright, William Heinemann, Australia, 1987, pp128-144 and *The Mitrokhin Archive*, Andrews and Mitrokhin, Allen Lane / The Penguin Press, London, 1999, pp 532-538.

serious danger. Life would never be the same again. It was a strain to pretend to my mother that all was well and discuss arrangements for her visit to us...I pleaded a busy day ahead, in order to go to bed early and be alone with my thoughts.' Unknown to him, arrangements were already in hand for an SIS officer to fly to Beirut and inform Gillian. The cables crackled between Nicholas Elliott's former London Station and his current one at the British Embassy in Beirut.

On the Thursday, as SIS was debating what to do with Blake for the weekend, came the breakthrough. Everyone had become on more familiar terms. The questioning had softened into dialogue, with Lecky and Shergold discussing the more 'conceptual' forms of spying. The discussion rambled through the psychology of espionage. What makes a spy, what induces loyalty; do some spies change sides for a feeling of belonging to the Greater Good? In what appeared a genuine puzzlement as to his motives, they put it to him that they bore him no ill will. He had been tortured by the North Koreans, made to confess he was a British intelligence officer and under pressure had revealed secret operations.

It was too much for the idealist in Blake. 'I felt an upsurge of indignation and I wanted my interrogators and everyone else to know that I had acted out of conviction, out of a belief in Communism, and not under duress or for financial gain. The feeling was so strong that without thinking I burst out: "No, nobody tortured me! No, nobody blackmailed me! I myself approached the Soviets and offered my services to them of my own accord!" '.

As Blake went on to account for his ideological conversion, the word was flashed to Washington via CIA station in London. One can only imagine the reaction of Bill Harvey, former head of CIA Berlin and 'proprietor' of the Berlin Tunnel when he realised that the note-taker of the original plans for OPERATION GOLD as far back as 1953 had been a dedicated Soviet agent. At one of those meetings, Harvey had pointedly said he hoped there were no Philbys present, to which the Scottish George Young, Head of 'Y'

Section, had gamely responded that 'we don't want to be caught with out kilts up...!'

Harvey, at the best of times impatient with, as he saw it, British prissiness, would be in no mood for conciliation. It was a tense time in East-West relations with the Cold War already hot as a cauldron and threatening to conflagrate. America and Russia had rafts of missiles with nuclear warheads pointed at each other, while Britain, France and Germany had bases with round-the-clock bomber readiness. Within months the Wall would go up in Berlin, Russian missiles would be placed in Cuba and the world would tilt into nuclear crisis.

In an effort to hold the Americans at bay and to gain time to manage the inevitable prosecution, it was decided to move Blake out of London for extensive de-briefing, while Dick White, the 'C' of SIS consulted with colleagues on the Joint Intelligence Committee (JIC) which reported to the Cabinet. Harold Macmillan, who had succeeded Anthony Eden as Prime Minister, was already bruised by the serial failures of the Intelligence Service and had requested more regular briefings; in effect he wanted advance warning of likely embarrassments. Accordingly, he had been told of the Blake enquiries. Once the extent of the damage became apparent, he consulted with his Home and Foreign Secretaries, taking soundings on the wider political implications. Coming so soon after the Philby whitewash and Portland Spy ring, Macmillan needed time to put the best face on another disaster. One avenue of damage limitation to the Americans would be if Blake gave a full account of his KGB contacts and operational methods.

With a view to fulfilling this requirement, Blake was driven in a service car to Radlett, where he collected clothes and told his mother he had to leave for a work conference in the country. Departure for Beirut would be delayed. On the morning, he was driven back up to Carlton Gardens, from where a retinue of black cars drove in convoy to a Hampshire village where he would have the palliative of English domestic life. Harry Shergold's country cottage came replete with pancakes in the evening and birdsong outside his bedroom window in the morning.

Blake's sense of irony and affection for English life helped him cope with the personal disaster awaiting him but was compounded by worry over his wife who was eight months pregnant and his failure to return in time for his son's birthday: 'Everyone acted as if this was an ordinary week-end party among friends and pretended not to notice how the cottage was surrounded by Special Branch officers. A police car drove slowly behind us when we went for a walk. It was a situation which struck me as very English — I should say endearingly English'. Blake making pancakes for a Sunday meal, which was conducted in a civilised, conversational fashion compounded that Englishness. At night, John Quine, with whom Blake was on good terms, shared the bedroom. 'He spoke a lot about my family and wanted me to tell him again about my motives for doing what I did...he was trying hard to understand'. Quine, it would emerge, was one of the senior officers who made a case for Blake to receive immunity in return for full co-operation. There was a precedent for such amnesty[*]. Over the weekend, other voices prevailed.

On Monday, 12th April 1961, George Blake, described as a 'former government official of no fixed address' was charged with offences under the Official Secrets Act, in that 'for a purpose prejudicial to the safety or interests of the State he communicated to another person information which might have been directly or indirectly useful to an enemy'. It was a catch-all offence. The remand hearing at Bow Street was in the late afternoon, when court reporters had departed — otherwise such key words as 'safety of the State' and 'useful to an enemy' would have generated coverage beyond the minimal paragraph. The much-vaunted judicial system was bending to the requirements of 'national security' —

---

[*]Both Blunt and Cairncross, members of the Cambridge ring, were 'amnestied' in return for co-operation with the security services over a prolonged period. So was Labour MP Tom Driberg.

journalists did not connect at that stage 'George Blake — former government official' with the much-photographed return of hostages from Korea nine years before.

The Crown had a month to marshal its case. More to the point, The Secret State in its machinations with the Cabinet Office, had four weeks to work in tandem with the Attorney-General's office, to mount a prosecution which would tell the public as little as possible about the nature of Intelligence operations, while at the same time seeking a maximum penalty which would deter any future defectors from that often onerous and dangerous work. In Beirut, meanwhile, John Quine had the unpleasant job of counselling Gillian and making arrangements for her return with the children to Britain. She was in a state of deep shock, not lessened by the reaction of her father who was of the old school of SIS, where patriotism was an everyday virtue. She visited her husband in prison, where she brought messages from his mother. Both women were in a 'safe house' in the country. Time would bond them in support of each other and of Blake. To his relief, there was no reproach in her demeanour when they had a stilted meeting before his appearance at The Old Bailey on 2nd May.

Meanwhile, in Crawley New Town — urban endorsement of Macmillan's 'never had it so good', one immigrant from a former colony who personally never had it so good was preparing to throw it all away in a fit of pique at the police.

CHAPTER THIRTEEN

TRIALS AND PUNISHMENT

It was against a background of heightened world tension that George Blake came to be tried at the Old Bailey in early May 1961. The fear of Russian invasion of the West was very real — so real that many countries had prepared Doomsday scenarios, with the public alerted to emergency measures in the event of nuclear war. The 'four-minute warning' became part of everyday life, with instructional films on how to survive a nuclear attack. In some Western countries, the better-off businessmen built shelters in the countryside.

In Britain, secret regional seats of Government had been established, stocked with supplies and communications for specially trained military and civil defence units. In London, an entire area underground from Holborn to the Courts of Justice in the Strand had been so equipped, with accommodation for the Cabinet, senior civil servants and military advisors as well as diplomatic staffs from selected embassies[*].

As with many NATO countries, American bases had been established in Britain with retaliatory strike capability. Bombers were stationed in East Anglia, Lincolnshire and in Yorkshire where CIA and SIS also constructed a SIGINT (Signals Intelligence) listening post to monitor wireless traffic in the North Atlantic. The bases had attracted the interest of protest groups, leading to the formation of CND (Campaign for Nuclear Disarmament) whose leading lights carried a pedigree across the mainstream of English life, which did not make them immune from monitoring by MI5.

The campaign's offices at 146 Fleet Street were 'miked and wired', the office staff followed and the post opened. Among the prominent supporters of CND were the distinguished playwrights John Arden, John Osborne, Robert

---

[*] Access was via the Courts of Justice and a Territorial Army Hall in Chancery Lane.

Bolt, Arnold Esker and J B Priestly, journalists Michael Foot and James Cameron and the Nobel scientist and philosopher Bertrand Russell. They were supported by thousands of 'ordinary' citizens; teachers, nurses and clerks who marched in protest outside military bases. Among them, three who would play a part in this story, Michael Randle, a teacher, Anne Randle, a nurse and Pat Pottle an antiques dealer. They had serious concerns about Britain hosting nuclear bases. Although traduced by the right-wing press as 'communist sympathisers', the vast majority of CND members were opposed to Communism and were motivated by a desire to have their own country free of nuclear weapons, thereby hoping not to become a target in the war that was expected.

That was the political climate that pertained when George Blake ascended into the dock in the Old Bailey. A minor player, it might seem, on the stage that was dominated by heavyweight powers in the flux and flow of perilous world events. But in the three weeks between his arrest and trial, those powers had managed to link him to those very events, which threatened world peace. Specifically, in the sanctums of the American and British secret establishments, there was no mood of mercy for George Blake. The British were still smarting over the rash of recent spy cases, while the escape of Burgess and MacClean rankled with the Americans. Bill Harvey, in particular, wondered out loud to colleagues why Kim Philby seemed a protected species in Beirut. The 'Third Man' to the other two Cambridge spies, suspected by CIA of tipping them off, worked as a correspondent for the British *Observer* and *Economist* — Harvey was sure he also continued to work for KGB.

This unease was active in the offices of CIA in Grosvenor Square, a mere 'walk and talk' across St James's Park to the offices of the JIC which occupied the curved-wall elegant house on the corner of Downing Street and which accessed both the Prime Minister's office on one side and the Cabinet Office on the other. In both, the gathering extent of Blake's confession demanded some exemplary retribution.

The trial of Blake was notable for a number of reasons. The most important from a Jurisprudence point of view was that most of the hearing was not in open court, thereby confounding an accepted tradition of Justice 'be not only done, but be seen to be done'. Added to that was a subsequent D Notice which limited the media coverage. Both the D Notice and the Indictment came under the Official Secrets Act, regarding '...information communicated to another person for a purpose prejudicial to the safety or the interests of the State'. In effect, news editors and proprietors were joined to the charges against Blake and felt themselves constrained to limit their coverage under threat of gaol[*].

Accordingly, Blake was at a considerable disadvantage when the trial opened on the 3rd of May 1961, before Lord Chief Justice Parker, who had already presided at the Lonsdale, Kroger and Gee trials. The trial was in Court No 1, being taken by the Lord Chief Justice of England, which said a lot for the gravity of the case, as did the presence of the Attorney General as Chief Prosecutor. The Attorney General, was a physically massive man whose credentials of Eton and Oxford were similar to other Establishment figures present, including the Head of SIS, Sir Dick White and the Head of MI5, Sir Roger Hollis. Between them they presented a formidable array of Government power, their presence likely to be noted by the trial judge. The fact that Blake had signed a confession would make it all the easier.

In the dock, Blake appeared demoralised. His own recollection is that: 'I was absent from the proceedings'. The implications of his exposure had impacted upon his usually professional demeanour. He had no contact with his Soviet controllers, correctly assuming that heightened MI5 monitoring had been placed upon the London KGB station. Gillian's distress, bravely borne, cut into his confidence that he would be able to endure the inevitable long prison sentence. He cherished family comforts and he was beset by self-blame at not having followed his instinct to tell her and

---

[*] Full Title: The Services, Press and Broadcasting Committee. In theory made up of media representatives, in effect controlled by Cabinet Office.

hope she would defect with him from Beirut. As he recalled: 'If only I had followed my hunch, I would not have come back to England'.

It was an England about which he had mixed feelings, exemplified by the trial. He liked the counsel assigned to him, Jeremy Hutchinson QC, whose lean asceticism appealed, in contrast to the 'pillar of the Establishment' Sir Reginald Manningham-Buller, the Attorney-General whom Blake thought of as '...an unprepossessing figure...with his wobbling crimson cheeks and the apoplectic, bulging eyes of the over-indulgent...'

Whereas, The Lord Chief Justice appeared kindly, 'His small wig, pushed forward, almost rested on the golden rim of his spectacles and made him look slightly old-maidish.' '...busily taking notes hardly ever looking up, I wondering what there was to write. For him it was now so simple...he knew the facts, I had already written them all down for him.'

The Lord Chief Justice was making notes for his speech in sentencing. The set pieces had to be delivered. The charges were read, five counts under the Official Secrets Act 'that for a purpose prejudicial to the safety of the interests of the State, you did communicate to another person information, which might have been useful to an enemy.' The five charges rocked Blake — he had been initially remanded under one, that of the Official Secrets Act. With five to go on, the State was clearly intent on hitting him hard. ...*might have been useful to an enemy* left a lot of leeway, which Manningham-Buller took up in florid style. The charges were very serious, he said, but he made no effort to define their seriousness under any statute of Law. Instead, he referred to documents which the Lord Chief Justice had in front of him, the depositions of evidence by police and which a court would normally require to be proven or disproved. There was no attempt by Blake's counsel to test these as evidence, because Blake had made a confession, provoked by his need to declare his ideological beliefs. Faced with this piece of prime facie material Jeremy Hutchinson QC could only fall back on a plea of Mitigation.

In trying to mount a plea for leniency, Hutchinson had privately asked Blake if he would express to the court some measure of regret. He had refused, saying he would not try and evade the consequence of his actions. He had spied for the communist system because he believed in it for the future of mankind. Had he not been caught, he would have continued spying — would have continued to pass to his Soviet controllers 'every document of importance' as he had done for the past ten years. Faced with this obduracy or blind belief, Hutchinson opted to plea for mitigation on the grounds of Blake's Intelligence work, which by its nature involved deception on many levels, so that a man might easily lose sight of where his loyalties lay...

The Attorney General outlined Blake's professional history. How he had volunteered, as a British Subject, to fight in the war, how he had served in the Royal Navy until 1948, how since then he had been 'in Government service'. But about ten years ago, his political views underwent change — he held the strong conviction that the communist system was the better one and 'deserved to triumph'. He resolved to join the communist side in establishing what he believed to be a balanced and more just society.

Mannigham-Buller continued: 'Having reached this conclusion he did not take the course of resigning from the government service. What he did was to approach the Russians and volunteer to work for them. His offer was accepted and to use his own words, he agreed to make available to the Soviet Intelligence Service as much information as came his way in the course of his duties in order to promote the cause of Communism. For the past nine-and-a-half years, while employed in the government service and drawing his salary from the State, he had been working as an agent for the Russians, as a spy for them and communicating a mass of information to them...'.

As the Attorney General made the case, Blake's foreboding increased. Although the actual information could not be divulged in open court, it was, said the Attorney General, 'of very great importance'. He would elaborate in closed session and when the court heard it, they would realise the magnitude of his offence. Blake had been engaged in betraying his country. After which Manningham-Buller lowered his considerable weight onto his bench and awaited the response of Defence Counsel, Jeremy Hutchinson. Hutchinson made no attempt to challenge the secret court, other than to say, 'I am told that much of what I have to say should not be said in public — in those circumstances, my client wishes, in spite of the disadvantages to him, that, I should have complete freedom to address your Lordship on all matters.'

Perversely, the 'complete freedom (for)... all matters' could only be done when the court was cleared of reporters and public. Heavy wooden shutters were placed over the windows (would the Russians be listening outside?). Lord Chief Justice Parker heard Hutchinson's plea of mitigation.

The accused was essentially a humane and good man, as his Lordship would glean from the testimony of some of his colleagues in the 'Intelligence Branch of the Foreign Office'. He was the father of a young family, with an addition imminent. He had not acted for monetary gain, but out of ideological conviction. In that respect he was different from the other lamentable cases, which his Lordship had so recently heard in this same court. He urged his Lordship to take into account these factors when determining sentence. Listening to this plea, Blake once again wondered why the judge continued to write. Lonsdale had got 25 years, Kroger 20 and the Ether Gee 15. His must be somewhere along those lines. If he received 18 or 20, with remission he might be out in twelve or fifteen. His children would be grown up.

As the press returned to court, the Lord Chief Justice of England began his deliberations. According to *The Times* reporter, Blake appeared sun-tanned, fit and composed, listening with 'alert demeanour'. What he heard drained the colour from his face. The Lord Chief Justice, calmly summing-up what had been said by both lawyers, went to the nub of the case. 'You have said in your confession that there was not an official document of any importance to which you

159

had access which was not passed to your Soviet contact. The information communicated has rendered much of this country's efforts completely useless'.

Reviewing evidence heard in camera, Lord Parker said the offences were 'akin to treason', that Blake had betrayed the country of his adoption, that 'the graveman of the case' was that, when his political loyalties changed, he had not resigned from the Service, but had stayed in a position of trust so that 'you could continue to betray your country'.

He fully realised that it was unfortunate for Blake that many matters urged in mitigation could not be divulged, as to do so would 'clearly be against the national interest'. However, for his traitorous conduct over many years there must be a very heavy sentence. He sentenced fourteen years on each of the five counts, three of the sentences to run consecutively, making a total of forty-two years. There were gasps and furious scribbling from the press benches, weary silence from the Heads of SIS and MI5.

The evening editions of the London *Evening Standard* claimed it to be the longest sentence imposed in legal memory. A life sentence for murder was indeterminate because remission was often granted — whereas 42 years, made up of three by 14 years, with another two by 14 concurrent, meant that release, even with full remission for good behaviour, would be not be before 1999. Without remission, the earliest release would be in the year 2003 when he would be aged 81. Between the time of his remand and the trial, three additional charges had been proffered, making five separate charges under the Official Secrets Act. What heavily influenced the Lord Chief Justice in secret session were these additions, based on Blake's confession and which referred to specific dates. According to his confession, Blake in Korea in 1951 had given to KGB Chief of Maritime Province, the operational structure of SIS and the identity of officers operating under diplomatic cover. A charge from September 1953 to April 1955 covered the period of the Berlin Tunnel and another covered part of his time operating out of Berlin Station, during which he revealed the identities of hundreds of Western agents within the Eastern Bloc.

Presiding over this secret trial during the tension of the Cold War, one can see why Lord Chief Justice Parker sought to make an example of Blake who clearly had put in peril agents acting on behalf of Western secret services and of Western democracy. On the other hand, as Blake saw it, if one were a communist, one had a duty to subvert those agents of the Imperial powers who were intent on destroying the first Socialist state in human history. These feelings became distant as he was brought in a van from the Old Bailey to prison in West London, seeing on the news stands along Fleet Street his own visage from Korea staring back at him. The trial had taken a little over an hour. At Wormwood Scrubs he surrendered his clothes and personal belongings and became a Category A, Special Watch prisoner. He was facing the rest of his life being spent in gaol, though he buoyed himself up with the fantastic belief that he would not serve that stretch.

The Political Storm breaks...

In spite of the trial being secret, the newspapers made enough of it to alarm a handful of Labour MPs who pressed Prime Minister Macmillan for a response. Macmillan was already an adroit hand in dealing with the Intelligence community, whom he privately believed to be dangerous and volatile — to himself. He had already set an 'enquiry' in train to quell unease after the Lonsdale, Kroger and Ghee trials. Composed of three peers one of whom was a Privy Councillor and another who had served on secret liaison with Washington, the ostensible brief was to examine vetting procedures related to employment in defence. Their political function was to appease both British public opinion and American foreign policy planners who were becoming increasingly reluctant to share intelligence product with Britain, given the rash of spy scandals[*].

Now, a day after Blake's conviction, Macmillan had to bat on the same sticky wicket. Though briefed by the JIC that the less said the better, Macmillan, who had turned down internal pleas of mitigation from SIS and personally decided on hitting Blake with the full weight of the Lord Chief Justice, made a statement in the House, designed to render further questions redundant. He said 'Blake was a British subject by birth' and that 'Blake did not have secret information on defence or atomic matters' — which begged the question as to what, then, could he have information upon? Macmillan wished to say no more 'in the public interest' but offered to share information in private with Hugh Gaitskell, Leader of the Opposition, as a means of defusing what other Labour MPs were claiming to be a security disaster. Gaitskell accepted the compromise. The Labour Leader also agreed with Macmillan that 'it was very difficult for the House to deal with these security matters...'.

Other Labour MPs were not so easily appeased. What kind of secrets had this 'Foreign Office official' betrayed? Was it not true, as was reported abroad, that he was a spy, employed by the Secret Intelligence Service? or as one MP, Dick Marsh quaintly put it, 'a member of the Foreign Office Intelligence'. Macmillan again offered to include Opposition Privy Councillors in the private briefing to Gaitskell. Mollified, Gaitskell agreed to accept private assurances and not press for another, deeper enquiry into the security services. During that meeting, which took place a week after Blake's conviction, Macmillan put to Gaitskell and the Privy Councillors that, Blake deserved every day of the sentences for the damage he had done to Western defences against Russia.

----

[*] Chaired by Sir Charles Romer, it included Sir Harold Emerson former Permanent Secretary at Dept. of Labour and Sir Geoffrey Thistleton-Smith, late of Joint Services Mission, Washington.

Macmillan then delivered a trump card, one familiar to Parliament. Because of the seriousness of the Blake case, he would set up another formal enquiry into security matters, even though the Romer enquiry had yet to report. When The Radcliffe Committee was announced, the heads of SIS and MI5 were relieved. Although chaired by Lord Radcliffe, who had an impressive legislative record as a Law Lord, the other members of the enquiry were 'friends of the firm'. They included Frank Deakin, onetime Special Operations Executive in Europe and now Warden of St. Anthony's College Oxford, a college, which unknown to the public, supplied the 'officer class' to MI5 and Kenneth Younger, who was a Labour Privy Councillor who had processed intelligence material at both Home and Foreign offices. On the face of it, the establishment of the Radcliffe Committee seemed to close the parliamentary chapter on Blake.

Meanwhile the man who caused the enquiry was adjusting to prison. In the early weeks, life was difficult. Having to surrender his civilian clothes brought back memories of Korea, though the conditions were infinitely more humane. Assured by the Governor of 'The Scrubs' that he would be treated properly, he was given books and access to the library. He was placed on twenty-four hour watch, to observe how he was adjusting and whom he was befriending.

'Gordon Lonsdale', whose conviction had preceded Blake's and whose role as one of the most successful KGB agent-runners in Britain had influenced Blake's sentence, made a point of making friends with him and assuring him that all would come right in the end. Lonsdale predicted that Blake and he would be special guests at the 50th Anniversary of the Communist Revolution in Red Square in 1967. Blake was sceptical. Had he fully realised the laxity of the prison security, he might have had cause for optimism. Although the home Security Service (MI5) had warned that Blake and Lonsdale should not fraternise, the prison service, unused to dealing with such weighty espionage operators, misinterpreted this to mean both should be on 'special watch' and be grouped together.

Lonsdale was a died-in-the-wool 'illegal', a long-term penetration agent whose service had begun when a boy. Through the influence of his aunt in Canada, an ideological communist, he was 'spotted' and surrendered to the Comintern conspiracy. By training, false identities and eventual placing in Britain, with an ostensible Canadian business background, Lonsdale built-up a business in Britain as the importer of jukeboxes. Playing vinyl records of pop songs in burgeoning coffee bars of the 1950s, the jukebox became the centrepiece of new town leisure. Co-incidentally Sean Bourke's impact on the 'teen-scene' of Crawley was through his technical knowledge of jukeboxes, though there is no evidence to suggest that he personally knew Londsdale.

Such was the growth of pin-ball and juke boxes however, in Macmillan's 'never had it so good' England, that Londsdale found himself actually making millions from their import — a piece of perverse history about which he would later boast, that he ran a profitable Capitalist company financed by a Socialist intelligence service. The fact that his KGB technical training equipped him to provide a reliable back-up service enhanced his sales. When he was finally rumbled by the same defector that had fingered Blake, the MI5 investigators found a string of agents so equipped with advanced radio that it took the redoubtable Peter Wright of MI5's technical section many months to comprehend their capacity to transmit British defence secrets to Moscow.[*]

This, then, was the nature of the initial support, which Blake had as he adjusted to prison. He found the company of Lonsdale a considerable morale-booster as the hearing of his appeal approached, though he had little faith in the process. Remarkably, The Appeal hearing was expedited being heard about six weeks after the conviction, as against the usual twelve or eighteen. Again, the part of it that might have most weight was heard in secret. Again, too, his counsel made mild protest but was overruled by the Judge, Mr Justice Hilbery.

---

[*] *Spycatcher*, Peter Wright, William Heinemann, Australia, 1987, pp 128-144.

He also resisted Jeremy Hutchinson's claim that three consecutive sentences of 14 years, was questionable in law, delivering his view that they had a threefold purpose 'to be punitive, to deter others and to safeguard this country'.

With Parliament mollified, the Establishment had another stratagem to ward off remaining unease. Included in Macmillan's confidential briefing of Labour's Privy Counsellors, were some who might later hint to journalists that Blake's sentence of 42 years represented 'a year for every agent he had betrayed to the communists'. When that version duly appeared in the press, much of the Labour indignation subsided. Blake was left to face into the long tunnel of his sentences. It took him some months to recover his composure.

In Crawley New Town, meanwhile, events unknown to Blake were settling into a pattern that would have profound effects on his life. On Monday 18th September 1961, in his home in Snell Hatch, Constable Michael Sheldon unwrapped a mailed parcel of what appeared to be a presentation coffee box. Noticing screws protruding, he quickly held it at arms length. It exploded, giving him a bad fright and burning his arms. Within hours of reporting to his police superiors, detectives visited Sean Bourke's lodgings. The landlady told them he was on holiday in Ireland, having departed the previous week. Detectives conducted a thorough search of Bourke's bedroom. When he returned to Ifield road, he was arrested, questioned and charged. What they had found in his room and among the refuse bins would form the bulk of the case against Sean Alphonsus Bourke. He was charged with the attempted murder of Constable Michael Sheldon, by sending him 'an infernal machine' through the post.

Bourke was returned for trial in early December, pleading not guilty. He was described as a factory clerk. According to the local newspaper, he appeared in court in a neat blue suit and answered the prosecution questions with a 'calm astuteness'. No, he had not sent the bomb; yes he had the expertise to construct such a device from his time in the RAF. The Crown's case strengthened, with evidence of components of the bomb being the same as those which Bourke used to construct the quiz-panel for the Army cadets. Screws, nails and electrical wiring similar to those used in the quiz-panel had been recovered from his lodgings. According to the Police Laboratory, the scrapings from a biro used in the writing of an inscription inside the box matched a biro found at his lodgings, while the spelling of the inscription caused some quiet merriment in court. The Latin exhortation *Requiescat in Pace* on the lid was mentioned by a detective as having been in a test of spelling during Bourke's interrogation. Would he care to spell it? Bourke had hesitated, asking was there an 'ie' in the word and had spelled it incorrectly, twice.

When Bourke's defence counsel addressed the jury, he made much of this inscription, saying that 'Rest in Peace' did not amount to a clear intention to kill, as the sender intended the recipient to read it. The sender would also have loaded a greater charge into the bomb — had he murder in mind. Whoever sent it had intended it to frighten and possibly injure, but not to kill. Bourke's defence also listed his client's good name among colleagues in the Metal Box Company and in his work for the Army Cadet Force, calling upon a senior officer, Bannister, who said he believed Bourke was a person of the highest character who would not commit such an act.

The Prosecution made much of the items found in Bourke's lodgings and at his work place, including a typewriter whose characteristic keys matched the typing of the address label. All of which on their own did not amount to guilt, but taken together as found in the bomb, were capable of only one conclusion. 'When one looks at the things which link the bomb with Bourke, it is right to start with suspicion and end with certainty'. The jury accepted this reasoning but accepted also the intention to injure rather than to kill. Bourke was found guilty of the lesser charge of sending a device intended to cause grievous bodily harm. Some of those who attended the court felt Bourke was taking a perverse pleasure in the proceedings, as if he was fascinated by — and learning — how the Justice system worked.

When the sentence of seven years was handed down, he stood rock still, with a clear military bearing. There were some in the court who thought it a waste of a talent, while others were shocked at the list of previous convictions which had been read out. From his boyhood in Limerick when he had been convicted of petty thieving of jam and biscuits from the railway, to the later larcenies in the RAF, it amounted to ten separate convictions. He was now about to enter the company of convicts with an even more impressive criminal pedigree, but of some also who had transgressed the law for the most ideological of reasons.

CHAPTER FOURTEEN

LIFE IN 'THE SCRUBS'

Insofar as prisons reflect the wider society, Wormwood Scrubs gaol told a lot about Britain of the 1960s. Built in the previous century to a style favoured by the War Office for military barracks in the far-flung colonies, its gothic towers set down among the fields of West London expressed Victorian theories that fresh air and hard work would incur reform among the criminal classes. By the 1960s, it was an institutional anachronism. Inmates earned three pounds a week sewing mailbags. Outside was a world of 'swinging' London of mini-skirts, Carnaby Street and The Beatles, of pot-smoking and anti-nuclear protests, of a soccer-mad proletariat and a sanguine Establishment.

Within this time-warped regime, George Blake and Sean Bourke made accommodation. Both were intelligent men of the world, skilled in coping with systems. Each had been imprisoned before. They were also keen to make good use of their time. Blake received Home Office permission to continue his Arabic studies, though the exam papers were vetted by MI5, which led him to wonder what hapless academic had been assigned to monitor the texts. Bourke pursued tuition in tailoring and telegraphy. Both signed up for London University postal studies in English Literature, which was augmented by visiting tutors. In the classes, they were to meet as varied a collection of eccentrics as England of the 1960s could provide.

Among the 'intellectuals' of the prison, there numbered an army officer convicted of murdering his lover's husband, a financial fraudster whose activities spanned several continents, two Russian spies and peace protesters gaoled for illegally demonstrating against Britain's 'collaboration' with America on providing bases for nuclear bombers. By 1965, Bourke had become editor of the prison magazine *New Horizon* and Blake had become a trusted guru, whose advice was sought by prisoners and warders alike. They had bent the regime to their liking and led lives of privilege. Blake ran the prison shop, where his disbursement of tobacco gave him leverage on other prisoners. Bourke had become Head Cutter in the tailoring shop and as editor of the magazine had his own office. But they were in gaol. The 'offices' were prison cells.

Outside, much which had influenced their personal histories continued to evolve. The Cold War had solidified with the building of the Berlin Wall. Because millions of unwilling communists voted with their feet and fled to the West as refugees, the regime had built a massive wall that sundered families as well as the city. Those trying to flee were shot down by border guards. As seen by Western leaders, Communism had failed on its ultimate frontier with the Free World as an ideology maintained by the gun and not by conviction — a failure exploited by President John F. Kennedy in a Berlin speech that became a fable of American willingness to fight for a free, capitalist world. In gaol for his beliefs, Blake continued to believe in a system, which was increasingly maintained by oppression.

For Bourke, the good life encountered in Macmillan's England continued even in gaol. Running a coffee bar in Crawley had given him a taste of media profile, which he managed from within the prison. Well spoken and articulate, he so impressed prison management that he rapidly progressed to becoming a 'trusty', being literally trusted to escort other prisoners on medical and compassionate visits.

As Editor of the prison magazine he commissioned articles from other prisoners, some of which he made sure were noticed in the national press. As an actor in several of the prison plays he found himself reviewed in the tabloids. How he managed that coverage said much for the cunning with which he manipulated an image of notoriety.

The tabloid *Daily Sketch* was hoodwinked in an elaborate ploy. As Editor of *New Horizon*, Bourke had access to prisoners. He enjoyed the role, replicating his days as a Boy Sergeant in the RAF. He also repeated the same abuse of his authority. As each edition of the magazine came off the small printing press, Bourke and a group of other trusties distributed the copies. Invariably he sought compliments upon the contents. *New Horizon* was closer to the left-wing *New Statesman* than to a prison magazine. It published articles on politics as well as cleverly worded profiles of the 'screws'. Sometimes an editorial addressed the weighty matters of British foreign policy. One article 'Morality of Spying', made the case that spies were paid by governments to do in peacetime what soldiers did in war. The Humanist Group made a case against organised religion. All very 1960s topics.

The *Daily Sketch* received a letter signed by 'Five dissatisfied prison officers' and enclosing a copy of *New Horizon*. 'A disturbing letter, written on notepaper headed 'Wormwood Scrubs Prison' (which) came from five prison officers who are angry and embittered by what is happening in this gaol', the tabloid reported. It accused the editor Sean Bourke, whom the *Daily Sketch* said is 'often to be seen taking tea in George Blake's cell...another regular at these cosy tête-à-têtes is Kenneth De Courcey, the financier who was gaoled in 1963 for fraud, perjury and forgery'.

Had the Sketch done some further checking it might have avoided a subsequent appearance before the Press Council on behalf of one Sean Alphonsus Bourke, prisoner, who formally indicted the paper for publishing false allegations about himself. He claimed he never had tea in George Blake's cell and had never conspired with Kenneth De Courcey to 'whitewash the crimes of George Blake'. The allegation that the prison magazine was being used 'for dubious purposes' was a slur on his own character, as he held a position of trust in the prison. Moreover the edition cited by the *Daily Sketch* was a forgery, claimed Bourke — a fellow prisoner who had access to his office probably perpetrated it. In fact, claimed Bourke, the article criticising religion had been authored by the Humanist Group and he, as Editor, had written the article on the Morality of Spying, which had been cleared by the prison Governor. He sought damages and an apology from the *Daily Sketch*.

The Press Council complained to the Home Office, whose investigation revealed the letter from 'the five dissatisfied prison officers' to be forged on out-of-date prison paper. Enquiries within the prison pointed at Bourke as the instigator of the entire affair, but the Home Office was content to let the *Daily Sketch* fry in its own difficulties. The *Sketch* had made much of recent escapes from gaols, claiming Home Office negligence.

The Press Council severely reprimanded the tabloid for not checking the facts. A reader of the *Daily Sketch* would have assumed the 'five prison officers' were known to the paper and that their 'dissatisfaction' was genuine, said the Council whose reprimand was prominently published in *The Times*. There was satisfaction among the 'intellectuals' who had conspired to deceive the tabloid; at the instigation of their master manipulator Sean Bourke.

He relished seeing his name in print, cast in a role of his own devising. Some of it was due to the cinema imprinting of his Limerick boyhood, where it was common for youngsters at the Saturday matinees to get up and act out the on-screen drama. The buccaneering heroics of Errol Flynn were replicated with shoot-outs and ambushes inventively conducted along the cinema aisles and occasionally spilling out in the foyers of the cinemas. It was part of picture going for Limerick youngsters, formative in actor Richard Harris and writer Frank McCourt. A taste for performing came with the Saturday matinees.

Bourke's own performing had been enhanced with the South London Shakespeare Society and the wider theatre culture, which was undergoing radical change during the 1960s. Plays by John Osborne, Arnold Wesker and Alan Sillitoe portrayed lone working-class heroes pitched against the Establishment. These new dramatists influenced political thinking of the 60s, though the Home Office balked at their work being performed in the prison, preferring mundane light comedies.

Bourke was not a regular actor, invariably providing a twist of mischief to even the most banal of roles, and he was not above making overtures to some of the visiting professional actors. In the case of the drama *So Many Children*, a professional actress, Yvette Wyatt, was taken aback in rehearsal when Bourke proposed marriage. She was even more put out when the tabloid press asked if she was having a romance with a prisoner, Sean Bourke. Her emphatic denial did not merit as much prominence as the fact that she had appeared in *Emergency Ward Ten*, one of the popular soaps of the time. Had she known more of her fellow 'character actor' she might have been less surprised at the coverage.

Blake, too, was making his mark within the prison. Once he appeared to accept the longevity of his sentence, he structured his day effectively, engaging in work on behalf of other prisoners and long bouts of study. He did Yoga and pursued his studies of Arabic. Among other prisoners he was highly regarded and managed to teach several of the 'hard men' French and German — his cell sometimes resembled a classroom, wherein the sound of French grammar with Cockney syntax could be heard. Both he and Bourke helped the less educated with letters to their families. Blake relied heavily for his morale upon the regular visits of his mother and wife. He appeared to be the forgotten spy who had accepted his grim future. In fact he was playing possum.

The security agencies had suggested to the Home Office that he be moved to a Birmingham gaol, to avoid a concentration of convicted Russian spies being in one place.

Once MI5 was alerted to the 'comradeship' of the two KGB agents, it asked they be sent to different prisons. However the Home Office did not accede to the written request of the Director of MI5 for Blake to be moved.

It may have taken a compassionate view of the travel duress, which a move would have placed upon his wife and mother, upon whose regular visits his mental welfare was dependent.

By May 1966, Blake had served five years of his sentence and appeared to have accepted that he would grow old in the Scrubs. He felt he would not be exchanged in one of those secret East-West trade-offs, whereby captured spies were repatriated to their own countries. 'Gordon Lonsdale' had secured his freedom in exchange for SIS agent, Greville Wynne, who had been caught posing as a businessman in Moscow. But Wynne and Lonsdale were natives of the exchanging countries. Although a British subject, Blake was foreign. Britain was also vulnerable to American pressure because of the long list of traitors within the British service. Unless he could ordain release from within his own resources, he would become a pensioner in prison. Forty-two years seemed very, very long.

As a respite from sewing mailbags, the 'intellectuals' re-worked their ideological concerns. Active in those debating groups were peace activists whose protests at nuclear bases had become part of British politics of the 1960s. Inevitably, Blake brought realpolitik to these debates and forged friendships with Michael Randle and Pat Pottle, who had been prominent members of the anti-war radicalism. When Randle asked Blake if he ever thought of escaping, Blake replied; 'I think about it every day'. Randle's colleague, Pat Pottle, had a history of non-violent direct action, having been prominent in campaigns against political oppression in China, Greece and, latterly, against the nuclear bases in Britain. Pottle had a pedigree of dissent. His English father and Irish mother had met on the Jarrow Hunger march and brought up five boys to believe that 'The rulers rule us by consent — and we can withdraw that'.

As their sentences finished, Blake understood that should he consider escaping, he could rely upon their help.

Blake had tried a few dummy runs, which left him with no optimism. One inmate had promised co-operation, but had gone to the police instead. Blake decided that he could not trust the criminal classes.

Randle and Pottle, on the other hand, were ideological prisoners and had been prosecuted under the same Official Secrets Act. While not being communists, they were sympathetic to his situation and, if anything, as Englishmen, were more indignant at the severity of the sentence. By the time he received a second coded Christmas card asking if he remembered their 'conversations', Blake had decided that Sean Bourke, was probably his best bet as a go-between. Bourke had an overriding hatred of institutions and had impressed Blake with his mental dexterity and 'ability to dissemble'. Having been imprisoned twice before in Spain and Korea, Blake had some sense of who would be most useful to him. In Spain he had allied himself with the Poles, in Korea, with the missionaries. In the Scrubs, it was 'the intellectuals and ideologues' — and one maverick Irishman.

Before approaching Bourke directly, Blake sought the view of the fraudster Kenneth De Courcey, whom Blake thought an acute judge of character because of his share rigging. Blake was told that 'If you get the right kind of Irishman he will go the ends of the earth for you. The problem is knowing which side he is on...'

For Bourke, his wildest ambitions were being realised. Since a teenager he had seen himself in some heroic role — which had usually ended in gaol. Yet he yearned for some higher glory, which maddeningly had not been defined. Now the ingredients were put in place — he would release a Russian spy from an English gaol. How he would relish the adventure. Boy, would the world know about it...

When Blake approached him, Bourke's reaction was immediate. As Blake explained that he could not rely on 'exchange' of spies that he would have to organise his own resources and suggested Bourke might like to think about it, Sean interrupted: he would not have to think about it. 'I'm your man'.

Thereupon he dedicated himself entirely to the enterprise. Having been given a date for his own release in July, he concentrated upon laying the groundwork. To ease their return to civilian life, the prison had an enlightened system for convicts coming to the end of long sentences. Outside work was obtained and they stayed in a hostel within the prison. In this halfway house where Bourke stayed while he worked in a factory in nearby Acton, he set-up an observation post on the top floor. He surveyed the prison. He could see over the prison wall, which ran along into Artillery Road, the wall he hoped Blake would ascend — and beyond the gates of Hammersmith Hospital. He calculated the distance from the end of D wing to the wall to be a mere matter of 15 yards. He logged the roster times of wall patrols, experimenting with diagrams of prisoner and guard movements.

Initially he communicated with Blake by using 'Trusty' prisoners who moved between hostel and prison. A series of notes were passed, as Bourke articulated his research. One note, passed in error to the embezzler De Courcey, caused Blake panic when De Courcey informed him of it — but the fraudster promised secrecy in return for being privy to the progress of the plot. Blake had no option but to agree, though he fed De Courcey snippets of his own choosing, not enough for the fraudster to know the full mosaic of preparations.

Other mishaps with messages led Bourke to ponder on improving communications, solved by a visit to Piccadilly where he became riveted by walkie-talkie radios, not available to the public when he had entered prison. The salesman took one out into the hub of London and Bourke, hearing him quite clearly within the shop, was convinced of the practical usage. Adopting the manner of a gentleman farmer for whom it would be invaluable on his country estate, Bourke purchased a set for £25, probably the most effective investment of the enterprise. Within days, from within the hostel he was talking to Blake in his cell.

A call-sign was devised, based on an Irish folk legend and Richard Lovelace's poem about 'stone walls do not a prison make...'.

As Bourke's period in the hostel ended, he found a room in Pennryn Road, about a mile from the Scrubs. Continuing his reconnaissance, he walked miles of pavement by terraced houses. He crossed roads and timed traffic lights; observed motor car routes and frequency of visitors to Hammersmith Hospital which lay on the other side of the wall that he and Blake had already decided would be the one to go over. It was across from 'D' Hall, where he had done his time with

Blake, Randle and Pottle. The visitors to the hospital would provide cover for two men on a dark winter evening. Bourke knew the routine of prisoners attending the Saturday evening cinema show, the melee of men going to various landings and cells afterwards, the impossibility of the few duty warders keeping track of any one prisoner among the mass of similarly attired men, before they were 'banged-up' for the night. Warders would see a mass of blue denim jackets and trousers.

Before the locking of the cells, Blake with the connivance of other prisoners, would move to a landing window whose struts would have been broken and repaired to seem secure. Blake would detach them again; ease his way down onto a sloping roof and from there to the ground. Still within the prison, he would make for the wall, at a time when the internal patrols would be on the far side. Fifteen yards to freedom.

The plan, for a night in October when weather would be murky and wet, was that Bourke would be on the far side of the wall and throw over a rope ladder that Blake would clamber up, with Bourke taking the strain until Blake ascended the top of the 20-ft high wall. Then Blake would swing down the rope, which Bourke held. It had seemed childishly simple when Bourke had recited it to Blake's mother and sister, so simple they had dismissed it as unworkable. Now, in many meetings in Randle's home in Kentish Town during June and July, the details were fine-tuned. Pat Pottle reminded them of how in prison, a common refrain among convicts had been 'if only...' If only a minor detail had been double-checked... . Anne Randle came up with the idea of knitting needles to strengthen the 'steps' of the ladder, to prevent it tangling under Blake's weight. Michael suggested a hook on the top, which would grapple onto the copingstone on the top of the wall, and allow Blake to descend on the far side. Such plans were formulated in many meetings throughout the summer of 1966.

Pottle, in line with his peace convictions, emphasised there should be no violence. They would not be armed. If caught, they would surrender 'with a struggle'. As a printer, he would provide fake passports for the pair, as Bourke intended to go to Russia as well, and from there to Ireland, where he would claim some kind of political asylum. Randle pored over the logistics, making timings and diagrams of how long it would take before the alarm was raised, suggesting an immediate hideaway within a mile or so of the prison, so that Blake would be off the streets by the time the search started and removed from the happenchance of discovery. It was decided that Randle and Pottle, as known friends of Blake within the prison, would not participate in the actual escape, as the security services could be expected to check on them immediately.

Bourke would also be high on the list of suspects, but if the daring escapade worked, he would go to ground and lay a false trail, ostensibly having returned to Ireland after his release. Before the escape, he would go to Limerick, where he would lay a legend of not returning to London.

Randle and Pottle would take over the arrangements for spiriting Blake out of Britain, once the hue and cry had died down. Bourke would disappear in London. There were many discussions on how best to conceal Blake. They thought of dying his skin black, inspired by a magazine article in which a journalist had changed his colour to find at first hand conditions of discrimination against Blacks in America.

By the summer of 1966, although the main logistics were in place, there was a stark problem of finance. Monies were needed to buy a motorcar that afterwards would be abandoned; there would be no trade-in value. Monies were needed to rent a separate flat for a period beforehand, and if all went well, for weeks afterwards. (There would be no return of the deposit). At Blake's suggestion, Bourke had met with his mother, by now a housekeeper to a wealthy Home Counties family. Mrs Behar was nervous, did not trust Bourke and asked her daughter for support. When Blake's sister, Adele, met Bourke, she insisted on knowing the detail of the plan before agreeing to fund it. A tense meeting in a London hotel ended in mutual disappointment as Bourke told how he intended to release her brother. Adele refused to contribute, saying it was foolhardy and not likely to succeed.

For a time, Bourke lost heart. In the region of £12,000 was needed (at to-day's values) an amount well beyond their combined resources. Michael and Anne Randle had a young family and he was training to be a teacher while Anne worked. Pat Pottle had a small printing business, which mainly produced material for the anti-war movement. Bourke had some savings from the factory in Acton, but most of his wages had gone across pub counters. Six double whiskeys in an hour was not unusual. Between them, they could muster only a fraction of the costs. Eventually, among the Randle's friends, a Socialist sympathiser donated an inheritance, sufficient to fund the enterprise.

Thus financed and with the first steps for Bourke to 'disappear', he told his landlord he was returning to Ireland, moved out of his bed-sitter and joined Pat Pottle at his home in Hampstead. They were burly and gregarious men and while Pottle made strenuous efforts to be agreeable, the Irishman tested his patience by returning at times drunk. Pat Pottle, with a taste for conspiracy and military training from his conscription days in the RAF, insisted on thorough security. Bourke, on the other hand, thought Pat 'excitable'. When Pat asked him to change the motorcar, which he had apparently bought in his own name, Bourke demurred. When Pat repeatedly urged him to sell it and buy another under a different name, Bourke said he had done so — but later could not provide details of the new transaction. Randle, Pottle and Blake would have been more concerned had they known of an incident in a pub in St. Martin's Lane in the West End, where Bourke had become drunk and insisted on telling anyone within hearing range that he was about to 'shake the Establishment to its foundations'. In another incident in the same pub, a pistol was produced by someone drinking with Bourke, impatient to hurry-up the bar service. It was not an auspicious start to an enterprise that required calm heads and cool nerves. When sober, however, he was polite, concerned and courteous. Pottle had to take the rough with the smooth, but his unease continued.

Blake, meanwhile, was becoming stressed as the planning culminated. There had been several scares in the prison. Bourke had used a wave band close to the police one. A whisper had reached the Governor of communication by walkie-talkie radio between a prisoner and the outside. Searches failed to turn up Blake's set, which he kept concealed in the prison shop, but some electronic 'sweeping' of the perimeters alarmed him. Word spread among more prisoners of the likely attempt. Surprisingly none appeared to have grassed, though warders may have overheard garbled gossip. Taken with the earlier escape of two prisoners over the wall at the spot selected for Blake, the mood was sufficient for the Home Office to order a review of security.

Among the measures, was the installation of a hut on each corner, with telephone, for a static officer to monitor the wall at night under improved arc-lights. Also, the end gable windows in the gothic towers were to be reinforced with strong wire mesh. If installed soon, that would be the end of the plan, as Blake was to squeeze through the church-like windows, made-up of panes of glass. Bureaucracy was on the side of the conspirators. By September the landing windows were being meshed, but in the traditions of the civil service, the workmen began with Block A and worked regulation hours. None of those events helped Blake's state of mind. He drew more heavily on his Yoga exercises to maintain his equilibrium, as he urged Bourke in their weekly talks by radio, to bring forward the date.

Bourke conferred with Randle and Pottle. A date of Saturday October 22 was set for the escape. Randle and Pottle would find something to do that evening which involved other people as alibis. Bourke put his part into operation by flying to Shannon airport and getting the bus into Limerick. As he arrived in the city of his birth, bitter boyhood feelings surfaced. Along the street of the mad, the bad and the dead, he glared at the limestone faces of lunatic asylum, gaol and 'holy statues'. In the cemetery, he found a friend; also back from England, tending his father's grave. He was moved — but not so much to change his view that Limerick was a dump and would always be one.

The closets in the public toilet were piled high with shit, while a printed notice exhorted men to keep their thoughts pure. He remembered toilets in London where the notices informed customers of the nearest VD clinics. 'The Irish fear you sin when you put your cock in hand' he told a friend, 'the English assume you already have and direct you to where they'll scrape the scabs off...'. He found his mother visibly older and tired, but overcome with love to see him. He gave her money and deflected her queries about his past five years. During his time in The Scrubs he had written to her via a brother in Manchester, but knew she was not fooled.

She urged her son to do nothing against 'John Bull'. 'If I was depending on the heroes up in the Dail I'd be starved long ago.'— a reference to the British Army pension which the residents of Bengal Terrace enjoyed from service in two world wars. He drank in The Munster Fair Tavern, which was the local pub and paid for liberal rounds for those companions of his schoolboy days who frequented The Tavern, which was known for the free-flowing quality of its Murphy's stout. He was saddened by their condition and angry as what he saw as the State neglect, even malice, which had exacted such attrition. To those who cared to listen, he held forth on the superiority of the British welfare system, disbursed monies and was privately exalted at what would become public in a few weeks. He visited many old haunts, had a drink with a lay teacher from his Sexton Street school, Jack Danaher, a humane man who told him that 'The Brothers' were less sadistic nowadays and tried to explain their harshness as being part of their own small farmer upbringing, where as boys themselves they were up at dawn to milk cattle, mend ditches and were often subjected to poverty and beatings. A 'religious vocation' was a passport to status from a life of servitude.

Mollified at being treated as an adult by a former school teacher, drinking quality pints, he mellowed over a few days of childhood recall. He lingered by Garda stations and school gates and was left with a confusing jumble of feelings — childhood resentments vying with adult control. He made a point of visiting the Courthouse where he had many appearances since the age of ten. Now he was a spectator and recorded the defendants' excuses in drink cases. Being a good mimic, with an eye for the dramatic, he later regaled an audience with the appearance of a man '…with the grand Christian name of Sebastian found asleep on the roof of an elaborate grave. At one o'clock am, acting on information received, Gardai surrounded the Protestant cemetery in St. John's Square and the accused was lying on top of the flat roof of a tomb. He smelt of drink and told a Garda "I felt like a climb" '.

He also looked up some who had been in Daingean Reformatory with him, all of twenty years before. On a personal note, it was in the company of one of those from my own street in Limerick that I met Bourke, in the George Hotel in early October 1966. I had been working in London and was back on a break to see my family. With my brother I went to 'The George' and met there a neighbour from a few doors away, who had often been in trouble with the law. He was polite, though known locally as a 'hard man'. Many of us worked in London which gave us conversation on digs, the vagaries of landladies and the route of the No 7 bus, which went from London Bridge to Acton, which I had worked as a conductor. It also passed the front gates of Wormwood Scrubs. As an aspirant journalist, I was struck by Bourke's erudition. When I jocularly asked him how he liked being 'back in a Christian country' he surprised me by the ferocity of his invective. 'Christian fucking country' he spat... 'My arse'.

Some weeks later, I was to recall that encounter in the Limerick hotel, when the man with 'erudition' stared at me from the front pages of the London newspapers.

CHAPTER FIFTEEN

OVER ONE WALL...

On Saturday 22nd October 1966, Sean Bourke sat in a Humber motorcar in Artillery Road by the wall of Wormwood Scrubs. A wet drizzle had descended. He was tense, nervous and determined. The immensity of what he was attempting now came to him, at a few minutes past six on a wet Saturday. On one side of the car was Hammersmith Hospital, on the other the 20-foot high wall of The Scrubs, behind which a senior KGB agent waited. A select audience of prisoners went about their evening ritual with the studied ease of extras in a film.

In the wider world, from which he had now removed himself, Pat, Michael and Anne were also waiting, in North London, hovering by telephones, unable to concentrate, sharp in their responses to their friends, yet needing to appear normal and sociable. Since returning to London a week before, Bourke had rehearsed the journey from a flat in North Kensington, to the prison. He had found the hideaway at 28 Highlever Road, a street of two-story houses divided into 'flatlets'. Even the hall had been divided with stud-board in the practice of the sixties to give private access to the flatlet on the ground floor. There were thousands of such conversions and Bourke reckoned that such an ordinary looking terrace would not be high on the search list.

The landlady lived some houses away and gave him keys on production of his deposit. He had given her a false name and address in Croydon. From the beginning of the week, he had a list of tasks to be performed every day, upon which he reported to the others. He bought a Harris tweed jacket and cavalry twill trousers for Blake in 'Jackson The Tailors', stocked up his larder with tinned foods and bought a radio and television for the news. He and Michael Randle visited chemists to buy doses of Meladinin, the drug that would dye Blake's skin dark. With Pat's false passport, it was intended to create a new identity for travel to Egypt, from where it was presumed Blake would contact KGB about his future. It will be remembered that Blake had spent a formative adolescence in Cairo.

They had all been so focussed upon the escape that the logistics of how to get Blake out of the country had not received the same planning. Buying the dye, they found was not easy and required prescriptions, as did the sun lamp, which stimulated the treatment. They got the Meladinin with forged medical notes. Bourke managed to persuade a chemist to sell them a lamp without a prescription and tossed the receipt over his shoulder but Randle became nervous of their fingerprints and went back later to retrieve it. He would have had a seizure had he known that Bourke had *not* sold the Humber car, (registered under his own name) but persisted in the fiction when questioned. Bourke, for his part, had taken to wearing disguise, which was more comic than convincing. The German-born landlady, becoming suspicious of 'Mr Sigeworth' complained to the local police station that her new tenant sometimes wore a beard and sometimes not — all in the same day. Her call was received by the desk sergeant along the lines of 'keep taking the pills, Madam...'.

Bourke had not actually done a dummy run on a Saturday evening along Artillery Road between the hideaway and the hospital, whose evening visiting hours began at seven. He had done many solo runs from his previous flat but having returned from Limerick and found the Highlever flat, had not done a first-hand run in the wet, wintery conditions now facing him. He found the traffic more dense than expected and was running late.

In the week since his return, the conspirators had intensified their involvement. The prisoners who were necessary as support had been briefed by Blake on their various roles. The escape was timed for the hiatus between the end of the Saturday film after six and the 'banging-up' at seven — the roll call of inmates for the night. One prisoner would hang blankets over the railing of the first floor, to mask the view of the two warders below, as switches were made between cells and the walkie-talkie was produced for

Blake. It was common for blankets to be hung out on Saturday for cleaning.

Another would break the window on the landing, return and signal it was done; yet another would keep watch on the warders below in case suspicion arose. Others would monitor the end of the film, pass the word along it was due to end, then would form a 'goal defence', loitering on landings and stairways, to obscure the view of the warders. Above them Blake would move along the gantry to the gothic window. Among the items concealed had been a wooden mock-up of the window frames, which he had practised negotiating in his cell. Once the breaker had done his job, the pressure of Blake on the swivel upper pane would expand into the damaged frame-struts below to allow him to squeeze through.

Outside in the rain, Bourke waited in a country that in the past few months had become politically volatile. After England's euphoria in winning the football World Cup in July, Harold Wilson's Labour government was encountering a series of disasters, natural and man-made. In August, right by the far boundaries of the prison, three policemen had been shot dead as they approached a suspect car. Bourke had to postpone his preparations for a month, resuming with the lessening of police activity.

It had not helped his confidence that one of the suspects, Harry Roberts, had fled to Ireland and that Scotland Yard had placed a premium on information from the Irish police and the London underworld.

In September, faced with almost half a million unemployed, Prime Minister Wilson had brought in an income freeze. In the wider political scenario that interested Blake, many former colonies were in active negotiation for independence. The Empire was winding down to becoming a Commonwealth, while America, having learned little from the Korean experience, was bogged down opposing Communism in Vietnam and unable to set a date for withdrawal. And on this Saturday in Artillery Road, a driver in a car outside the side entrance to the hospital appeared to be sniffing a pot of chrysanthemums which doubtless he was about to present to a patient.

Sean Bourke was speaking into a microphone and instigating his call sign with George Blake:

'This is Fox Michael calling Baker Charlie. Fox Michael calling Baker Charlie. Come in please. Over...'

Bourke pressed the receiving button.

'This is Baker Charlie to Fox Michael. Receiving you loud and clear. Over...'

On-cue inside the prison, the chatter of the prisoners increased, as cover. Although they had done it many times, Bourke again went through the full call sign, which embraced a poet they had studied in English Lit. classes:

Bourke: *'Stone walls do not a prison make, nor iron bars a cage'*

Blake: *'Minds innocent and quiet take this for a hermitage. Over...'*

Bourke: *'Richard Lovelace must have been a fool. Over'*

Blake: *'...or just a dreamer. Over'*

Although Blake had been irritated with Bourke's insistence on going though the entire sequence, he answered with relish. Whatever happened, this would be the last time to recite Lovelace over a private airwave. Smartly, he was out on the landing, with the burglar who was to break the struts, their position masked from the warders below by blankets and his radio talk obscured by deliberate chatter from prisoners waiting outside cells. But there was silence — nothing coming back on the radio from Bourke.

For a while Bourke was off-air but came back, apologising for being late. He gave the signal for the struts to be broken. Within minutes the burglar was back, having done the job with his boot. There was a growl of approval from supporters as Blake padded off to the landing window in his plimsolls. The embezzler Kenneth De Courcey held Blake's copy of *The Koran* and intoned his own form of prayer that Allah might favour his disciple.

The radio was tucked into his sweater. He called Bourke but got no reply. With an ease that surprised him he was out the window and onto the roof of the covered passageway below. He dropped down and tucked himself into the lea of the Gothic tower. It was raining steadily and he was quickly soaked as he waited for the rope to come over the wall. He could see clearly the spot through the frazzle of rain under the arc-lights, the place opposite the tower where the rope would dangle...It was about fifteen yards from him. On the other side of the wall, Bourke had placed his car opposite that tower, facing away from Scrubs Common and into Du Cane Road, which would be their exit. *'It is coming over now...'* Bourke said. Blake waited...and waited...becoming wetter and wetter... No Bourke on the radio and no rope over the wall... It was so wet that even the watchman on the corner could not see him.

'I must have been there for fifteen or more minutes. It seemed longer', he recalled, noting the distance from tower to rope to be about twice the length of his Moscow kitchen 'I kept calling him up: *"Baker Charlie to Fox Michael, Baker Charlie to Fox Michael, come in please...Over"*. No reply. *"Baker Charlie, I'm out in the yard, come in please...Over..."*. No reply'. Neither could Bourke radio Blake with the simple explanation. As he was about to throw the rope ladder, he had been interrupted by a security patrolman checking the wicket gates into the sports ground at the end of Artillery Road. Something in Bourke's demeanour had caused the patrolman to be curious, most likely the car's proximity to the prison wall, forty-five minutes before hospital visiting time. Visitors to the hospital mainly parked nearer the main road and not that close to the wall. The patrolman had decided to take a second look at Bourke, bringing out his Alsatian dog as protection. In fact, the patrolman had a number of dogs to exercise and was waiting for one of them to finish sniffing in the park, when he noticed Bourke.

They stared each other out, until Bourke blinked and drove away. It would have invited disaster to proceed with the patrolman staring at him. Bourke steadied himself with a drive to a roundabout, turned back and parked in the same spot. The dog-man had gone. He had been gone about eight minutes. As he turned on the radio, he heard Blake's plaintiff pleas: *'Fox Michael, Fox Michael — are you hearing me...You must throw it now...now...you simply must'*.

'I'm out in the yard' — Bourke responded: *'Rope coming over now'*. Then, as before at the critical moment — a car came down the lane with headlights on, illuminating Bourke as he was about to take the ladder from the boot.

Before that a car had pulled in and a courting couple had stymied him, until like a voyeur, he had stared at them until they moved. Now this car with full headlights. Third time, unlucky. Again, he waited until the lights were switched off and the occupants walked back to the front entrance of the hospital. Another attempt: again a car. He was in despair outside the Humber, hearing Blake desperately calling to him from the radio which he had left on the passenger seat. He could not risk answering it, got back into his car and steeled himself. Four interruptions — more could be expected. Now or never...five to seven, the film would be over, the roll calling started. Now or never...from the radio, Blake: *'Fox Michael, you must throw the ladder, there is no more time. Please Fox Michael, are you still there...?'* Stuck in the drenching rain by the tower, Blake could hear the babble of noise above him as the prisoners made their way to cells in 'D' Block. The shouts of screws — 'Alright on The ONE's Sir'. Military precision. The counting had started.

Suppressing his own panic and taking command, Bourke buttoned: *'Fox Michael to Baker Charlie. The ladder is coming over now, no matter what the consequences, the ladder is coming over now...'*. Bourke was under the wall in the rain, whirling the rope like a cowboy lassoo. On the other side of the wall and directly in line with him, Blake heard him again coming through the radio. Suddenly, there was Bourke's voice again, full of determination: *'I'm going to throw the rope, I'm throwing it now...'*. 'I had my eyes fixed on the top — there it was, this thin nylon curling down like a snake. I knew then that nothing could stop me. I made a run for it, saw the steps and climbed them up...'

Bourke jumped onto the boot to throw the ladder. He had devised two heavy knots before the rope divided into ladder to provide purchase on the coping as he took the weight of Blake. But even as he felt the weight, he wondered if it would be Blake — or a decoy to land him back inside for a longer stretch. Looking up he saw Blake's face come over the parapet. 'Hurry, hurry, drop down and jump' Bourke ordered. Taking a moment to get his bearings, Blake heaved the final few feet, fell flat on the top, looked down, swung his legs over, and then hung by his fingers. Bourke was beneath him, between the car and the wall. 'Jump, jump, for Christ's sake, jump' Bourke hissed as the road was lit up by yet another car's headlights.

In a classic case of mistaken intentions, Bourke moved directly under Blake to break his fall. George, trying to avoid Sean, twisted in mid-air and landed clumsily on the gravel, breaking his wrist and banging his head on the gravel. At the last moment he had thought that if he hurt Bourke, he would be at bay in London, not knowing where to go. Now Bourke dragged the dazed Blake into the back seat of the Humber and told him to put on the hat and mac, which lay beside him.

Disguises, and their amateur attempts, were to prove hazardous. Bourke had perfectly good eyesight, but since the beginning of the week had taken to wearing spectacles with the false beard. Trouble was, he sometimes forgot to wear part of the combination when leaving the flat. He was more in danger with the spectacles, which he put on as they drove away. With condensation building within the car, he took them off...too late. Turning into Du Cane Road, he pranged into a car outside the main hospital entrance. As the driver signalled to pull over, Bourke put the boot down and passed him, causing Blake to urge him to slow down. 'Please, Sean, you will undo everything...take it easy'.

Bourke swore belligerently. Blake again urged calm. As they headed for the hideout, Bourke gave Blake the address of the flat and provided its keys. He turned to look at Blake in the back seat and realised that he would have to stay with him. Blake was practically fainting from shock and pain, keeling over, and hanging on by willpower. And his face looked a sight.

They had departed the prison a few minutes after seven, the time when the screws were looking through keyholes and counting inmates. By twelve or fifteen minutes past seven they were walking in the door of Highlever Road. Sean showed George in the back, the welcoming fire already lit. He cleaned-up his face. The wrist had an ungainly lump protruding. It was clearly broken, though Blake made light of it. They stood awkwardly in the small room, unable to put words on what they had done, unable to comprehend the magnitude. Bourke suddenly felt claustrophobic. He needed air, he needed to talk to himself, but more so, he needed to move the car from the next street. He had no means of knowing whether the suspicious patrolman had noted the number. Would he recall the car when the alarm was raised? Would he blame himself forever for not having acted on his instincts? Maybe, thought Sean, he had memorised the back number plate, which had a light over it. The urgency was to move the car. Oh — and celebrate.

Before leaving the house, Bourke imprudently called Michael Randle from the coin-box in the hall. Conscious of the other occupants invited in the house as alibis, Bourke told Randle that things were good, very good — 'I threw him the bait and he took it, hook, line and sinker.' 'In fact, he's right here with me.' Bourke also told Randle of a problem which could wait until the following day. Michael would talk to Pat. They would have to be ready to help with George's broken wrist.

Walking up the middle of the road like a prize-fighter re-living a title win, Bourke laughed, and 'effed and blinded'. He was hysterical with pleasure and longed to shout out into the night that he, Sean Bourke, had sprung the spy George Blake. To himself he repeated: 'I've done it, I've done it!' He wanted to bang on the doors and have everyone come out into the street. Instead, he got soaked, had difficulty starting the car and drove aimlessly, finding himself on the Bayswater Road, heading towards the West End. There was a pub in St.

Martin's Lane where he dearly wished to watch the BBC Nine O'clock News on television. Instead, he drove north towards Paddington, onto the Harrow Road, which is a long road, and off that found another long road, more deserted than usual. He had come down from his high and noticed he was in Kilburn. He would leave the car here, reckoning it would not come as a surprise to Special Branch to find the suspect car in an Irish part of London. He made for a pub on the corner. Watching the clock, he left with the warm glow of a few whiskeys inside him and two bottles of spirits for 'domestic use'.

As Bourke left the pub, all of a mile away, there was consternation in The Scrubs. The warder who had found Blake's cell empty could hardly believe it. Maybe Blake had taken ill. Maybe he was lying on the floor below the spy-hole. Or doing Yoga, standing on his head, out of sight. Unlocking, an instant view showed the cell bare. Worse, a sense of the occupant *not* coming back. From other warders, came a smatter of suggestions. Maybe Blake was still in the tuck shop — that was closed. Maybe he had stayed behind at the film — no. In the library, in another cell? Somewhere? As the panic spread, the screws felt the prisoner's amusement, their unspoken knowledge that the worst *had* happened. This night, there was no routine cry of 'Alright on The TWOS!'

Along the gantries and landings, a steady chatter arose to muted cheers. The word was passed by whisper, signal and then a shout that said it all: 'Old Blakie's had it away!'.

As the Assistant Governor ordered another, thorough search, in the Home Office not far from where Blake had served his early time with SIS, the late-night duty officer answered the phone. What he heard galvanised him into a string of phone-calls. By eight-thirty, the formal statement was released. By nine o'clock it was the lead item on the BBC News, the mug shot of Blake filling the screen, the broadcast seen by millions including two men in a small bed-sitter less than a mile from the gaol. Uncorking the bottle he had brought from the pub, Bourke raised a glass of whiskey to Blake's brandy, remembering a line from the South

London Shakespeare Society; 'Mischief thou art afoot —
take what course thou wilt'.

CHAPTER SIXTEEN

... AND ANOTHER WALL

For Pat, Michael and Anne, the problems were beginning. With their connivance, Bourke had borne the brunt of both planning and execution of the escape. Now, with the injured fugitive hiding a mile from the prison, the next stage was imminent. The problem was, 'the next stage' had not been thought out, beyond the idea of changing Blake's skin colour. Clearly he would have to be moved soonest. Bourke, too, would have to be moved, not least because his chronic inability to stay indoors increased the chances of a random encounter with a prison officer. Though the authorities had not mentioned anyone other than Blake, they knew it was only a matter of time before 'the intellectuals' came into the frame.

By the Sunday morning, Randle had received two phone calls from journalists asking for his recollections of Blake in gaol. Articles he had written for *Peace News*, in which he mentioned his Scrubs experiences, had found their way into the cuttings library of the dailies. Working much the way police do, but with more efficient use of the telephone, journalists trawled through their files of CND protests and court cases. Other prominent 'peaceniks' were also phoned. Totally oblivious of Randle and Pottle's involvement, they in turn rang the two to tell them of the escape of George Blake, as if it was not already plastered all over the Sunday front pages. It required some acting ability by Michael Randle to fend off these enquiries, a situation not helped by seeing Sean Bourke walk up to his front door on Sunday morning, the day after the escape. Bourke seemed incapable of sticking by an arrangement when something unforeseen intruded or he had a better idea. In this case, Blake's broken wrist required urgent attention. Still, Sean's arrival to Kentish Town alarmed Randle. It was possible that Special Branch already had them under surveillance. The arrangement had been not to meet for a few days and use the telephone only sparingly. Sean had broken these rules, but reasoned that the medical need was paramount. He was also bursting to tell the others his story, the hazards of the dog patrolman and the prang with another car. When he suggested taking Blake to a hospital, Michael decided he would have to see for himself. As every hour passed, the buck was being passed to Randle and Pottle — they would have to deliver the next phase in order for the overall plot to succeed. Bourke would become a liability unless the next phase was taken out of his control, they reasoned. For Randle and Pottle, then, the Sunday after the escape was entirely taken-up with trying to cope. Securing a doctor became the priority, after they had visited Highlever Road and saw George's condition for themselves. He was heartfelt in his thanks, but in pain. The pleasure of re-union was drastically submerged under the need for decisions.

What Sean had led them to believe was a self-contained flat turned out to be little more than a bed-sitter, with shared a bathroom. Comings and goings would be observed by other occupants in the house. The room was cleaned every Wednesday; they would need to be gone by then. But they had not actually worked out those moves. On hearing of the high doses of Meladinin required for a colour-change, Blake was less than enthusiastic and taken aback to realise that in fact there were no definite plans to move him out of Britain. One suggestion that he be 'dumped' over the wall of the Russian Embassy in Kensington he thought naive in the extreme. He told them that MI5 surveillance of the embassy, though never foolproof, would now be rigorous. It was also likely that SIS had someone inside — within minutes of arriving, the authorities would know.

He would become the centre of a diplomatic stand-off, an embarrassment to the Russians who may well wonder if they were being set-up — no, that option was out. Other means would have to be found. As the four of them drank tea and whiskey, interspersed with awkward silences, it became clear that some serious thinking — and action — were needed. Blake finally dispensed of the Embassy notion by saying he would rather go back to the Scrubs than be a burden on the Soviets. With that idea out of the way, the priority was to have his wrist treated. Michael tasked himself with finding a doctor, while Anne and Pat went through a list of their friends who might shelter Blake in the short term. And Bourke, too of course. It was asking a lot of law-abiding English people who, while happy to march against Nuclear Weapons, would balk at harbouring an escapee — especially one whose name was all over the front pages and news bulletins.

Michael found a doctor who knew instantly the identity of 'the patient'. He assured them it was his duty to help. Along the way, they picked up setting plaster from another sympathiser who worked in BBC Television Drama. It was used as a prop but serviceable. When they arrived at Highlever Road, Bourke was in a state of high anxiety and gabbling. Examining Blake's arm, the doctor said he understood that the patient was allergic to hospital. In the circumstances, he would attempt to re-set the bones. Did the patient agree? He asked for warm water, used the kitchen table as his surgery with the Sunday papers as a tablecloth. He gave Blake an injection and manipulated the fractured parts together. Blake braced himself against pain, his own image staring back at him from the Sunday newspapers. The doctor appeared not to register this blatant connection and worked the plaster into the bandage. Shortly, Blake felt the relief of the bones being re-set. 'I was no longer in pain'.

As the doctor was tidying up, the TV news came blaring with the Blake Escape still the lead item. Sea and airports were under watch, as were Eastern bloc embassies. Widespread police activity, Home Secretary informed, Prison Service under scrutiny, former prisoners being interviewed — in the huddle of the bed-sitter, they agreed it was standard practice for the police not to release all they knew — they could be knocking on the front door any minute. The doctor refused payment, packed and left, their effusive thanks trailing behind him. Now, they had to re-group and assess the future. As Blake remembered it 'It was clear that nobody had a plan beyond where I was at that moment'. Again, in a panic, friends were called. A couple agreed to take Blake on his own. But first they sought a promise he would no longer spy for the Soviet Union, an undertaking impossible either to give or receive with conviction. To ease their consciences, Blake assured them he no longer possessed information of significance to the Soviets.

His host's composure did not last. When he arrived at their house he found them in a tense state. With mass media speculation as to Blake's whereabouts, the pair's fears increased. After two days they asked him to move. Blake was not sorry as he had felt more restricted than in prison. The couple had insisted he stay in bed all day, use a bucket as toilet and then demanded he go to the basement. Remembering it all much later in Moscow, Blake gave a wry laugh: 'The basement was actually the foundations of the house — rubble and sand. I was worse off than in prison. No heat, no light and a terrified couple upstairs'.

Again, the circle of friends was tried and again, a reluctant offer was made, this time by a married couple. But the husband did not inform his wife — who was of nervous disposition, of their new lodger's identity. When Randle told her, after Blake had been there for a few days, she hit the roof and remonstrated with him. She had believed the men were deserters from the American army in Vietnam whom the Committee of 100 regularly helped, by finding shelter in Britain en route to asylum in Sweden. While this argument raged, the husband said they should know his wife was undergoing therapy, which required her to be completely honest. As a result, she had told her analyst she was harbouring a prison escapee, the spy George Blake. A 'delusion' which the analyst deemed the result of watching too much television. But the tale was enough to have them pack their bags again.

It was a week after the escape and they were floundering. No secure place to stay — and for Pottle still the nagging question of the Humber car.

Pat Pottle had been sceptical when Bourke had told him, before going to Limerick in early October, that he had disposed of the car and bought a replacement. Now it became clear the Humber had been used in the escape. Bourke felt the car was lucky, he had gotten to like it and the aerial for the car radio suited his purposes — he could unscrew it from inside and feed the walkie-talkie output into the socket. Apart from the deception, Pottle was concerned: the car had been registered in Bourke's own name. It was only a matter of time before it was found. As for its location, Bourke admitted he had left it in Harvist Road, Kilburn.

The admission put Michael and Pat into a spin. When they looked to retrieve the car, there was no sign of it. They drove up and down Harvist Road, but no Humber Hawk. The next day's papers revealed that the car had been found, that an Irishman was a suspect and that the Scotland Yard officers had visited with his mother in Limerick. What the conspirators felt had come to pass — Special Branch had moved quickly to identify a prime suspect and had kept information back from the media until it was operationally useful to release it. Though not named, the police had added Bourke to the plot. They would have been much more troubled had they known that it was Bourke who had led the police to the car.

On one of his numerous trips away from the others, he phoned Scotland Yard from a coin-box, giving the location of the Humber. Their trawl in Harvist Road had come after police surveillance finished. Bourke was getting out of control and becoming a danger to the enterprise. Such was his hatred of authority and his visceral dislike of police that he wanted them to know he was behind the escape. Around this time, too, he made plans to send a letter to Constable Sheldon, letting him know he was released from prison and would return to Crawley to complete the job he had failed to do with the exploding biscuit box. None of the others knew of these subversive actions by Bourke, but they sensed there was more to his activities than he told. His drinking, initially regarded with indulgence as a 'making-up for lost time', a post-prison excess, began to threaten their safety. Blake realised Sean had become a liability — in prison he had no way of knowing of his predilection for alcohol. At the same time, he wanted to keep on good terms with him, so he urged Pat to restrain Sean. Initially Pat balked at the idea — he did not see himself as 'Sean's Keeper'. How could that be done, unless they all lived together...?

After many conversations Pat Pottle relented. Bourke and Blake could stay in his apartment in Willow Buildings, Hampstead. It was an old tenement, currently being re-furbished and had three rooms. Bourke would stay in Highlever Road until Pat had put in place some elemental security and he would take Blake first.

Blake arrived on the first day of November, accompanied by Anne and Michael with their young sons. To anyone giving them a second glance, they appeared a family, with the down-at-heel uncle in tow, unremarkable in the bloc of working-class tenements. Free of the unpredictable Bourke for a couple of days, Pat and George got to know each other. Both were deeply political yet having strongly different views on espionage, nuclear weapons and welfare of populations.

They had invigorating discussions over evening meals which Pat hurried home to cook. He had a small printing business whose clients were mainly on the Left and had to work a full day to keep up repayments on the machines. Over meals and wine, they came to respect each other's viewpoints. Although Pat was sympathetic to the ideals of Communism and several of his relations were active supporters, he opposed the creed as practised, especially in its denial of personal freedoms. Blake, though defending the ideal as best he could, was acutely aware that only in a liberal democracy such as England, with its tradition of tolerance for the individual, could the 'Randles and Pottles' have organised his freedom. In the Soviet Union they would have been sentenced to long gaol terms, perhaps even executed. But he was unwavering in his belief that Communism, when properly practised, was mankind's only hope for salvation. Quite how it should be practised led to much discussion between the KGB agent on the run and the English radical who believed in non-violence.

When Sean arrived, the atmosphere changed. He seemed insecure and felt left out. After a week or so, his various antics had tried Pat's patience and tested his proclaimed 'non violence'. Added to his misrepresentation over the accommodation in Highlever Road and his downright lying over the car, came an evasiveness over his movements. That was how Pat and George saw it, but not Sean. He frequently absented himself when Pat had gone to work, in spite of George's entreaties. Blake then complained privately to Pat to remonstrate with Sean, so the ingredients for an 'odd threesome' were in place. When Pat took it up with Sean, he was told the conditions were becoming worse than The Scrubs. The riposte stung Pat, who was already feeling the strain of harbouring the two most wanted men in Britain. He could not be sure his home was free of surveillance. Neither could Blake reassure him from his former career that the State's security services were not already engaged in prolonged surveillance before making an arrest.

How either would have reacted can only be imagined, had they known of the extent of Bourke's restlessness. Shortly after he arrived to Willows Buildings, he walked into a photographer's in Hampstead. The pictures were intended for the fake passport which Pat was manufacturing from a discarded one of his own. Sean held one back, having other ideas for its use.

They reviewed their options. The Meladinin dye had been ruled out by Blake, mainly because he did not wish to risk being 'a half-caste for the rest of my life'. He would not go a Soviet Bloc embassy in London because he did not wish to become a 'Cardinal Mindszenty', who had become a hostage in an embassy and a political issue for years between East and West. Either way, he did not want to curtail his future ability to lead a normal life. After much discussion, it was decided Michael Randle would smuggle him out of Britain in a camper van, which would go aboard a standard ferry sailing to France and drive him to Berlin. When he demurred at this, saying he could not put another family at risk, his espionage having already cost him his own family, Sean volunteered to drive, but by now none of the others trusted him.

Anne then said she would accompany Michael; she wanted to be with him if it went awry. Anne going meant the young children going — out of that family dialogue the plan was refined and Blake's objections overcome. More funds were sought from the supporter whose inheritance had paid the bills so far. Michael bought a camper van and with a skilled carpenter from the 'circle of friends' devised a false compartment under the bed for the children. The bed was essentially a pull-down platform, resting on cupboard doors which opened out underneath. If the cupboard was substituted with drawers of lesser depth, space would be created for Blake to lie behind. In camper vans, with space at a premium, the furniture was multi-purpose. A family with two young boys in bed, travelling through France and Germany near to Christmas, would be unlikely to provoke a search by police or customs. They set a date of Saturday 17th December, with Sean to follow two weeks later.

Again, Bourke railed against this plan and argued he should be allowed to return to Ireland where he would announce himself and resist the inevitable warrant from Scotland Yard. He was confident that Extradition laws would find in his favour. He would argue that freeing Blake was 'a political offence' — a definition which had been used in the Irish courts to avoid handing over fugitives on IRA terrorist offences. The others were not as confident and when put to a vote, Sean reluctantly agreed to follow Blake behind the Iron Curtain. For all his bravado, he was as much in thrall to the Western view of KGB and sought assurances from Blake that he would not be 'eliminated with extreme prejudice'.

The mood became sombre in the days before the 17th. In spite of Sean's sometimes abrasive presence, all realised they were coming to the end of an epic adventure. Whatever befell them afterwards, none would be the same again. During several celebratory meals they made toasts: 'to absent friends' (for the wider helpers) 'to the future — of The West, Russia and Mankind'. George was moved and somewhat awkward in trying to express his appreciation of what they had done for him — putting their own liberty at severe risk. He would, 'never forget' them, he said emotionally.

Bourke entertained them with media coverage of the escape, of how the army of journalists had used titbits to keep the public agog. How the papers had pieced together the 'mystery of the pink chrysanthemums' — the pot which he used outside the hospital, to conceal the microphone and with which the tabloids fascinated readers by suggesting KGB had used 'flower pots as signalling antennae'. Television used stand-up 'experts' to convincingly claim the escape had, variously, been a plot by SIS to dupe the Russians into believing Blake was on their side, or that the real George Blake had never been in the Scrubs, but had been replaced by a decoy.

Other aspects intrigued them, such as the bank wrappers for thousands of pounds (wrappers only, not the money) found in the glove compartment of the Humber car — in fact from the previous owner's business. The sightings of them in Dublin, East Berlin, London and Portsmouth amused them, but they would have choked on their laughter had Bourke owned up to some of his drunken antics in the pub in St. Martin's Lane. Unknown to them, Special Branch had put Bourke on their search list within hours of the escape, when officers interviewed Blake's mother. She readily told them of Bourke's plans and visits. From their underworld 'snouts', CID were getting Bourke's name as well, from whispers in the Scrubs.

Blake's departure on Saturday evening, 17th of December, was timed to merge into the pre-Christmas traffic at the port of Dover. He said goodbye to Pat who laughed off his thanks, climbed into the space under the children's bed and settled on a foam mattress, with a hot-water bottle for urination. It was a four-hour drive to Dover. Nearing the port, however, Blake became overcome with fumes from the

200

rubber hot-water bottle. Retching and dizzy, he resorted to the emergency drill by knocking loudly on the side of the van, which Michael did not hear above the engine. Blake was close to fainting when Anne, hearing the knocking, insisted Michael pull over on a quiet stretch of road. Recovering with some stiff walking and gulps of air, Blake went back into his lair, sans bottle. The children, half-asleep, were tucked back on top. With the minimum of checks the camper van and its occupants clunked aboard the car ferry. The family left for the upper deck while Blake reclined his way across the English Channel — and out of the jurisdiction.

In the morning, they journeyed from Ostend through Belgium with Blake now sitting up — just another British-registered family van trying to make it to somewhere for Christmas. The journey was not without its own hazards. The driving was arduous on Michael who resorted to stimulant pills to keep from falling asleep at the wheel. The windscreen wipers failed and George and Anne took turns to manually operate them during rain. The children became cranky as the miles wore on — in many genuine respects it was a family saga, having all the pressures of a husband and wife with two children driving a long distance in winter. Michael and Anne had bouts of irritation with each other over road signs. A couple driving a long distance test their relationship as much as their navigation skills.

Persevering, they arrived at the West German border by Sunday evening. It had been a long haul. Apart from the few hours aboard the ferry, Michael had been driving for the best part of twenty hours. He was at the end of his tether as they approached the dual checks of exit from West Germany and entry into the communist sector. By the time they traversed the final check, the journey took on a surreal imagery; watch-towers with machine guns posts, barbed wire and grim frontier guards reminded them of the regime that George had served — and a foretaste of where he was entering. Anne and Michael grew solemn, with the imagery of border guards shooting down those unwilling citizens of Communism who had decided to flee the regime. Here they were, surrendering a man whom they had got to respect, to that same regime.

Although the Eastern checks were more severe, the children's bed was left alone. On a clear stretch, they stopped where Blake had instructed, within sight of East Berlin. Blake, now more confident of his future, warmly took his leave and promised that someday all would be celebrated with champagne. As in other momentous times in his life, he was conscious of his enigmatic place in history. 'For an instant in time I was free and alone in the dark night, poised between two worlds, belonging to neither'. And as in those other moments, he had recourse to the Scriptures:

'To everything there is a season and time to every purpose under heaven. A time to weep, and a time to laugh; a time to mourn, and a time to dance. A time to get, and time to lose; a time to keep, and time to cast away'.

Casting away, also, was Sean Bourke, now also a displaced person. He had wanted to go back to Ireland, but had been persuaded otherwise. Becoming a hero in his own country would have to wait. On New Year's Eve, December 31st, holding a passport forged with Pat Pottle's graphic skills, he boarded the overnight boat train from London to Paris. As the passports and identity checks were done at Victoria Station, the others accompanied him to the departure lounge. Their last sight of him was of his jaunty posture, raincoat open and pork pie hat askew, making banter with the customs official as he passed through in a light haze of whiskey. Their solemnity would have deepened had they known of his parting gifts. Old habits die hard. One of the passport photographs had been posted earlier that day to a Fleet Street newspaper, with the address of Highlever Road on the back. Another letter was addressed to Constable Sheldon in Crawley and promised next time there would be no bungling.

As they waved him goodbye from the barrier, his mentors had no inkling of the surprises he had left for them.

CHAPTER SEVENTEEN

PRIVILEGES OF COMMUNISM

When Blake arrived at the communist checkpoint, he had a long period of waiting. Although speaking fluent German and Russian, the lack of documentation made the guards suspicious. It was Christmas week, when many Germans took risks to see their kinfolk on the other side of the Iron Curtain. When he prevailed upon them to call the Soviet Control at Karlshort, his knowledge of the chain-of-command persuaded them to provide him with accommodation for the night. With no paperwork and dishevelled from the travel, he presented as an impostor for the man whose exploits had been on the front pages for weeks. The phones buzzed along the frontier and in the morning, as he was having his breakfast, the door burst open and one of his former KGB controllers in London shouted 'It's him, it's him!'. Sergei Kondrashev, his onetime London handler had been in Berlin on business when the word came that a man claiming to be George Blake had turned up at the Berlin checkpoint.

The celebrations were overwhelming. KGB had been as puzzled as SIS by his escape — all of two months earlier — and had practically given up trying to contact him. Although they had heard from within the British Communist Party that he was 'being looked after', they did not know the manner by which he was safe. Now, here he was in Berlin, the city where he had served them so well with his early revelations of the Berlin Tunnel.

The reigning Head of KGB at Karlshorst and the General of Soviet Group Forces Europe, regarded his arrival as a feather in their caps and made him feel welcome. Within days he had a driver and a villa at his disposal. Agent DIOMID had come home...

Bearing out, once again, a dictum of the service that it looks after its own, elaborate arrangements were made to fly him to Moscow as a VIP. Expensive clothing was purchased in West Berlin and he was given a generous allowance of

East German marks. Quickly he realised the duality under which his admired communist ideology functioned. While officially disdaining 'Western Capitalism', the comrades regarded Western goods as desirable for an agent of his status. An elaborate apartment was provided and the services of a housekeeper. After six days he was flown to Moscow in a military aircraft, landing in a 'sanitised' zone and installed in the kind of luxury reserved for senior functionaries. He met others of his former contact, including Dozhdalev, the KGB man who had recommended his recruitment in Korea after Blake's approach while in captivity. He was feted at a KGB dinner and made to feel he had 'come home at last'. Problem was, he had never been in Russia before.

Neither had Bourke. The day he crossed Checkpoint Charlie on the 2nd of January 1967 he made himself known, as 'Mr Richardson', as previously agreed with Blake. Although fortified with a sense of personal adventure — and a bottle of wine from the night before — he was apprehensive. The Iron Curtain turned out to be more grim than he imagined — a series of checks, no smiles, watchtowers, soldiers with machine-guns — no smiles. A hazard of concrete barriers, 'where the two halves of mankind met each other in enmity'. It was not until he had cleared five passport controls that he was met with something approaching friendliness.

Two senior KGB men, who spoke excellent English (in an American accent) were waiting in black cars which cruised alongside him after he walked some distance away from Checkpoint Charlie and into the waste land of the Eastern Sector. They stopped; invited him to enter the nearest car (he did not have much option). They told him they had immediately recognised him as the 'Mr Richardson' whom they were expecting and escorted him to the Karlshort compound. With a sinking clarity, he became aware of the freedoms of the territories he had so virulently disdained, now that he was leaving those democracies.

The main man introduced himself as Vladimir. Bourke felt it was all straight out of Central Casting and fell into actor mode, one part of him playing the hero, while the other part was terrified. Though the men were affable, he was under no illusion that his life had become confined by the iron realities of Communism. It was a creed in which he had no belief — though now was not the time for philosophical debate. He was given quarters in the same villa Blake had occupied and a protection detail of border guards. He could hear no sounds in his quarters among the Karlshorst compound, though he noted rather dramatically that a guard's gun-barrel '...glinted in the pale moonlight'. He felt afraid and slept fitfully. In the morning, directed with formal courtesy aboard a military aircraft, he was flown to Moscow, accompanied by a KGB officer and an armed guard. At the military airport, he was given VIP treatment and put into a convoy of black cars. Asking apprehensively about Blake, he was told George was well and was looking forward to meeting him.

In London, meanwhile the main English conspirators were recovering from a narrow escape over the New Year holiday. As soon as Bourke was in Paris, en route to Berlin, he telephoned Michael to say he had arrived safely — and warned him not to go to Highlever Road. 'I have been in contact with my former address. I phoned the landlady. The police are there. They're awaiting my return. For God's sake make sure our friend does not go back there'. Alarmed and wary, Michael said he would 'pass it on' — a reference to the rows which Pat Pottle and Sean had over security. Pat felt there was incriminating evidence in the bed-sitter — walkie-talkies and probably lots of identifying prints as they had left in a hurry. Pat had argued for the place to be cleared out. Sean had resisted before leaving London — now he used the fictional call to the landlady to cover his own sending of the spare passport photograph to the newspaper, with '28 Highlever Road, W.10' on the back. Had the others known, they would have been in serious disarray.

Bourke wanted the police to find the hideaway and to connect him to it. His ostensible reason, as he afterwards claimed, to lead police away from Randle and Pottle, would always remain unconvincing to them. They did not appreciate his addictive need to bait the police, to have the authorities know that it was he, Sean Bourke, who was the main mover of the escape. On Sunday, the day after they had seen him off at Victoria Station, Pat and Michael debated the dilemma posed by Sean's warning. Feeling the need to go there, in spite of the risk if Sean was telling the truth, they drove in the camper van to Highlever Road and scouted the house. It did not appear under watch. Nervous and alert, they entered with Sean's key. To their relief they found the walkie-talkies. To their consternation, they found a hoard of other evidence; pictures of the prison taken from inside by Bourke with a miniature camera, plans and drawings of routes, timings of traffic, their own phone numbers (coded as minus one digit) and old letters between Blake and Bourke which made clear reference to themselves. All the technical logistics of the plot, sufficient to send them away for years, had the police found them.

Expecting at any moment to be pounced upon, they removed that array of items and wiped the surfaces. Only years later would they realise — when they read of Sean's letter — that the prolonged New Year holiday had saved them. Bourke's giveaway missive to the *Evening Standard*, posted in Hampstead before he left London, stayed in the sorting office over the holiday and did not reach the paper until Tuesday, two days after Michael and Pat had cleared out the bed-sitter. By which time Bourke was in Moscow and the 'circle of friends' had ceased to function as an escape committee. They were for the time being in the clear, by the narrowest of margins. They were not to know — though they suspected — that Special Branch were now looking more closely at their own circle. As the police investigation eliminated criminal gangs and the IRA by the 'word coming back' from police agents within, by the same sensitive means came the whispers that pointed to the Committee of 100 — in particular to those who had contact with the nefarious Sean Bourke within the Scrubs. In tandem with police interviews with prisoners which named the CND activists, covert tapping of phones by 'F' branch of MI5 showed a gossipy buzz among the Committee of 100 that within months would make the plot known to the security services.

In the meantime, both the security services and the conspirators could let the escape Enquiry take the flak. Headed by Lord Louis Mountbatten of Burma[*], the enquiry was designed to placate public unease in the wake of the sensation and identified a series of security lapses in Wormwood Scrubs, including the mix-up which allowed Blake free association with other Soviet spies. Anticipating the Mountbatten recommendations, there was a rash of escapes from several gaols, which diluted the media attention on Blake. KGB spies William Vassal, Harry Houghton and Helen Kroger were moved to higher security prisons. As Randle and Pottle resumed their civilian lives and the search faded from the front pages, in Moscow the two men at the centre of the most sensational escape in modern British history were finding themselves in another kind of gaol.

Re-union and regret...

When Sean Bourke arrived in Moscow he felt the cold. Vladimir's purchase of winter clothes had not prepared him for the packed ice and military guards on the runaway, the sheer greyness of everything. He noticed the bulky women clearing snow in the streets, the pervasive gloom, everywhere. The city into which he was entering had defeated two of Europe's dictators by its own dogged winters which clogged everything in snow and bogged down the foreigner. Even as he was driven through seemingly endless roads and then the wide streets northwards through Moscow, Bourke felt despair. He was sure he was not going to like this. He had been persuaded against his will to come here, for the safety of the English conspirators. They were at home in

---

[*]Lord Louis Mountbatten, hero of the Pacific naval war against the Japanese. Assassinated in 1979 by the IRA — as a close friend of the British Royal Family, he presented a 'soft target' while on holiday in Ireland.

the warmth of their families: Michael and Anne, whom he admired, with their children in Kentish Town, Pat in his bohemian flat in Hampstead. He began to feel alone and un-cared-for. The best efforts of Vladimir, constantly asking if he needed anything only deepened his gloom. Pat and Michael would be recovering from celebrating New Year, so would the gang in the Salisbury pub in St. Martin's Lane, so would millions in pubs everywhere. But not he, Sean Bourke, instigator and progenitor of the Great Escape. His reward was Moscow in winter, the opposite of Oscar Wilde being exiled to Paris for his sins.

Moscow is a vast, concrete city and The Leningrad Hotel sits on one of its many large squares across from three railway stations which service local, national and international routes including the Peking-Moscow express. As Bourke was delivered outside Leningratski Gestinitsa, a grey high-rise of baroque subtlety, his minders took up his suitcases to his room on the second floor which had ornate furniture and ponderous piped heating. When he suggested a drink in the bar Vladimir looked embarrassed. Bourke could not be seen in the bar as he might be recognised by Westerners. His meals and anything else he might need would be brought up to him. It was not an idle promise, as Sean was to discover, but for the moment he was further depressed. Even the supply of vodka in the room did not alleviate his foreboding. He would have liked to celebrate his arrival with them and with George. But that was promised for the morrow. Vladimir left, with a reminder that Sean was now 'Robert Garvin' — he would be addressed as such by everybody.

In the morning, looking out the hotel window, he had the distinct feeling of being somebody else. The square could only be Russian. When the phone rang, the American accented voice of the receptionist addressed him as Mr Garvin. When Vladimir rang, he called him Robert. Repeatedly, he checked that his holdall had not been rifled: he secured the tapes he had made of the conversations with Blake across the wall of the Scrubs. They would be his insurance policy, if he could manage to leave after a reasonable time. He was itching to tell the world of his part in The Great Escape. That would not be possible here. His moods swung between being excited and being depressed. At least he would meet Blake and see where they might go from there...

KGB had placed him in 'The Leningrad' because it was a couple of blocks from where Blake was staying, in an extensive apartment with a housekeeper. Blake had impressed upon KGB the importance of Sean's well-being as well as his volatility and the need to have him close at hand. Privately, Blake feared that Sean might not settle and was concerned for the safety of the conspirators in England, to whose risk-taking he owed his freedom. As he did to Sean. But now that he had arrived, Blake was uneasy, remembering how difficult it had been to restrain him in London. 'I had not realised in prison that his excessive drinking could be a problem. How could I? There was no alcohol there. Later I did realise, when we were in Pat's flat — he would return in an intoxicated condition and be argumentative. Now that he was going to live in Moscow filled me with apprehension, because I had already observed how much alcohol was consumed in everyday life of the Russians. But my primary concern was the safety of the people in England. I had already broken up one family, my own, by my activity. I had no intention of doing the same to Anne and Michael and their children. So I had to look after Sean. We had argued before leaving London that it would be foolish of him to return to Ireland after the escape, as the British Government would request his extradition and the Irish authorities were likely to grant it.

Sean cited cases where the Irish courts had refused to hand over IRA people because of what they deemed 'political offences'. But we all felt that the Catholic judges were not as likely to show the same sympathy for helping a communist (myself). That was the argument, which we had used to prevail upon him, rather unwillingly, to come to Moscow'.

In spite of these unspoken tensions, the initial meeting was celebratory. When Sean was brought by his new minder Stanislav to Blake's apartment, he was greeted warmly by Blake, whose housekeeper had a meal prepared. There was plenty of champagne and many salutes of *nastarovia*. To the obvious fascination of Colonel Stanislav, they went over the details of the escape and their subsequent adventures as they were moved from one sheltering household to another. As they laughed at the incidents, it was clear that KGB were puzzled by the situation in Britain, which had allowed the fugitives to move around London. The Russians had difficulty in grasping how much of the operation had been conducted by walkie-talkie and on the telephone. Moscow was a city in which only senior KGB (police and military) had access to radio telephones. As for standard domestic telephones taken for granted in the West, in Moscow only an influential minority of the citizens had telephones in their homes — which were regularly monitored by State security. Such a domestic reference as the London Telephone Directory, listing millions of people by name, address and phone number was unheard of outside KGB registry. In any group of six or more friends, one was a likely KGB informant. So why had not the British security service found them? As for fooling British 'border controls' with a passport — that was beyond belief, as Soviet citizens needed KGB permission to travel outside the USSR.

Though Blake tried to hide his surprise as his hosts revealed the reality of life in the Soviet Union, Bourke quickly perceived the awesome gap — and Blake's uneasy laughter. The evening set a pattern that persisted for weeks: Bourke staying cooped-up in The Leningrad Hotel during the day, unable to frequent the public areas, his social life reduced to an evening meal with Blake. Sometimes the pair were introduced to a carefully limited circle of people. Bourke sometimes managed to slip out a delivery entrance of the hotel, and get lost in the railway station across the square where the Peking Express came in promptly at the same time every morning. East met West but Bourke could not go in either direction. And he found his lack of Russian a complete handicap.

Blake, meanwhile, was writing to his mother, with letters posted in Egypt to give the impression he was somewhere in the Middle East, correctly surmising the letters would be opened in Britain. In fact by now she had become friends with her Special Branch detail and she felt sorry for them on their roster in cold cars outside her cottage. She took to inviting them in for tea as the night shift began. Her son meanwhile had been taken in hand by a section of KGB which specialised in identity papers, false trails and such — nonetheless, word had leaked to the German press that he had been seen crossing Check Point Charlie. Interestingly, on foot of these reports and the stated unease of CIA, the British Government appears not to have pressed the Soviet authorities as to Blake's whereabouts, thereby avoiding a diplomatic incident. It is likely that SIS and MI5 had accurately gauged the conspiracy, via the leg-work work of Special Branch. As one of the investigators put it 'The big fish had got away — they didn't really want him back — what was to be gained in pursuing the little fish?'.

It seems to have suited the Foreign Office not to pursue the matter, Prime Minister Wilson was keen to have good relations with the Soviets and at cabinet meetings was wary of the behaviour of his volatile Foreign Secretary, George Brown. On the global front, unease in Czechoslovakia would become a crisis within a year as premier Dubcek's liberalising measures were regarded by The Kremlin as yet another satellite trying to break free of the centre. Britain had a similar colonial problem with premier Mintoff in Malta negotiating for Independence, deflecting Britain from its main foreign policy thrust of joining the European Community. The Big Powers had much to pursue other than the whereabouts of a spy who was a product of the Cold War. Blake, from whom nothing public was heard, would hopefully recede into obscurity. But in Moscow, the volatility of one Irishman was threatening to upset the blind policy to the escape mutually adopted by Britain and Russia. Sean

Bourke was finding it increasingly difficult to settle and was chafing at the restrictions.

By early summer of 1967, Bourke had left the hotel and was sharing Blake's apartment, an arrangement designed to ease his isolation and help him settle. Though well intentioned, it turned out disastrous. As recalled by Blake: 'We had too much time on our hands and not enough to fill it. In the beginning I was busy writing my account of the escape for the Russian authorities and then working as a translator in a publishing house. Although Sean was also offered work, he did not take it up — it could have been as simple as correcting English-language proofs because he was very grammatical, but he did not take it up. So both of us were in my apartment for long periods and we got on each other's nerves. I found I was doing all the housework and washing up — I am by nature a tidy person, whereas Sean was the opposite and soon I began to resent him. I thought at least he should do some housework...'

There were wider differences of temperament, as Blake conceded 'Sean was too much of an individualist to settle in the Soviet Union which was then a very authoritarian state. He was completely lost here. Cinema, theatre, newspapers were all in a language he made no effort to understand.

Compared to the West, the greyness of it all depressed him. There was no outlet for his streak of anarchy, except for the Russian tolerance of excessive consumption of alcohol. But even then as an Irishman he missed the conviviality of the English pub — people here drank to excess in the streets or in parks, which didn't really suit him at all. He missed the cosy English pub'.

'Our positions were completely opposite. I was not blind to the shortcomings of Soviet life — the constant queues for things like bread and milk and meat, the dourness of the people in shops — I had to make the best of it because there was no going back. Whereas Sean wanted to go back; to claim his dues, as it were. Indeed his idea all along had been to write a book about the escape and he desperately wanted to have his reward by boasting about it to his friends and drinking companions in Ireland. Or, if he were extradited, in England...'.

Blake began to realise that for Bourke the escape would be a justification of his life, being both revenge and redemption for his Limerick childhood. He would use the book to explain his attitude to authority, recounting his Daingean experiences and his career in Britain.

Blake had sympathy with this view, believing that all things fit a pattern, that our fate is pre-ordained, made up of the good and bad. As Bourke applied himself to listening to the tapes and making notes, it became clear he was serious about publishing his version of events — which made Blake very uneasy.

Bourke got to know Moscow well from his long daily walks which depressed him further. Whatever imprinting he had from the walled city of Limerick was put into parochial proportion by the walled Kremlin. Set down as a commanding fortress in the middle of Moscow, its granite blocked walls took a full day to walk around. From inside, practically half the world's population were controlled in their political beliefs and in their personal futures. During the day, when Sean went for walks, George wondered if he had managed to make telephone contact with some publisher or newspaper in England.

'Sean's desires clashed directly with the security of our friends in England. I was faced with an agonising choice: either to support Sean in achieving his personal wishes, which if carried out would expose Michael, Anne and Pat to prison — or to ensure their security by opposing Sean's intentions'.

Pondering the choices within a moral framework was not strange to a man whose youthful ambition was to become a Lutheran minister, but who had brought ruin on his English family by replacing it with communist convictions. Deciding that his loyalty was to the friends in England meant relations between himself and Bourke could only disintegrate. By the summer they were hardly on speaking terms. Bourke's insistence on writing up his account upset Blake, who was himself not in the best of moods because of the news that Gillian had received a divorce in London, an event deserving of a couple of paragraphs in the main British newspapers. While in gaol, he had given her the option of divorce, seeing her for all practical purposes a widow to his forty-two years gaoling. She told him she had become involved with another officer in SIS and they were contemplating marriage, which would give his three young boys a stable family unit (privately, he had hoped she might have deferred it, but he could not tell her about his escape plans during visits).

He had hoped against hope the affair would end and she would in time join him in Moscow and re-make their marriage and their family. The newspaper coverage of the actual divorce put him into a depression. He felt even more alone. And much of Soviet society irked him, with its drunkenness on the streets, shortages in the shops and lack of joy among the population. He had to make an effort to look on the better side. As in many instances before, his religious sense helped. Although textbook Communism saw religion as 'opium of the people' and dismissed the old aristocracy as 'oppressors', Blake, nurtured in older European tradition, was consoled by the remnants of these cultures. '...I liked everything that was old in Moscow, from the quaint little back streets, the courtyards with their one or two storeyed merchants' houses, the fine old palaces of the aristocracy, the many churches with their golden or blue star-sparkled domes...'.

He and Sean needed lifelines. They came in the form of a visit from his mother and a diverting tour of watering-holes for Sean. Both were orchestrated by Col. Stanislav. Since his arrival in Moscow, Blake's mother had received regular letters from him and in anticipation of a meeting had returned to live in Holland. Contacted there, she thought she might go to Egypt to meet him, but was asked to travel to East Berlin, where 'Stan' met her and accompanied her to Moscow for a re-union with her son. She brought George's well-cut English suits and personal belongings which Gillian had given her, messages from his children and a farewell gift to herself from her Special Branch watchers — an album of Dutch Old Masters — as a thank you for the many cups of English tea which the spy's mother had given them as they monitored her in the aftermath of her son's escape.

For George and his mother, it was their third re-union after as many imprisonments — the Nazi invasion of Holland, release from captivity in Korea and now again free from being a casualty of Cold War espionage.

To allow them time together and to ease the tensions over Bourke, KGB organised an elaborate itinerary for the Irishman to tour the republics of the Soviet Union. There were many stopovers at breweries, vodka distilleries and watering holes where local KGB invited young female officers to some active 'swallow' training, using Bourke as both pleasure and bait. The junior officers did not need much tempting. With his ready wit and melodious singing voice, Sean was the classically handsome buccaneer of espionage legend. As the majority of Russians did not have a clue where Ireland was — and to avoid giving intelligence tittle-tattle — the devised cover story was that he was an English communist who had been deported from South Africa because of his opposition to Apartheid.

When Bourke performed his party pieces of song and story-telling, the traditional image of the Englishman abroad, often caricatured in text-books which the young women had studied at school, came in for re-valuation. Bourke enjoyed the steady supply of agreeable young women, some of whom spoke fluent English. He was relieved by his release from his 'odd couple' existence in Moscow and indulged himself. During the summer of 1967 he drank, sang and copulated his way though the resorts of the Black Sea. Bourke was accompanied by another KGB Colonel, 'Slava', for the first leg of the tour, then by local officers who in the interests of faith and fatherland participated in many encounters with 'swallows'[*].

---

[*] Known as 'Honeypots' by Western Intelligence services, whereby female agents traded sexual activity to compromise their targets.

The reckoning was at hand on his return to Moscow. Although both men were refreshed from their break and Blake in particular had deeply enjoyed the company of his mother, the enforced re-union provoked a discussion on Bourke's future. According to Bourke's later account, it became a fraught encounter. The KGB officer patiently explained that it had been decided Bourke should stay in the Soviet Union for at least five years, in order to protect the English 'friends', whom he said numbered about ten. Bourke exploded at the suggestion he would betray them if arrested and berated the hapless Colonel. Bourke accused him of doing Blake's bidding. The KGB officer was adamant that generous arrangements would be made to accommodate Bourke: 'Every town in every one of the fifteen republics of the Soviet Union is open to you. And we will give you every assistance to pursue a worthwhile career in publishing'. Bourke flouted the offer.

With his determination to return to Ireland souring his relations with Stan and George, he took to eavesdropping on their conversations. As he recollected, he overheard an intention to 'eliminate' him, should he not comply. With some flights of fancy, powered by fear and alcohol, he imagined his own end:

'How would they do it? They would hardly shoot me here in the flat. No. There would be a drive into the country. That would not look suspicious. We had driven into the country many times during the Winter and Spring and we had gone for long walks in the forest...'. 'They would allow me to walk ahead, there would be a whispered instruction behind me, a rustling of clothing, and then oblivion. Would Blake come with them? Yes, he would have to, otherwise it would look suspicious. The grave would already be dug and waiting. A dark damp hole deep in the forest, the freshly dug clay piled up around the edges, and lying crumpled on the bottom a still-warm body dressed in a smart English suit. No coffin. The wet clay would be shovelled in on top of the soft flesh. And the only sign of any disturbance in the calm autumn forest would be a small patch of fresh earth standing out briefly against the back cloth of yellow autumn leaves'.

The taste for self-drama might be explained by Bourke's profound isolation. He had rarely felt so alone, not even when waiting under the wall of the Scrubs on a wet Saturday, in a car that he could hardly drive. Now, the man whose freedom he assured on that night was no longer a friend and was, as he saw it, threatening his life. According to his own account he saw a different George Blake to the one he had known in England:

'The only thing at stake for Blake was his personal vanity, his only motive an insatiable thirst for power. Blake needed the KGB a lot more than the KGB needed him. The KGB was his muscle, his strength, his backbone. Without the KGB he was just a weak, insignificant little man. Blake likes to play God. For years he used the KGB for his own ends, to enable him to wield the power of life and death over stronger men than himself. This was the only way he could ever achieve power. This power had not been a means to an end but an end in itself'.

Bourke omits to credit Blake's overriding interest in securing the safety of the English conspirators. As a man driven — and riven — all his life by agonising decisions of conscience, it seems clear to me that Blake was motivated by those concerns rather than by malice towards Bourke. However once he had had opposed Bourke leaving Russia he fell into the role of enemy and thence forward became an object of Bourke's obsessive derision. Not much different from previous objects of his pathological attention, such as the policeman in Crawley or the escape itself. Both men were responding in character under the pressures.

Furious arguments ensued with George defending their life in Russia and Bourke deriding it. When Blake said Sean would not be free should he return to the West, Bourke responded by saying the Russians did not understand the meaning of freedom as it had never been given to them — The Party did all their thinking for them. When Stan warned that the intelligence services in Britain would give him a 'truth drug' to reveal the names of the English plotters, Sean was angered that such a transparent threat should mollify him. To Blake he said he would rather take his chances — even if he were extradited from Ireland to Britain, he would rather spend 'five years on porridge than live in the USSR on champagne'.

CHAPTER EIGHTEEN

FEAR IN THE FOREST

Bourke became increasingly paranoid. Withdrawing from social relations, he eavesdropped when Blake was on the phone and listened to conversations when Stan visited. He quietly opened the door of his own bedroom, where he was ostensibly writing his account of the escape, to hear what was being said about him. Most was in Russian, thus his later published version must be treated with caution. He had made little headway with the language and had feelings of persecution since his adolescence. A perverse situation evolved — the professional spy was being spied upon by the amateur. Both men were trapped in their anxieties — Bourke that he might never get back to Ireland, Blake for the welfare of the English conspirators. He believed Bourke's return would imperil them, though he insisted he would never reveal their identities. Blake believed otherwise — he had seen how garrulous the Irishman became when inebriated.

Their relationship foundered during August as Bourke's drinking magnified in his mind the (imagined?) threat to liquidate him. He had no one to turn to — nobody with whom he could talk out his fears. He felt very alone. The more he tried to reason with Blake that he should be permitted to leave, the more he was countered as to why he should not. He turned against Blake, seeing him as a merciless agent, whose strength derived from being both spy and betrayer. 'At the height of his power and glory he had contrived to work for two Services so that he might have a *double* measure of power'.

Blake's attempts to humour him fell on stony ground. When the spy told him how his SIS office has been known as The Wimbledon Club, because it was all 'rackets and balls', Bourke did not find it funny. Nor was he impressed on a walkabout in Moscow when Blake made an ironic comparison upon the dreaded Lubyanka being next to the Moscow emporium for children's toys. 'All this Secret

Service work is so utterly childish' he reports Blake as saying. For Bourke, his own freedom to return to Ireland became so pressing that in early September he embarked upon a ploy that forced the stalemate to a crisis.

Leaving the apartment to go for a walk, as he told Blake, he scouted possible places of refuge. One was the Journalists' Club, frequented by English-speaking correspondents of Western newspapers. Another was the Intourist Hotel on Ulitsa Tverskaya, where he might meet British tourists and somehow purloin a seat on a coach to the airport. But surveying both, he realised identification would be required — he needed a passport. Although he had lived his adult life in England, he thought of himself as Irish — and Ireland had no embassy in Moscow. He walked on through Red Square, thinking out where he might get a passport. He observed the tourists by the magnificent St. Basil's Cathedral, watched the ritual of the Guard of Honour at Lenin's mausoleum and thought that desperate situations needed desperate remedies.

Across from Red Square was the British Embassy, set back from the embankment road that ran beside the Moscva river. An imposing building of ornate character, redolent of an English country mansion, it beckoned to Bourke with the allure of the master towards the recalcitrant servant. Thoroughly monitored by KGB from nearby buildings, it had but a routine external presence of Moscow police in a guard hut outside. Realising the guards were gossiping among themselves at the 'entry' driveway, he skipped sharply up the 'exit' side and made his way to the front of the building, where he announced his identity to a receptionist, saying he was wanted by Scotland Yard.

Unfazed, the receptionist directed him to Administration, in a nearby building. He insisted he could not risk it as the police outside were now observing him with some alarm. He told the receptionist he preferred being returned to another police force — in Britain. He was asked to wait and presently two young functionaries approached, whom he took to be SIS people working under Embassy cover. He repeated who he was and — according to his own account — they considered his proposition. Then told him, with some measure of satisfaction, that he could not be helped by the British Embassy. Ireland had no representation in communist countries. He was on his own. Bourke pleaded for help...

Eventually they called an Attaché who appeared more sympathetic and took Bourke's details and date of birth and promised to ask the Irish Foreign Affairs in Dublin if they would facilitate the forwarding of a passport. Call back in a week, the Attaché suggested. A week? — Bourke said he would be dead within twenty-four hours of leaving the precincts of the British Embassy. The officials again listened patiently as he recounted the saga of the escape, emphasising that Soviet Intelligence services were in no way involved: it was a one-man effort by himself, with the financial help of friends. He told them he and Blake had immediately flown from Britain to Berlin, where they had crossed Check-Point Charlie with false passports, now in the possession of KGB. He had no way of leaving. Instead, he was being hunted. He insisted he had heard Blake urging KGB to kill him.

When they questioned him on specifics of the escape, he became wary. He would answer no more questions, he said, unless they could give him asylum. If they refused his blood would be on their hands. The Attaché repeated the Embassy position. Asylum was out of the question, as the Embassy would cause a diplomatic incident by sheltering a fugitive who was not their citizen.

With a dramatic flourish, an exasperated Bourke made a speech towards a ventilation grill, denouncing Blake. In his spy-reading imagination he assumed the air-duct was the microphone conduit for KGB monitoring. Back out on the pavement he was accosted by the policemen who demanded to see his passport. Claiming to be an English tourist, he told them that The Leningrad Hotel held it, as it was standard practice for hotels to retain visitor passports until leaving Moscow. They let him go.

Where to now? Within a short time, he felt sure, both Blake and KGB would know of his visit. The gamble had not paid off. In fact, he had made things worse. Now he felt really hunted. He wandered around Moscow streets, then approached the club frequented by the international press corps. His courage failed when he realised those entering spoke Russian. He wandered the streets again, until — unable to bear his own desperation — he telephoned Blake and told him he had visited the British Embassy. The reaction, as expected, was an explosion of disbelief and outrage. Then he gave Blake a piece of his mind, letting his pent-up frustration spill out in telephonic abuse: 'You know, I can't understand *you*...I can't understand you at all — *comrade*. Any other man in your position would be standing up and waving flags for me. Any other man in your position would be shouting at the top of his voice, "Let him go, let him go! If the man wants to go home for God's sake let him go! He had done me a great favour and he is at least entitled to that much!" But not you, oh no, not you'. Blake asked what right Bourke had to speak to him like that — in response, Bourke blustered, becoming wary that the call might be monitored. He put the phone down. He would have to forage for himself. He had closed off his options.

As in his troubled childhood he had wandered in the fields from school and police, he headed now for the countryside outside Moscow, where an abundance of forests soaked up the capital's pollution and were favoured by early-morning mushroom pickers. Trekking into Izmaelovo Park, he spent the night on a bed of bracken, covered by newspapers. Whatever about purveying the truth to the communist states, Pravda's[*] thin pages, were not sufficiently robust to keep out the cold — he awoke several times and did prison exercises to keep warm. In the morning, head down, he joined the mushroom-pickers. He became depressed by his situation. During the day he walked in circles through the forest, reviewing his life, calling to mind his childhood and court appearances, the brutality of Daingean reformatory. All of it had led him to this mess. Yet he could see no way out, short of surrender and what he imagined was execution. Two

---

[*] 'Pravda' means 'truth' in Russian.

nights of this privation focussed his mind on a choice between dying of malnutrition and a KGB bullet. By the third day he decided to surrender. Reluctantly, he realised only one person could mediate some kind of reprieve — George Blake.

He made his way back to the apartment, called from a nearby phone-box and heard Blake respond with relief. When Bourke said he would return, Blake's ease was palpable. On arriving he found him smiling and welcoming, in the company of an armed KGB man, whose presence was explained on the grounds that the authorities had no idea in whose company he might return. They feared he had revealed Blake's address: any attempt to capture him, would have resulted in a gunfight. George was genuinely glad to see him safe, called him 'Sean' instead of 'Robert' and to Bourke's immense pleasure, cooked him a hefty breakfast of bacon, eggs and tomatoes, washed down with a pot of English tea — a foddering which put him into a receptive humour when Stanislav arrived.

As the senior KGB officer, Stan's own job had been jeopardised by Bourke's absconding, a situation which he emphasised in a heart-to-heart talk. Bourke responded that he was trapped in Russia, that Blake's influence would keep him there indefinitely. Stan listened, said he was sorry that he had not found Russia to his liking — and to his surprise, told him that arrangements would be made to return him to Ireland. But that it would take some months. In the meantime, he would deem it a very great personal favour if in return Sean promised not to go near the British Embassy again. The promise was readily given and Stan further told him that an extensive tour of the Soviet Union would be given to Blake and himself, as the Western intelligence services were now aware that both were in Moscow and that a joint CIA/SIS operation to seize them could be expected.

Even if that did not occur, as a result of his visit to the embassy the British Government could now be expected to formally apply to the Soviet Foreign Ministry for their extradition — which would upset his bosses. KGB would now supply an armed protection detail, housed in an adjoining building, which would monitor both the fugitives' movements. Stan took his leave with some sadness, leaving Bourke with the impression he had failed to honour a friendship. Until the tour was organised, he would have to live again with Blake in conditions of tension. Still, buoyed up with the promise that he would be able to leave for Ireland, Bourke set about mending bridges with Blake, though he had said too much of an abusive nature for relations to be fully restored.

Blake reached into the recesses of his character and restraint to cope with Bourke's re-instatement. Though he dearly wished to be rid of Sean's volatile, moody presence, his over-riding concern was for the safety of the English conspirators. When Stan discussed the projected tour, Blake had misgivings. He feared it would turn into another excess of drinking but was prevailed upon by Stan to co-operate. That section of the Foreign Ministry to which KGB reported required both the fugitives to be away from Moscow by the time the Western media got wind of the visit to the Embassy. The tour was scheduled for October, but a classic piece of espionage bungling saw the pair leave Moscow earlier when a joust between SIS and KGB in London erupted onto the front pages.

As far as the public knew, a Russian scientist on an exchange at Cambridge University had been put aboard a Russian aircraft at London airport, apparently in a drugged state. The police had intervened and taken him to hospital — but he discharged himself, sought the protection of the USSR Embassy in Kensington Gardens and at the Embassy's invitation, his wife told a press gathering he had escaped a kidnap attempt by the British authorities. Both were later escorted to an Aeroflot flight. The hapless scientist's misfortune was to have been targeted at Cambridge University by one of the resident SIS 'spotters' on the academic staff.

Torn between the promises of a new life in the West and his loyalty to his homeland, he had a nervous breakdown.

The Gatehouse at Wormwood Scrubs.... by the time he entered as an adult, Bourke was familiar with prison regimes (© Crown Copyright. NMR).

Above: Blake leaves Holland for Egypt with his sisters, mother and grandmother seeing him off, 1935 (George Blake).

Right: Blake in Mampo prison camp, Korea, 1951 (George Blake).

Blake relaxing off-duty in Seoul, 1949 (George Blake).

George Blake (L) with his wife Gillian, young sons, sister and mother on leave from Lebanon, 1960. It would be their last family holiday together (George Blake).

The picture that caused a rift.... From L, Ruffa Philby and Kim with friend (standing) R - Blake's son Mischa on his father's knee, with Ida, Blake's Russian wife. Blake allowed the picture to be taken as a favour to Kim Philby's son, John, visiting from England, for the family archive as he understood from Kim. He was angry when it was published by the *Daily Mail* ....

Two of a Mind.... Michael Randle and Pat Pottle, leaders of the English conspirators, discuss tactics during their Old Bailey trial, 1991 (© *The Guardian*).

The Breadline.... Elderly women sell paltry possessions outside a railway station. Moscow, 1996 (author archive).

An ordinary life.... Blake at a Christmas party and below with one of his granddaughters in 2001 (George Blake).

Blake and his Russian wife, Ida, on a visit to a monastery in Northern Russia, Summer 2001 (George Blake).

Dearly Beloved.... Blake addresses a select audience in Moscow 2001 (George Blake).

Staff from KGB London Residentura had sedated him in order to return him to hospital in Moscow. SIS, seeing their potential agent being ex-filtrated, ordered the police to halt the aircraft's departure. The débâcle made the front pages of the international press, with suggestions of SIS bungling. In Moscow, the Foreign Ministry regarded the episode as a propaganda victory but expected that Bourke's adventure at the Embassy would be used by the British Foreign Office to deflect attention from SIS — which duly happened. Briefings to London newspapers produced accounts of the visit, in which Bourke was variously described as 'dishevelled', 'down-at-heel' or 'unkempt' — living somewhere with Blake in Moscow but eager to leave Russia. He had been asked to return to the Embassy while enquiries were made with the Irish Government for a passport — but had failed to do so. As the Moscow-based correspondents were briefed by the Attaché who had met him, it emerged that a photograph of Bourke in evening dress, taken at a function in Crawley, had been sent to the embassy officials, who identified Bourke as the man who had called.

There was now little doubt that KGB would have to act quickly before either of the fugitives might be spotted in a Moscow street. It was the height of 'spy-mania' and legendary defectors were on the journalists wish list and any likely lead of encountering either Blake or Bourke would have led the correspondents to tramp the pavements in the hope of getting lucky.

As the correspondents filed more stories, Stan arrived to urge an earlier departure from Moscow. Blake found himself accompanying Bourke — a role reversal where the Irishman was becoming his gaoler. He had become a liability to Blake's desire for a peaceful life. Reluctantly, Blake agreed to the tour on condition they would have separate hotel rooms and letters from his mother would be forwarded to their various locations. He was also deeply concerned about contact with his estranged wife and children, from whom he would be out of touch. The tour began with the Baltic states and would travel as far east as Tashkent, a distance of many thousands of miles across the span of the USSR. All this to ensure they were not accidentally recognised by journalists or sharp-eyed tourists.

Meanwhile back in Britain, the conspirators whose safety Blake worried about were also deeply uneasy as the news broke of Bourke's rash visit to the embassy. Since his departure eight months earlier, they had engaged across a broad front of dissident activity. Pat Pottle had married Sue Abrahams, Secretary of the Committee of 100 and set-up married life in his flat in Hampstead where the fugitives had hidden. Pat, Sue, Michael and Anne and others of the Blake conspiracy were prominent in anti-war protests.

The group involved in the Blake escape were now organising an escape route to Scandinavian countries for American deserters from Vietnam, using the passport fabrication they had perfected for Bourke. They were prime movers in a wide range of anti-war protests.

One of those protests, against the military takeover by the 'Greek Colonels' involved Randle and Pottle being among a group storming the Greek Embassy in London, resulting in their arrest. Pat Pottle booted open the door of the police van and escaped. Michael Randle, however, was sentenced to twelve months imprisonment, which he was serving when he read of Bourke's visit to the British Embassy in Moscow. The clear message was that Bourke had become disenchanted with life in Russia and intended returning to face the charges connected with the escape. It spun the highly principled Randle into a spiral of worry — if Bourke were extradited to London, would he and Pottle feel obliged to volunteer their parts, rather than have Bourke take the rap alone? Michael had a young family and was already finding this gaoling more onerous than his previous stint in Wormwood Scrubs.

Oblivious to the worries back in England, Sean Bourke set out on a rejuvenation saga of his own, on a prolonged bout of wine, women and song, courtesy of the KGB. Towards the end of September 1967, he and Blake set off on their escorted tour of the USSR which would last for over a month. Beginning in Leningrad, they went onto the Baltic states and the Lithuanian capital, Vilnius, across to Odessa and Yerevan, ending in Uzbekistan. It offered as informative a view of the USSR as only the most determined of travellers could hope to find at the time. Bourke, then aged thirty-three, was in the prime of his health and perceptions. A robust figure who kept himself fit, even his excessive drinking did not dint his curiosity and appetite for both knowledge and sensations.

Blake, though twelve years older, was similarly curious about the terrain and populations they encountered. But they differed considerably in taste and discipline, so those patterns of their previous tour were replicated. Blake visited art galleries and those sparse churches that remained open as museums. Bourke spent much time sampling the breweries, champagne factories and the female guides. According to his own account, the cock-notches began at the first stop in Leningrad with the guide Valentina who invited him to inspect her apartment. After that, his conquests seemed to become a matter of routine, though the further East they moved, the less attractive he found the women. In one instance, their In-tourist guide sported a moustache, and hairy legs.

More distressing was the tension, which built-up between himself and Blake as the journey progressed. Bourke, giving way to his obsessive streak, still smouldered over what he took to be Blake's conniving at his 'extermination'. When they should have been celebrating the anniversary of the escape on the 22nd of October in Armenia, Bourke provoked a public row to the consternation of his minders. On other occasions he went out of his way to flout the agreed rules: for instance talking to Indian seamen who were temporarily stranded in the port of Odessa and letting them know he came from Ireland. There were other incidents which tried the patience of both Blake and the escorts. It was with some weariness they returned to Moscow in mid-November. Whatever reservations KGB had about him leaving for Ireland, one is left with the distinct feeling that, unofficially at least, they would be glad to see the back of him. From Bourke's point of view, maybe there was method in his madness.

Shortly after returning to Moscow, he was given permission to phone his brother in Scotland. Kevin Bourke was settled in Ayr with a family and a skilled job as an air traffic controller. Like Sean he had RAF service behind him but unlike Sean, Kevin was a model of propriety and had been upset at his brother's public notoriety. Nonetheless, he felt close to Sean, worried about him and was relieved to hear him speaking clearly down the line from Moscow in November 1967. In guarded phone conversations they embarked on a plan to interest the British tabloid, *News of the World*. The newspaper was enthusiastic. It would fund a visit by Kevin to Moscow, in return for an account of the escape and Bourke's adventures since leaving England.

Assuming their conversations were being monitored, Bourke was surprised that Stan raised no objections about Kevin's visit, scheduled to take place the following spring. Neither did the KGB Colonel ask to see the working manuscript of Bourke's account of the escape, which he had kept with himself at all, times. Those matters could wait until his departure. With their vast array of surveillance and interception methods, it would not be difficult to control what he could take out of the country, including his memory[*]. In the meantime, as Blake's mother had come to live with him for an extended stay and as cordial relations with Bourke were now very low, it was decided that he should have his own accommodation. An apartment would be got ready for him and a 'swallow' put in place — a female used by espionage services. The changes were welcomed by Bourke, now considerably improved in morale by the authorities'

---

[*] According to Intelligence authority Christopher Andrew, Bourke was fed a memory-impairment drug, organised by the section of the KGB which dealt with foreign espionage. This is denied by Blake (to author, Moscow, 2001). See *The Mitrohkin Archive* by Christopher Andrew and Vasili Mitrokhin, Allen Lane, The Penguin Press, 1999, pp 522.

change of heart and the impending visit of his brother. And then came Larisa...

CHAPTER NINETEEN

PARTING IS SUCH SWEET SORROW...

She was undoubtedly beautiful — long auburn hair, blue eyes and the kind of figure that stopped conversations among her student group at Moscow University. She was as fashionably dressed as young women of her background could manage in the Moscow of the late 1960s, which meant her skirt was not a mini but yet displayed sufficient for Bourke to feel the allure of lust. When she spoke English with the formality of the language student, her intelligence shone through as a further attraction for an Irishman whose recent deprivations included free-ranging conversation. He was smitten.

He did not know she had been carefully selected by the *Residentura* in her language year at Moscow University and approved by Colonel Stan as a 'swallow', with a view to wider activities of KGB. But little of these background machinations mattered when Larisa and 'Robert' embarked on a love affair, sparked off by an introduction by Stanislav in room 207 of the Warsaw Hotel. The age-gap of thirteen years provided chemistry to a student meeting a handsome older man whose place in world politics she understood to be heroic and mysterious. What twenty-year innocent would not succumb to the challenge of providing services to the Party, when the working conditions seemed so agreeable?

'Robert Garvin' for his part, was coping with his inner despair. The months of travel, drinking and fornication had provided a 'high' diversion from the prison of Moscow — he was now faced with the 'low' reality of hotel living. His weeks in the Warsaw Hotel had been lonely, compounded by drinking bouts in the bar. When Larisa arrived, his life took a turn for the better. Under the calculated image of a hard-drinking adventurer, his heart beat with new possibilities — with Larisa he might have a kind of life. She brought him to meet her student friends and on social evenings they went to theatre, ballet and art exhibitions. Gradually, he realised the relationship had profoundly bettered him. By the spring of

1968 they had become inseparable and had dropped the pretence of their contrived identities. A skiing holiday gave them time on their own and inspired Bourke to write lyrical letters to Kevin.

'I had never worn skis before and I must have been the worst pupil the slopes had ever seen — it took me four days just to learn to fall on my face. So much so that when Larisa saw me in an upright position she exclaimed: "Oh Sean, you're standing up!" The Russian countryside in winter and the forests are like works of Art. When I told her I was from Ireland, she talked about Shaw and Joyce and Swift...coming from a 20-year old student this says much about the education system in Russia'.

Their holiday also facilitated another visit by Blake's mother, who came for a lengthy stay. It was now clear to the KGB section in charge of defectors that Blake would make his life in Russia, whereas Bourke had to be returned to the West. When he again broached this with Stanislav, the calming effect of Larisa had favoured his chances. The free exchange of letters with his brother in Scotland was part of the process. At Bourke's request, The Foreign Ministry facilitated a passport application for Kevin to travel to Moscow in the summer.

In spite of Bourke's view that Blake was preventing him from leaving, my own enquiries indicate otherwise. Yuri Andropov, who was indeed a harsh head of KGB, was cognisant of Blake's gratitude to Bourke and acquiesced with the view that the Irishman should be afforded every protection while he was in Russia. Within a Foreign Ministry that dealt, day-to-day, with issues of population unrest, famine and political alignments across a sixth of the world's habitations, Bourke was not such a big fish as he imagined himself to be.

There was much else happening in the late 1960s, which engaged the leadership of KGB with profound change. Across Europe, Asia and Africa cracks were widening in the post-war order, as the USSR armed revolutionary movements in the former colonies. From the democracies of Germany and France, streets protests by radicals led by Rudi Deutsche and Daniel Cohen-Bendit inspired marches as far away as Londonderry in Ulster and Prague in Czechoslovakia — all concerned with increased individual rights.

The US, for its part, was caught in conflict at home and abroad as it attempted to sustain with money, arms and training channelled through CIA, regimes which were dictatorships or Right-wing repressive. The Western establishments were quick to label any protest movement as 'communist-inspired' and its leaders as 'Reds'. America focussed obsessively on the expansion of Communism, seeing itself as the bastion of Democracy — opposing Civil Rights for blacks in its own country while suffering massive casualties in Vietnam against Marxist advances.

Within the Foreign Ministry in Moscow, where the short-wave radio transcripts brought news of coups and countercoups in which it was intimately involved, the matter of one difficult Irishman could be solved more easily by deportation than by extermination. Andropov was coping with a system whose internal contradictions threatened the Russian hold in Europe. Communism claimed 'freedom of the proletariat' but sent tanks to crush the workers in Prague; on the pretext of 'defending Socialism' and curtailed the liberalising moves of Czech communist leader Alexander Dubcek, who had, for the first time since the war, encouraged open debate on the living standards of his people behind the Iron Curtain.

The policies, East and West, which had grown out of the Second World War were undergoing erosion. The systems which could absorb change would survive. Those unable to change would perish. Somewhere in the maw of these tensions, Bourke and Blake found means to adjust — Blake by his mother's visits and his religious beliefs, Bourke with the companionship of Larisa and the impending visit of his brother. In Scotland, meanwhile, Kevin was visited separately by Special Branch and *News of the World* representatives. Carrying messages from both, he arrived in Moscow in August 1968.

Kevin found Sheremetyevo Airport a gloomy cavern as he searched among the crowd for his brother. He was intercepted by Stanislav who greeted him warmly and brought him to Sean who loitered by the exit, wearing dark glasses. Necessary, he said, in case he was recognised by journalists for whom the airport was a 'marking'. Accompanying them to Sean's apartment by KGB car, Colonel Stanislav then departed to allow the twin brothers to catch-up on their lives. They had much to talk about, including the death of their mother, which Sean had heard about many weeks after the event.

Kevin's journey was financed by the British newspaper, which undertook to lodge monies in return for a version of the escape. Because of legislation in Britain which prohibited the monetary reward to criminals for their published stories, the saga would ostensibly be written by 'Desmond Bourke', to evade direct payment to Sean and to protect Kevin's job as an Air Traffic Controller, which involved sensitive work such as monitoring secret military flights over the North Atlantic.

For the brothers, it was a satisfying re-union as they re-lived childhood escapades, took stock of their lives as adults and soon fell into a familiar pattern of Sean regaling his more sensible sibling with his adventures since leaving England. He showed off his apartment, displayed the coat that had disguised Blake and explained, in a diatribe that was all too familiar to Kevin, how relations between he and Blake had disintegrated. While he made it clear that KGB had been good to him and promised to provide a wage equal to that of a university professor, he was determined to return to Ireland and publish his account of the escape. He would entrust Kevin to bring back the manuscript, hand-written in a bundle of school exercise books.

Stanislav and his colleagues made sure the brothers were entertained. A car and driver were at their disposal. Sean proudly introduced Larisa to Kevin, who accompanied them on walkabout in The Kremlin and to meals at the restaurants favoured by State functionaries, including The Praga and Arbat, scenes of key events during the revolutionary era half-a-century before. She was proud of the achievements of Socialism, pointing out how backward and oppressed the Russian population had been before the Revolution of 1917. As they stopped by buildings, which had sheltered the makers of the modern Soviet State, she gave them a crash course in political history, reading from the plaques commemorating sieges and confrontations. Kevin was impressed — but more concerned with his brother's uncertain future in Russia.

They seem not to have been security conscious about writing for the *News of the World*. Kevin took down from Sean the narrative of the escape, using as source the hand-written draft, which he had worked on since his arrival. Although it was kept locked in a suitcase, it was easily accessible when they were absent from the apartment. The newspaper account gave the impression Blake had flown out of London Airport, rather than being smuggled overland by Michael and Anne Randle. It gave other misleading information about their time on the run in London, which protected the English conspirators[*].

Although the reality was far from that trumpeted by the paper — **For the First Time — the Full Story of how the Master Spy GEORGE BLAKE got out of Britain** — it was sufficiently descriptive to cast him again into the media limelight — exactly what Bourke wished, as a lever for his release and a sample for the book which he hoped would keep him in clover in Ireland. As written by 'Desmond Bourke' and subbed with the flair of a tabloid editor, it ran as a racy sixties thriller, with such headings as: **Man who Sprang Spy Blake talks at last...Payment for Springing a Spy — a Life of Debauchery...**

Claiming that the puritan Blake was jealous of Bourke's success with the girls — (He has the luck of the Irish) — it reeled off Sean's sexual conquests: Natalia, Meela, Olga... Valentine — 'I woke up one snow-covered morning in Leningrad with a terrific hangover, to hear Valentine

---

[*] *News of the World*, Sept/Oct. 1968 and author's interviews with Kevin Bourke Ayr, Scotland, 1987.

whispering Shakespeare gently in my ear: "Shall I compare thee to a summer's day? Thou art more lovely and more temperate…" "My dear girl, let us not exaggerate!" says I, catching a glimpse of my bleary-eyed stubble-chinned face in a mirror. Valentine, not to be deterred, recited more poetry "For God's sake, pass me the bloody bottle", says I…'

Kevin Bourke found Moscow both intriguing and intimidating. Before leaving he had received from the Irish Embassy in London, a visa to allow his brother entry, on the strength of a birth certificate which he had secured from Limerick.

As to returning with the seminal account of the escape in the seven notebooks, Kevin wondered if they would ever see the light of day in the West. Though Stanislav and the other KGB officers were solicitous for their welfare — he thought Stan an honourable man — he knew them to be professional intelligence officers. He was relieved when departure day came. The notebooks were stored at the bottom of his suitcase and he was en route to the airport, accompanied by Sean and Stan.

Sheremetyevo Airport is about an hour by car from Moscow, on a highway connected by a series of ring roads that feed into the city. Kevin thought it was taking longer to get to the highway than he expected — then the car spluttered to halt with mechanical trouble. He felt panicky because his wife expected him home on the scheduled flight and knew of the delicate nature of his visit. Even though Sean assured him that KGB would speed him through the cumbersome checks at Sheremetyevo, he was relieved when Stan flagged a passing taxi. It had a passenger next to the driver and two in the back, so there was nothing for it but to say good-bye to Sean and grab the only seat to get him to the airport.

Although the flight had closed, he was ushered to Customs with his suitcase. The searcher went instantly for the notebooks, which were taken to an urbane, English-speaking official who explained they would have to be read by the 'Press Committee'. Kevin should leave quickly as his flight was being held for him. In his apartment, Sean waited to hear that Kevin had made the flight. The call came from Stan with assurance that all was well and Kevin would be home that night. Some days later, Stan called again, more in sorrow than in anger, to tell him that the notebooks had been confiscated and suggesting he could have organised their safe delivery if Sean had only asked! Moreover, he was wrong about Blake, Stan said. It was a pity he held such views, but that was his privilege and there was nothing the authorities could do to alter his impressions. Clearly, Stan had read the draft manuscript. To Bourke's relief he also told him that as it was now clear he would not be happy in Russia, they would make arrangements for him to return to Ireland.

During September he had a bittersweet time with Larisa, both conscious of his impending departure. University had resumed and Sean did not offer to make a life with her in Ireland. Kevin was in regular contact by phone and letter, informing him of travel arrangements. Granada Television in Britain would record an interview in Amsterdam where he would change planes for Ireland. There was also interest from book publishers. Stanislav told him that the Foreign Ministry would facilitate his leaving in October. It suited him to leave on the second anniversary of the escape, thereby providing an extra bite to media coverage.

Larisa and he gave a farewell dinner for Stanislav and a colleague. She presented him with a ring as a token for the marriage that would never take place. It was a trying and tearful time for them both, privately relieved on his part by the impending media coverage — and the new life — he was about to embark upon. Outside the airport, he said good-bye to her. He was given the VIP fast-track through the usual three checks and was not surprised to see Stanislav loitering in the departure lounge. In Amsterdam, the crew from Granada recorded the first television interview with the notorious Sean Bourke.

The lengthy interview, as later transmitted, would provide him with a wide media profile in Britain and Ireland. Shortly after it was recorded, he received a phone call from Kevin who, casting his professional eye over the weather charts, warned of fog at Dublin Airport and the possibility the flight might be diverted to London. Kevin was also concerned, as he later told me, that it might be used as an excuse by the British security service to instruct the plane to land in Britain, thereby putting his brother under arrest[*]. Heeding the possibility, Sean stayed overnight in Amsterdam, flew onto Dusseldorf and caught a transatlantic flight bound for America which would re-fuel at Shannon. He landed there, fifteen miles from his native Limerick, on the 22nd October to a barrage of cameras and questions: Why had he come back? Had he *really* sprung George Blake? How was he treated by the KGB? What were his plans now? Did he fear being extradited to Britain...?

He was urbane, patient and clearly reveling in the attention. He had returned, he said, because he was an Irishman 'and where would an Irishman settle — if not in his own country?'. Yes, he had sprung the 'Russian Spy', without the help of KGB or IRA but had the financial help of 'good Englishmen' who had not known what the money was for. No, he had not been paid by the Russians, all he had was forty American dollars given to him by Colonel Stanislav of KGB. Yes, he could have stayed in Russia and not wanted for anything, but he intended to settle in Ireland and make a career as a writer — all would be revealed in time when his manuscript arrived from Moscow.

Reading the reports in England, Michael and Anne Randle and Pat Pottle were nervous. Sean was being as flamboyant as they had feared. They hung on every word and analysed them afterwards as they presumed was being done by Special Branch. They thought it only a matter of time before the knock came on the door. The references to the English sympathizers alarmed them, though Sean had taken care to lay a false trail about the actual means of Blake's concealment, claiming that they had lived for two months in Highlever Road, before he constructed the hiding place in the van, which he drove himself to Germany. They were puzzled

---

[*] Interview with Kevin Bourke, Ayr, Scotland, September 1987.

by this contrived detail — at variance to his recent tabloid versions, which had both fugitives leaving by air. The conspirators suspected the security sleuths would reconstruct it, confirming what they already knew, leading to them being charged. Since Sean's departure nineteen months earlier, both Randle and Pottle had again come to the notice of Special Branch on a range of marches — against the military takeover of Greece, against the American war in Vietnam and against the Russian invasion of Czechoslovakia. Michael Randle had been gaoled over the Greek Embassy invasion. He did not relish another stint.

The Granada programme, aired next day, did not ease their fears. Sean elaborated on their involvement, with transparently 'misleading' detail: they thought it would not be difficult for a desk officer in Tintagel House[*] to glean the reality. By now Randle and Pottle were well known by MI5 to have socialized with Bourke in the prison. Pressed to explain how such an operation could be funded 'with £1,000 from friends', Bourke said he did 'not give a damn what you ask me or how un-frank you think I am. I am not going to tell you where I got this money from — I can tell you only this — I borrowed it from some of my very close and sincere friends and I'm not going to help you or anyone else identify these people'.

Bourke went on to explain that the money had been repaid by KGB, through means of which he was not aware. 'The KGB did not tell me how they achieved this, but I know the money has been repaid'. He stayed with his version of Blake and himself having flown out of the country using false passports. Contrary to his antagonism against Blake in Moscow, he took a more benign view now, saying that KGB had assured him not one of the agents of the Western secret services named by Blake had been killed in reprisal as Labour Foreign Secretary George Brown had claimed to the *Daily Express*.

---

[*] Building on South Bank then used by 'F' section of MI5 which dealt with internal subversion.

As for Blake now, he was living in Moscow but was not happy, as he was essentially a Westerner and found it difficult to adjust to the harsh realities of Soviet life. But he had no option, said Bourke, because he was a devout communist. He ventured that Blake had 'great delusions of grandeur', citing how Blake would '...stride into my room in his dressing gown, brandishing a bottle of champagne in one hand and two elegant glasses in the other, and say in his cultured Foreign Office voice, "I say, Robert, what is your attitude to a glass of champagne?" '.

Meanwhile in Moscow, sans dressing-gown and more importantly Bourke, Blake was feeling a weight lifted from his life — he was reading the manuscript and deleting the sections which could identify Randle and Pottle.

Bourke's bout of instant fame lasted into the weekend. Arriving on Tuesday, 22nd October 1968, he was world famous by the Sunday, with coverage syndicated to many continents. His fairytale of himself was coming true — he might yet become a prophet in his own land.

CHAPTER TWENTY

BOURKE: HOME IS THE HERO

Bourke's reception at Shannon Airport temporarily sated his appetite for notoriety. Before a battery of interviewers, he accounted for his last two years. He was at pains to assert the escape had been 'an amateur effort', unaided by KGB who had been 'as surprised as the British — who had made the mistake of thinking it was the Russians who organised it'. In spite of being repeatedly pressed by reporters to identify his back-up team, he batted back with aplomb, saying variously that they were sincere people...University-educated...persons of conviction...' No, he would give no further details – 'I am not a police informer'.

He cut a debonair figure in a well-cut gabardine coat, with a hat perched cockily to both his past and present. Russia was then a closed society and his views on living standards and individual freedoms were widely reported, particularly his account of the poverty of the mass of citizens. As for freedom of expression, The Party did the Peoples' thinking for them. It was not, he felt, a society in which someone used to Western standards would feel happy — which was why he had come home. He had been well looked after, as someone who had done the communist State a service and could have lived out his days in luxury. But Ireland was his home; 'I wanted to be safe and secure — if an Irishman could not be safe in Ireland, where could he be safe...?'

He had returned with only the essentials of travel and had not been paid for his services. Brandishing the two twenty dollars bills which Stanislav had given him, he said that was all the money he possessed, though he hoped to make a living as a writer, once his book was published. Naively in the circumstances, he did not ask for fees for media interviews. But somewhere along the line, monies were placed at his disposal, though Granada Television later denied any payments to him. Within weeks of his arrival, a literary agency in London sent an emissary to Dublin to negotiate terms for his book and pay an advance against expected sales.

Equally alert were the police authorities in both countries. Dossiers were compiled and a steady exchange of information charted his movements in Dublin. Ten days after his arrival, the Extradition Warrant was duly delivered to the Irish legal authorities, naming him as Sean Alphonsus Bourke and requesting he be delivered to representatives of the British Attorney-General. He was arrested by the Irish Special Branch at The Gresham Hotel in the capital's main street. Brought before a lower court, he nominated John Gore-Grimes a prominent Dublin solicitor to represent him, who promptly went to the High Court and achieved a stay on the Extradition Order until the legal issues could be heard. He was released, pending the hearing at the first sittings of 1969.

The Extradition Act had been amended three years before and contained many provisions which had their roots in British legislation designed for the protection of political refugees who had fled to Britain from Europe during the turn-of-the-century upheavals. Some of those provisions had been amended into Irish law, such as the refusal to hand over someone charged with 'a political offence or an offence connected with a political offence'. It had been used successfully by IRA gunmen on the run from attacks made on the British state in Northern Ireland. Bourke's lawyers advised that he should establish in the mind of the court that Blake had acted out of political motives — therefore his lawyers would plead that aiding the escape of George Blake came under the same 'political offence'.

That should not be difficult, the advice went, as he had admitted in numerous recent interviews his role in the escape. It would be sensible for Bourke also, when on the stand, to make clear his sympathy that Blake had been given an excessively long sentence for his spying — which could be held to be political, as inferred by the comments of the Old Bailey trial judge, in saying he 'had rendered much of this country's work useless' — meaning Blake's work for the

Secret Intelligence Service of the British Foreign Office. It would be up to the lawyer for the Irish State, acting to effect the Extradition Act, to cast doubts on the 'political' interpretation of Bourke's motives and portray him as a criminal who was motivated by hostility to the police — that in effect Bourke had used Blake to hit back at an Establishment he detested. If the court accepted this version of Bourke, the way would be clear for him to be extradited. This was the scenario for an exploration of legal, political and criminal definitions, whose relevance was not lost on the wider world.

Much of that world was in political turmoil at the beginning of 1969, in student-led protests in territories as diverse as communist satellites and Western democracies. In Czechoslovakia, students protesting at Soviet invasions were hailed as heroes by the populace and defined as criminals by the communist State. In London, radicals invaded the embassies of South Africa and Rhodesia, in solidarity with black majority populations deprived of civil rights, while nearer to Bourke's trial, the British Protectorate of Ulster was under siege from marchers demanding votes, jobs and housing for the minority Catholic population who had not accepted the legitimacy of the two states resulting from the partitioning of the island. Even Dublin, the capital of the 'Catholic Republic' had seen radicals on the receiving-end of police batons when demanding houses for the homeless.

Against this background, Bourke ascended into the witness box, neatly dressed and keenly interested in the proceedings. Advised to cast himself as humanitarian in aiding Blake, he caused his lawyers some consternation by playing that role to the wider gallery.

Many of his answers were acerbic, lengthy and — to the media — quotable. Excerpts provide the flavour of the tussle between Bourke and the State lawyer, Niall McCarthy (SC), who was seeking to establish his 'criminal' motives while the effort of Bourke's counsel, Declan Costello (SC), to show the 'political' nature were sometimes sabotaged by his client's responses.

By the second day of the hearing, with the facts of his recent history established, State Counsel probed Bourke's motivation.

'Would it truthfully express your basic philosophy to say that nobody ever crosses you and gets away with it?

— I would say invariably not! —

And is it your philosophy in life?

— I would hardly exalt it to a state of philosophy. It is my attitude —

Are you capable of a deep and burning hatred?

— Very capable —

Do you have a deep and burning hatred for the British police?

— I do —

Does your deep and burning hatred extend to the British Establishment?

— It does indeed —

And would you be prepared to take very drastic action for the purpose of harming the British police or an individual police officer?

— I would have to have very good reason for wanting to harm a British police officer —

Have you got a very good reason for wanting to harm Mr Sheldon?'

Apparently unaware where this line of questioning might lead, Bourke replied that he had been 'framed' by Constable Sheldon, on the charge of sending him a bomb, for which he had been found guilty and sentenced to seven years. Citing the background that Sheldon had implied he was homosexual and that he had failed to get a retraction, he went on to claim that PC Sheldon 'had sent the bomb to himself'. He wanted Sheldon sent away for a very long time. Asked about his state of mind before the escape, Bourke said the success of the mission would embarrass the police and 'give me immense pleasure'. After further exchanges it became clear that State Counsel had reasonably established that Bourke was motivated to spring Blake in order to gain revenge on the police. Too late, Bourke realised he had been boxed into making an admission which might go against him.

Neither did he see what lay ahead when he was asked to explain the discrepancies in various accounts he had given of the escape — to Granada TV he said he drove the Dormobile, having hollowed out the drawer to conceal Blake. In court he had said one of the English conspirators drove it. Did he believe in the Oath he had taken in court to tell the truth? Well, as much as any man, he replied. Did he believe in God as a witness...? Yes, but that did not mean he had to like Him: 'God is the type of person I would hate to be seen drinking with in a pub. I believe in God, but I do not like Him very much'. But yes, in spite of that he had taken an Oath under God to tell the truth.

Asked to elaborate, he delivered a tirade:

'...I believe in God, but as I say, I do not like him very much. I think he is a cruel, vindictive and selfish God. A God who is more on the side of the rich and powerful than on the side of the poor and the weak, God was on the side of Nazis in Europe and the Black and Tans in Ireland. He was on the side of the British in Africa and he is now on the side of the Americans in Vietnam, as the American Catholic bishops are telling us. I was born and went to school in Limerick city in this country, I went to school barefooted in summer and winter because my parents could not afford to buy me any shoes. If I was one minute late through the school gate the Christian Brothers would beat me black-and-blue in the name of Christianity. At Mass on Sunday morning the well-shod and well-fed priest would solemnly mount the pulpit and tell me and others like me that far from complaining we should give thanks to God for our poverty. He told us poverty was a gift from God, a virtue and a means to sanctifying grace. Well, of course, the only people who derived any comfort from those words were those priests' friends, the rich employers. They rejoiced on hearing these words, because they knew the weak and humble peasant and labourer would not go on strike for more wages or complain about his bad working conditions because this would be tantamount to rejecting God's divine gift of poverty. So you see, even in insignificant Limerick, God was on the side of the rich and powerful!'

When pressed to name the other conspirators, on the grounds he should 'tell the whole truth' as per the Oath, he refused (Counsel's reasoning was to test the 'political' motivation of the other conspirators). Probed at length about his political views, he said he was not a communist, indeed he was opposed to the USSR before the escape not least because of its invasion of Hungary in 1956 and its more recent invasion of Czechoslovakia. There followed long exchanges to define 'political prisoners', in which Bourke said he was not automatically sympathetic to that category — 'If Ian Paisley asked me to spring him from gaol, I would refuse'. Asked if he would agree that of all reasons given, 'your real motive had been compassion and feelings of a humanitarian nature? Bourke agreed 'Yes, it is fair to say that...'

The probing continued over three days, playing to a full public gallery and extensive newspaper reports. After each day, Bourke held a further court in his Dublin hotel to an audience of journalists and hangers-on. To the despair of his legal team, he became volubly indiscreet in that raffish company, admitting that he had sent the bomb to the policeman, in spite of denying it in court. Neither had Blake been of any current use to KGB because during his five years in gaol, much had changed. In drunken sessions he offered to act as conduit for the IRA to get guns from Russia, saying that KGB were probably shadowing him even as he spoke, which provoked some of his impressionable retinue to stare at hapless hotel customers. He promised more sensational revelations in court.

His solicitor found him both exasperating and amusing, as he presided over the day's aftermath, paying lavishly for rounds of drinks and referring to his Counsel, the respected lawyer Declan Costello, as 'My Honourable Queen's Counsel...'. He was showing himself to be that peculiar mixture of the Irishman whose formative years had been spent in British penal institutions, not unlike the writer

Brendan Behan, then a legend in his own booze-time — a role Bourke overlaid with flourishes of Wildean wit. It was an act he could not resist, but one which his legal team hoped could be restrained until the verdict. Not surprisingly, *The Irish Times* headed one day's hearing as 'James Bond and Theology in Extradition Case'.

The proceedings were avidly followed by the English conspirators, bemused at Bourke's exhibitionism, uneasy at the prospect of untoward revelations. Troubled by the detail which Bourke had given in court, they felt it was only a matter of time before Special Branch fitted the remaining pieces of the jigsaw. Michael Randle got a fright when he answered the phone at home and heard Sean's voice. He asked Michael to post him the small open-reel tapes of his conversations on walkie-talkie across the wall of the prison with Blake. Nervous of his phone being tapped, Randle declined. Days later, Bourke rang back with the same request.

Randle and Pottle now felt that Bourke was getting too close for comfort. The tapes were given to a courier from Dublin who turned up on Randle's doorstep shortly afterwards and extracts duly appeared in tabloid and television reports later in the year. They had a further uneasy time as they awaited the verdict of the Irish court which was delivered in early February 1969. The political pundits who had predicted Bourke would not be extradited were proved correct, though Mr Justice O'Keefe did take aboard the State Counsel's efforts to establish that Bourke himself had not acted out of political motives.

However, in reviewing the evidence, the judge said he had no difficulty in coming to the conclusion that because Blake's original offence was 'political' — Bourke's offence was clearly 'connected to a political offence'. He refused therefore, the application of the British Attorney-General. Outside the court, the plaintiff in the action found himself surrounded by spurious well-wishers. Although ODCs[*] were returned to Britain almost as a matter of course, the

---

[*] Ordinary Decent Criminals.

Republic's legal system was sensitive to extradition cases with 'political' overtones. Invariably, judges leaned towards demonstrating the independence of the native judiciary in matters relating to the legal demands of its former imperial ruler.

It was a heady time for Bourke. Since his return almost three months before, he had regularly featured in the media, vying for space with such notable events as the musical 'Hair' which extolled the new liberalism of dress and lifestyles, the orbiting of the moon by American astronauts and the cessation of bombing in Vietnam, ordered by the outgoing President Lyndon Johnson. Incumbent Richard Nixon vowed to exploit the lull with a lasting peace, while Beatle John Lennon led a world-wide chorus of teenagers to 'Make Love Not War...' and Norman Mailer's account of peace marches was required reading for a generation of Americans who wanted out of Asia. In Russia there were hardly any signs of liberalism — Soviet troops occupied the Czech capital while Russians could only read smuggled copies of the works of their monumental writer Alexander Solzhenitsyn.

By the spring of 1969, Ulster dominated the domestic agenda with widespread civil disorder. Refugees and fund-raisers for guns were common in certain Dublin pubs. In Groome's hotel, Government ministers jostled with villains and con-men, politicos and actors, writers and those looking for a good time. I was there one evening as Bourke arrived in the company of a retinue from the Gresham Hotel. He carried himself with an air of importance, surveyed the company and said: 'Holy Jaysus, Ireland's only hope'. He made for a corner with a tray full of drinks. Within minutes, he had received overtures from a couple of drunken Dail deputies, had his hand shaken by the inevitable boulevardiers who waited cravenly upon the famous — and proceeded to entertain the assembly with colourful abuse of the Fianna Fail Party which at that time was substantively funded by builders and businessmen.

As the members often wore mohair overcoats, Bourke entertained his circle with calls of 'Fur-coated Paddies' directed to the nearby Parliamentary table. 'I suppose none of you ever saw a shot fired in anger' he taunted, as they engaged in conversation with Northerners — 'and you certainly cannot speak the Queen's English — proper!' He lampooned the mantra of a United Ireland — 'Protestants join this Catholic slum — not likely, mate!' His mimicry of Southern accents was initially amusing to the gathering — but as he baited them with calls of 'Little Irelanders' and 'Sinn Fein — Me Fein', (Ourselves — Myself) unease gave way to a row. In attempting to get at Bourke, one Northerner knocked a table of drinks into the lap of a Dail Deputy. 'Only time he got his cock in the hard stuff' riposted a merry Bourke.

'Go back to England, you Limerick Ham... !' Shouted an aggrieved regular. The bar listened to Bourke remind the parliamentarians of their failure to legislate for anything of which the Catholic Church would disapprove — 'You are terrified of the belt of a crozier — infants in swaddling clothes instead of public representatives'. He mimicked a Customs Officer confiscating condoms from a British tourist 'Oh, what have we here now — dis is a terrible ting, do you put it on your mickey or what?' Others joined in a scene that was smoky, conspiratorial, teetering towards violence, reprieved by restraint. Bourke, I registered, had put on weight and was in his element: famous and infamous in his own country. The years of perdition seemed to fall away in a haze of good fellowship.

With the Extradition case in his favour he seemed set to make a new life. But now he had money and success, regular bouts of merry-making were the order of the day and night. The London literary agency pressed him on the promised book, which he assured them would contain revelations not in the public prints. Although the manuscript remained in Moscow, he had hopes that Colonel Stanislav, once the court reports routed from the London embassy had been read, would realise that he had protected the English conspirators and prevail on Blake to agree its release. This duly happened in the form of a wrapped package to his Dublin lawyer —inside was his handwritten manuscript. The references which could have identified Randle were, thought Bourke, deleted by the censoring hand of George Blake.

The literary agent who arrived in Dublin to peruse the manuscript found Bourke to be wary: as it happened he was a former Army officer and retained a military demeanour. Bourke outright accused him of working for the British security services: it took many phone calls to his London office and a day of thawing before Bourke agreed to hand over the manuscript. Five thousand pounds was lodged to his bank, the agent departed with the hand-written account in school exercise books, leaving the author a rich man by the currencies of the time. By the times, too, the windfall did not prove a boon. A more prudent person might have invested the money, or made himself scarce in a city of codgers — prudence was not Bourke's middle name. Within weeks, the word was out among the riff-raff that Bourke was hosting parties, paying for drinks in the Gresham and Groome's and eager for 'the knowledge' — of the 'haunts and habits' of Dublin's underworld. Old habits die hard.

By day he could be a model of decorum: well-spoken, entertaining and intelligent in conversation. By night, he changed, looking for the mavericks who infested Dublin pubs. Already he was perceiving that the Ireland he had romanticised from afar was essentially conservative. In fact, it was hard-working, devout, family-based with a bemused tolerance for the infamous like himself — but not willing to take him to its bosom, not into the hearths and homes redolent with fears of the outside world. He might provide an evening's entertainment in a pub and be generous with his money, but was rarely invited into the daytime lives of people he had caroused with the night before. He moved into a suburban apartment along the coast but found time heavy on his hands. His boom companions of the night were reticent or unavailable during the day. He fell back on his prison and RAF training, made his bed in the morning, had breakfast alone, read the papers avidly and went for long walks along Sandymount strand — and began to fear, rather like Blake in Russia, that his imagined home had become another kind of prison.

This restriction was brought home forcibly with the publication of his book, *The Springing of George Blake* in the spring of 1970. A friend recalled: 'he was absolutely over the moon about it. He could hardly believe he was at last an author — he was so proud'. As it was prominently on sale in some Dublin bookshops, he strutted about town with copies under his arm, lingered by bookshelves, indulged in liquid lunches to hear praise from those who had read the reviews. He could not, however, throw a launch party in London, where he would have liked to invite favoured inmates of The Scrubs, including some of the 'screws', as well as Michael Randle and Pat Pottle and for good measure some of the Special Branch officers who led the investigation. They showed much interest in the book, which confirmed their own re-construction.

He had, for instance, described the contacts with Blake's mother and sister and his failure to raise the initial expenses from them — which Special Branch had heard about when calling on Mrs Behar within hours of the escape. His raising the monies by calling on *Michael Reynolds* tallied with their knowledge of Michael Randle. Bourke's description of the house being about twenty minutes walk from Camden Town tube station was accurate, as was his account of *Reynolds* as '...about thirty, very slightly built, his face was rather pale and drawn...he would never be well off, for he was a Socialist at heart...but not a communist'. The description fitted Michael Randle closely, down to his mother being a Dublin woman and his father a Londoner. A similar English/Irish background was ascribed in the book to *Pat Porter* whom Bourke described as 'more vocal than Michael...impetuous and a little excitable'. No prizes for identifying Pat Pottle, maybe even with the sly Irish joke of Porter[*]. *Anne Reynolds*,

---

[*] Porter — now known as Guinness.

'pretty...practical, asking sensible questions' and mother of two young boys, could only be the Anne Randle who later travelled in the camper van, with the boys as disguise.

'Any intelligent boy-scout could have worked it out', one of their friends said, on reading the advance copy which had been sent by a journalist who knew that Michael's time in the Scrubs coincided with Blake's. The conspirators were in disarray. If a boy scout could work it out, what decision would be taken by the Security Services? Sue Pottle had moved with Pat to a village in Wales and was so concerned that she drove to London to buy a copy, rather than be seen in her local bookshop. Outside that foursome, there was also consternation among the wider helpers who had provided the back-up of safe houses or who had helped in material ways. As they read of their various roles (including the man whose wife told her psychiatrist they were harbouring a prison escapee) they all knew the significance of what they had done. Enough to gaol them.

The waiting gnawed at their nerves while the book was extensively reviewed in the broadsheets, who generally regarded it as a racy and entertaining if questionable account. It was used as a peg by the tabloids and television to recap the 'great escape' and its loose ends. Public questions hung over their identities, but as the weeks went by without visits from the police, they settled uneasily back into their civilian lives. They would have slept more soundly had they known the silence of the authorities would become eloquently important for their later liberty. Pat Pottle had become an antiques dealer in Wales, with a young family. Michael and Anne were living in Bradford: he teaching, she nursing. The political world continued to engage them, as it began to change from old Imperialism to new liberal democracies, helped by the influence of their movements — beyond what their small numbers at the time appeared to signify.

Across the globe, the old order liberalised, even as it appeared to resist the criticisms of radicals. A softening brought about by the combination of media, technology and liberal pressure groups. Although increasing his bombing of the Ho Chi Minh trail of supplies to the communists in Vietnam, President Nixon was already under intense pressure at home and was suing for peace, even as US troopers shot dead four students protesting against the war at Kent State University. Ulster was aflame and British troops given orders to shoot dead petrol bombers — but already MI5 had identified IRA leaders who would later secretly meet the British Government to sue for a process that would take another twenty years to copper-fasten. As far as the English conspirators were concerned, a watershed was best expressed through the death of Bertrand Russell who died at the age of 97. A philosopher and free-thinker, imprisoned for his CND activities, he had inspired a generation to non-violent action against the arms-race and nuclear threats of the Great Powers. He spoke for many of them when he defined the three passions of his life — the longing for love, the search for knowledge and pity for the sufferings of mankind.

CHAPTER TWENTY-ONE

BLAKE — A NEW LIFE (MARRIAGE AND THE SPIES CLUB)

While Sean Bourke was in Ireland trying to find a 'home', George Blake was also trying to make a home in Russia. With Bourke out of his life — and gone from Moscow, he had the undivided support of Colonel Stanislav in the onerous transition. He quickly found that without the active influence of KGB, as a vast state organisation, it would have been more difficult. Utilities easily available in the West took months to negotiate. In a capital of ten million people there was one cumbersome office to give driving licenses. It seemed impossible to find decorators or comfortable shoes or batteries for radios. He learned to become his own hairdresser after an encounter with a barber whose hand seemed more used to the vodka glass.

He was shocked at the degree of alcoholism in day-to-day encounters. Though he found Russians a warm and kindly people, the shortages of basic supplies made shopping into an obstacle course. He queued for hours to purchase one item, then joined another queue to pay, then tagged onto another queue to being the cycle again. For someone used to the bright lights of Oxford Street, it took some adjusting as he trekked to buy a foodstuff that might be randomly in supply — which quickly ran out, forcing him to start another shopping safari for sugar here or fruit there. Meat was badly cut and crudely wrapped, with generous portions of gristle. Even the most elegant of Moscow women carried a supply of folded bags, as they never knew when they might come upon a scarce commodity. He became used to frayed tempers as frazzled shoppers faced empty shelves.

To his surprise he found them making space for him as a foreigner, identified as such by his accent. He felt they took pity on him because the system was so perplexing to an outsider. They also believed Western articles to be superior to their own, an inferiority which maintained an enormous illegal black market in the goods of the Capitalist West, titular 'enemy of the State'. Though he believed in Communism with a religious zeal, he accepted KGB help in order to live, which, perversely, put him in the position of being privileged. While he believed in the liberation of the masses — and had suffered six years in gaol for that belief — his own tastes were not of the majority. Even the plentiful supply of champagne, which he had initially seen as, 'only the best being good enough for the people', he realised was produced by State distilleries in such quantities that required mass consumption — in a society where alcoholism was a major medical problem. But beef and bread were of poor quality.

To make life bearable, he found himself allied to the nomenklatura, the elite whose State contacts provided them with a living well above the mass of the ordinary citizens. Otherwise he would not have been able to stock his kitchen or enjoy the antique furniture which decorated his apartment. His mother, too, was a crucial support when she stayed on prolonged visits from Holland. She brought his well-cut English suits which had been part of his Foreign Office 'uniform' and which she had stored in the confidence he would someday use them. She mastered the daily saga of shopping and worked to make a home for him, conscious of his upset that his marriage to Gillian was finished. It came as a bitter blow that she had formed a relationship with another SIS officer, by whom she was expecting a child. This harsh news was communicated in a series of letters, which on grounds of compassion, were facilitated by both British and Russian Intelligence services.

Over thirty years after that final break, Blake's demeanour became solemn as he controlled the tremble in his voice. It had not been a happy time in those early months, he admitted. He had been confused, unhappy and privately fearful of his future. Though he had been forced, as he put it, 'to see Soviet life through pink-tinted glasses', to counter Bourke's damning views of life under Communism, he had been putting on a brave front. 'The news from Gillian, that she was with child by the man with whom she had taken up — a very bitter blow to me. I was aware of what I had inflicted — the effects of my gaoling on her father, who was in the Service — it caused a rift between them — the upset on her own family life and her relationship with former colleagues in SIS — and then the further blow of my escape — because of course I had not indicated to her during prison visits even the remotest possibility...',

'In spite of all that, I had secret hopes that she might yet come and join me in Moscow with our children. So when I heard of her starting another family — it was a very bad blow indeed...I was very disappointed'. Did he feel the marriage break-up was too high a price to pay for his allegiance to Communism? In answering, he reached for the comfort of Predestination: 'No, I never felt that because I believed that one thing flowed logically from another, all part of what was meant...even when I was in prison...'. He resumed with an ironic repeat: 'Even when I was in prison — it prepared me for life in the Soviet Union. Had I come straight from the West, from being a free man, life would have been much more difficult. But six years in gaol acted as a foretaste for what life was going to be like here'.

After Bourke left, his conditions appreciably improved, as restrictions were lifted on his 'prison within a prison'. He was allowed to galleries and theatres without KGB escort, though visits to the Bolshoi Ballet, heavily patronised by tourists, required him to be smuggled into a box not readily seen by the public. His mother was his main companion on outings and as they entertained each other with reactions to events, orderly domestic life was restored. Their sense of humour extended to Blake remarking, on seeing a neighbour on walks with her idiot adult son: 'We are just like those two!'. That domestic pattern changed for the better, some months after the numbing news from Gillian of *her* new life: his loneliness eased when he made the acquaintance, during a cruise on the river Volga, of a lively countrywoman, Ida, whose outgoing nature took him out of himself.

Ida had many similarities to Gillian (not unusual for second relationships). She engaged actively in outdoor pursuits; skiing, boating and forest treks. She had the same country tastes as his former English wife. When marriage was mooted, he encountered opposition from her step-mother, who had lived through The Terror, when contact with foreigners resulted in gaol. (The paranoid Stalin designated Foreigners as Enemies of the State — spies from the Anti-Soviet outside world). The knowledge that he had KGB 'connections' intensified her unease. According to Blake, when Ida said her husband-to-be was *Persona Grata* with the Party, the mother retorted that he might easily become *Persona Non-Grata* tomorrow — the comment of a Russian who knew the midnight knock at the door. It took some time to accept that her step-daughter was safe in marriage to Gorgi Ivanovich, the name by which Blake was known. The marriage took place in a town outside Moscow. The town had a good quality hotel, being a centre of Atomic Research. The marriage to Ida was a short civil ceremony.

Apart from shielding him in the aftermath of the Bourke extradition case in Dublin, the policy of KGB then was to not publicise the safe recovery of senior agents, so he was officially known as Gorgi Ivanovich when he joined a research institute 'from service abroad'. He settled into the role of an academic translator. Daily attendance was not required and much of the work could be done at home, though he would have preferred to be among busy colleagues and have the interaction of coffee breaks and the usual office atmosphere. The Institute seemed to be without goals, other than compilation of economic output, culled from published sources. Little of the work engaged him intellectually, though it gave him status and salary — staples of newly married life.

He was, however, bound to KGB instructions. Although the service looked after agents who had served them loyally in the West, their operational usefulness ceased on capture. Defection to Russia meant 'rest and care', during which their possible role as triple-agent or deliberate plant was assessed. Still, he had the company of Kondrashev who had been his case officer in London, to whom he had passed the seminal secrets of Operation GOLD, jointly run by SIS and CIA[*]. In the course of his cover in London, Kondrashev had assumed the persona of a dandy Englishman, dressing in blazer and slacks and appearing more like a bank manager having an after-dinner walk. Kondrashev, a warm and sometimes unwittingly amusing figure appeared to his former agent with the remnants of his cover, which in the dullness of Moscow, bordered on a character from an Ealing film.

In true old-soldier fashion, they reminisced in a Moscow KGB club, surrounded by senior figures who had also had lives of duplicity abroad. Another with whom he shared memories was Gordon Lonsdale, who had with unusual optimism forecast they would be both be in *Krasna Plochad* (Red Square) in 1967 to celebrate the fiftieth anniversary of the October Revolution, sacred to the creation of the first Worker State. Afterwards, there was the elation of fellow conspirators, the mutual recognition of each having survived capture in the West. Contradicting the widely-held view by Western analysts that Londsdale's prophecy in 1961 betokened a KGB hand in the escape, Blake explained Londsdale's uncanny prediction: 'I don't think he had any inside knowledge, because he could not know, any more than I could, how it would turn out...When Lonsdale made that comment to me in gaol, I had not yet met Bourke or the others. He said it because he was a Russian officer of KGB, and felt responsibility towards an agent who had been caught. An officer will always feel responsible for an agent, as indeed I did myself when an officer of SIS and handling agents in Germany'.

This distinction, especially in a communist intelligence service, reveals some interesting parallels with the espionage services of the West's great political powers. Essentially, a defecting agent comes to the end of their shelf life by being revealed, negating their primary value as an unsuspected source. Tellingly, the loneliness of The Spies Club in

---

[*] See Chapter Eleven.

Moscow did not distinguish between 'officers' and 'other ranks' in terms of human attrition, or the despair many felt, as the following brief case histories make clear:

(1)   Gordon Londsdale (Konon Molody) code-name *BEN* in KGB files.

Blake took to Lonsdale from their first meeting in The Scrubs in 1961 as one who had subsumed his identity to become someone else, for the 'greater cause'. Not indeed that Londsdale balked at the transition, easily adapting his Socialist beliefs to become a Capitalist entrepreneur who made millions of dollars importing juke-boxes into England at a time when that music culture was denounced as 'decadent' in Russia (the cynic might opine that jukeboxes did more harm to Britain's national morale, post-war, than the theft of state secrets by KGB). Neither did leaving his wife and children in Russia limit Lonsdale's capacity to enjoy the heady 'sexual revolution' of 1960s London, when Carnaby Street, The Beatles and The Pill became labels for a hedonistic age that a single, wealthy Canadian found to his liking.

Such sacrifices for the Motherland sat easily with an espionage agent whom Blake regarded as being among the first rank. 'In the Scrubs he was good company and had been a real support to me when I was at my lowest ebb. In Moscow, Gordon was re-united with his family and showed little signs of the strain of having been 'an illegal resident' which is among the highest calling of an intelligence officer. Being an 'illegal' means they have to give up their own life and become somebody else. Yet they must retain real nerve. Engaged in recruiting somebody who might be a plant — at the moment they put the crucial question — the 'illegal' risks their liberty or even their life in another country...'.

Blake concluded that 'Only a great cause can ask such a sacrifice from its officers...only an officer who believes very strongly in a great cause will embark on such a career'. However, Lonsdale, like many another returned operative, found that serving the great cause in Mother Russia was more grim than serving it outside. He too had changed in the course of living in 'the decadent West' — from the transition of being the dutiful son of a KGB officer in Russia, to being brought-up in Canada by an aunt, where the international facilities of the First Chief Directorate had purloined for him the identity of a deceased Canadian. Through calculated stays in different countries he was transformed from Konon Trominovich Molody to Gordon Lonsdale, arriving in London as entrepreneur and bon vivant. All part of a long-range plan of deep cover.

Living the good life in Macmillan's 'never had it so good' England transformed him to the point where the act became the man. On the surface, he was the most unlikely of Russian spies, well removed from the Boris caricature of the media. A suave, cheerful Canadian businessman whose electronic wizardry won prizes at trade fairs, a party-giver and serial fornicator whose very persona, according to intelligence expert Christopher Andrew, may have been too much for one of the long-term British agents, Melita Norwood. An English ideologue who became a fellow-traveller in the 1930s, she trundled bundles of technical research to KGB out of conviction that Communism was the correct political system. Lonsdale was her case officer for a time but she may have felt more comfortable with a more 'Russian' personality and Lonsdale ceased in that role. He was caught only because he was providing technical back-up for the Krogers, also serious KGB 'illegals' whose real name was Cohen and who were under MI5 surveillance because of the same Polish defector who had rumbled Blake. That surveillance led to Lonsdale and his gaoling in the same year as the Krogers and Blake. Though their capture and conviction was a coup for British Intelligence in 1961, all three would not endure their lengthy sentences but were to be delivered 'home' to Moscow by 1969 in secret exchanges for British spies or alleged spies.

In Moscow, Lonsdale quickly became soured of Russian life, alienated by its obstacles to comfortable living. The business acumen which had earned millions of dollars for the

Russian state in patenting juke-boxes, was reduced to ranting frustration at the lack of the free market. When he became critical of obstacles to business, he was reduced by his superiors to being a pen-pusher. Part of the problem, common to many of the Club of Spies, was that their case officers, with whom they had formed dependent relationships abroad, were no longer influential by the time the spies returned. Some Case Officers on whom the spy depended for support had disappeared in the periodic purges in KGB. By the time Blake met Lonsdale he was disenchanted. Indeed it became the turn of 'Gorgi Ivanovitch' to support BEN when he was relegated to trivial work. Blake made his life more bearable, boosted by the hospitality of his new domestic situation with Ida, where Lonsdale was always a welcome visitor.

Conscious of the debt he owed since the Scrubs, he provided realistic support for the disappointed former 'illegal' and allowed him to overcome many set-backs. According to Blake, Lonsdale's death when picking mushrooms with the family he had but recently lived with, was some kind of fateful release from his disappointment. Blake ruefully wrote that had Lonsdale lived to participate in Perestroika, his business experience in the West would have been put 'to good use', when Mickael Gorbachev, seeing Russia descend into chaos, became architect of the reform and urged his citizens to embrace the market and 'sell everything'.

(2) Kim Philby — *STANLEY*

More than the others, Kim Philby chaffed at being put 'out to grass' when he arrived in 1963 and complained about the restrictions imposed on him. His apartment near the Kremlin was wired, his mail and phone-calls monitored. He had to report any contact with foreigners and especially Moscow-based correspondents of the Western media who repeatedly wrote to him, c/o of the Central Post Office in Moscow, where the legendary spy regularly went to pick up his mail[*]. Colonel Stanislav, also a case officer with Philby until shortly before Blake's marriage, was much concerned with the Englishman's excessive drinking and bouts of depression. It is probable that he discussed with his superiors the potential good influence of the abstemious DIOMID upon the disintegrating STANLEY[**].

Like most Western spies, Philby found life in the ideological 'homeland' far from easy. Essentially an upper-class Englishman in mode and manners, the elitist tastes of his class had allowed him to mask his equally seminal adherence to Communism for thirty years. But after the relief of escaping gaol in England, his years in Moscow had been marked by intense home-sickness, barely relieved by *The Times* cross-word puzzle, breakfast with marmalade and ritual listening to the BBC radio World Service.

By the time Blake met him, he was in a state of advanced disintegration: 'Kim was in a very bad way when I first got to know him — he was badly depressed and was very bitter. We met at a dinner given by the Service in our honour. The Service made great efforts to accommodate him — for instance, it make sure he had *The Times*, which arrived in week-old bundles and which he carefully kept in sequence, so he could he check his cross-word solutions from day-to-day'. This most charismatic of spies, who in his heyday had demoralised and mesmerised both CIA and SIS, was reduced, in the words of one KGB observer to being a 'semi-employable pensioner...dependent on props of Englishness ...corduroy trousers and Jaeger pullovers'. Like many others who had romanticised Communism from afar, the reality proved different. Stultified by the bureaucracy of daily living, enraged by the Soviet treatment of dissidents which so profoundly offended his English liberalism, he was refused

---

[*] An anecdote tells how Philby was recognised by a former British colleague and followed into a cinema. Seating himself behind, the man was startled to have Philby turn around and say 'fuck-off Carruthers'.

[**] One of Philby's code-names in KGB. Another was SONCHEN-loose German for 'sunshine boy' or 'Sonny'.

intelligence work during his early years in Moscow. Later, at the suggestion of the officer whose description is quoted above and encouraged by Andropov, he lectured to trainee KGB officers on how to assume the cover of working in an English environment (one presumes he avoided Kondrashev's version of Burton's tailoring).

He had, nonetheless, managed to exert his malign sexual appetite upon several Western women, including Eleanor Brewer, wife of an American journalistic colleague in Beirut who followed him to Moscow. While she was on a visit home, he took up with Melinda Maclean, wife of Donald Maclean, another of the 'Cambridge Five', also a former colleague. By the time Blake met him, at the function organised by KGB, Melinda had returned to her husband, leaving Philby surviving messily on his own in an old-world apartment, where he drank excessively, smoked incessantly and felt suicidal. Yuri Andropov, then Chairman of KGB, admired Philby and the other agents from The West. Among his reforms, in the wake of mass expulsion of KGB officers from Britain, were steps to improve facilities for those ex-filtrated, to enhance their long-term care, in order to assure agents still in place that the 'homeland' would truly be home. Perhaps also, he sensed with political instincts, that the outside world would soon know more about how they fared, as the media age advanced even with the Soviet Union.

For Philby, an old die-hard communist whose recruitment dated back to the 1930s, it was too little, too late. To reprise his consummate career as a spy is to register, after his recruitment in 1933 to the Soviet intelligence services, as both 'agent and asset', that all his later working life seems to have been controlled by Moscow. Son of an eccentric explorer and Arabist, St. John Philby, he was born in the Indian 'colonies' and reared with a contempt for the British Establishment which his father ostensibly served but privately disdained. Sent to English prep school at the age of seven, he was academically bright and a sports-all rounder. He was a King's Scholar at Westminster School by age thirteen and won a scholarship to Cambridge at seventeen. It was a time of great poverty in Britain, during which the Jarrow marches seized the imagination of idealistic young men, encouraging them to bond with working-class politics, then rare in British society.

Like Blake, Philby read the Russian classics of literature, among them Tolstoy and Dostoevsky, long before he came under more overt influences of the University forcing-house for British spies. He had fallen in love with the literature of Russia before he read Marx and became active in the Socialist Society where he met many of those who, as they ascended the Establishment to which Cambridge provided privileged entry, would sabotage British actions against post-war Russia[*]. With other graduates, he engaged in support for Dockers and Jews in London's East End and saw at first-hand the massive poverty during the Great Depression, when, according to Marxist theorists, the Capitalist system of government exploited the labour of the hungry to over-feed the rich. He visited Austria and Germany in his twenties where he saw, also at first-hand, the street brutalities of fascists against Jews. Only communists presented the iron-fist of opposition to the Nazis in street brawls to save victims, a baptism of political warfare which forged in him an iron template of dissent. It is very likely that in the growth of Nazi street thugs into the machine of mass destruction that became National Socialism, Philby saw nothing that veered him from the correctness of that first political position. 'Bolsheviks and Jews' became the continuing hate-figures of the Nazis.

In Vienna he took up with a diminutive Jewess of great charm and sexual allure, Litzi, and together they embarked upon underground work to save Jews and dissidents from summary execution by the right-wing mobs. Kim and Litzi came to the attention of the Comintern, the ultra-secret council charged with 'exporting' the Communist Revolution from the 1920's. His return to London was noted and an officer code-named OTTO was tasked with the formal recruitment of Philby, 'to work for peace and Socialism'.

---

[*] Sometimes known as *The Magnificent Five* in KGB lore, though more than five. See Chapters Seven and Eight.

As a training exercise, aged twenty-two, he was tasked to leave the Communist Party in England, to which he and Litzi had become passionately attached. It was to be a test of his abilities to work underground, to become a real 'worker for peace'. The challenge was akin to the testing vows of chastity for a philanderer. He detached himself from the Party, while becoming adhered to its objectives, an indication of the steel to come. He seems not to have such qualms about his next tests, to copy his Father's private colonial papers and to join the Anglo-German Fellowship. Masquerading as a Nazi sympathiser, though he privately hated them, he found he could convincingly sail under many flags, thereby becoming addicted to that career of 'controlled schizophrenia' which marks the career espionage agent. Shortly after his 25th birthday, again as directed by Moscow, he used the 'old boy network' from his Cambridge education to get himself to Spain as a journalist for *The Times*. Accredited to Franco's forces in the Civil War, he wrote pro-Franco accounts, while secretly attempting to organise the assassination of Franco. Planning failures saved Franco, while luck saved Philby. Targeted in a rocket attack which killed his companions in a car, Philby would later have the ironic pleasure of being commended by General Franco for the quality of his reporting.

Perhaps his dissent began even earlier, possibly from his childhood in The Raj, where he had seen the inequalities of race and caste manipulated as props to the Imperial system which his father 'served'. As a youngster he toured Spain with Philby senior, a maverick, sufficiently far away from line management of the British Foreign Office to be described by one who read his reports as 'incorrigibly untrustworthy'. But like Blake's cousin in Cairo, who was a founder of the Egyptian Communist Party, the influence of colonial inequalities at about the same age upon the young Philby set a template upon which the theories of Communism found a ready acceptance. Like a religion, the Faith stuck. Though he would often deny he worked for Moscow when under suspicion, Philby would never privately renounce communist beliefs.

Such were his management abilities that he ascended SIS, becoming, after the war, Head of the Anti-Soviet section. In that capacity, he betrayed to Moscow a British-organised attempt to land Albanian resistance fighters opposed to that country's communist take-over, consigning them to Soviet torture and execution. He had a few close shaves when defectors from KGB informed SIS of moles within their ranks. One description of a senior Soviet agent within SIS included such an accurate description of Philby that when it landed on his own desk he realised it would have 'outed' him, had any senior colleague had the wit to match the pieces. But Philby's iron nerve was based on his own private contempt for what he later termed 'the intellectual gifts' of his colleagues. He remained active as a powerful KGB source in Britain throughout the war and afterwards, in spite of several approaches to SIS from those who suspected him of being a Soviet agent, including information from a former mistress and allegations from a junior officer.

Safe until the flight of Burgess and Maclean caused Bill Harvey of CIA, smarting after Blake's betrayal of the Berlin Tunnel, to 'sort through the cards', Harvey turned Philby face-up as the prime suspect in a string of operational failures, including Albania, which had involved CIA liaison with SIS.

Harvey persisted with his pressure on SIS, which eventually forced the British service to examine Philby, albeit in a manner so gentlemanly as to be useless. Hearing of his 'questioning' KGB dropped him in the autumn of 1951, at about the same time as they were, fortuitously, recruiting George Blake in Korea, to become a serious replacement for Philby. KGB were resigned to lose STANLEY and gain DIOMID.

And so to 1952 and his leaving SIS, in the most gentlemanly of English ways,[*] with a pension lump-sum of

---

[*] Said to 'C' on being confronted, 'I think you had better let me go...' (i.e. resign).

£4,000 (worth about £60,000 today) and re-location to Beirut as a foreign correspondent for *The Observer* newspaper. Unknown to all but a few, he continued to 'string' for SIS. Then, under American pressure, came the ill-fated journey of Nicholas Elliott to confront him with more evidence.

Such was the potential embarrassment of his being charged in court in London, in the wake of Macmillan formally clearing him in the House of Commons, that he was given much leeway in making up his mind whether to return to Britain. Rather than face a lengthy gaol sentence, of the punitive order of Blake's, he signalled his wish to KGB to go behind the Iron Curtain and was duly ex-filtrated by ship from Beirut, while back in London, the senior SIS management ostensibly waited for him to decide upon his future.

Blake for his part, always felt hurt by the contrast in treatments. Blake was lured back to London on a pretext of promotion, whereas Philby had been left in Beirut, to allow him time to defect, a difference which Blake put down to Philby's upper-class demeanour and membership of that old boys club which seamed through the British Establishment. Philby was allowed a weekend to think over his future, during which the Head of Station in Beirut, Peter Lunn, absented himself on a skiing trip. Elliott returned to London and a Russian ship came off course into Beirut harbour. Though Blake had been in Beirut at the same time, studying Arabic at the SIS school, and they shared a common employer, the two did not meet.

When they did, in Moscow in 1970, Blake was making another life for himself, while Philby was at the end of his tether. But Blake, out of kindness was to do Philby an immense favour that changed his life for the better. Blake's wife, Ida worked in an economic institute and among her close friends was Ruffina Pukhova. A warm and good-looking woman, she was unusual in that at thirty-seven she was unmarried — and not bothered by her lack of husband. Her mother was Polish; their family life was happy until her father paid a severe price for his wife's nationality when he was gaoled in a routine Stalinist purge against foreigners. When he returned to the family home his health was broken, as was his wife's spirit. 'Rufa', as she was known, became the breadwinner and homemaker, which did not leave much room for romance.

When one of Philby's sons visited Moscow, the Blakes invited Rufa as a companion on an outing. Kim Philby was smitten and when she visited with his son to the apartment, he resolved to see her again. Declaring his interest to the Blakes after his son's departure, they invited both on a long car journey, taking in the river Volga sights which George and Ida had encountered on their first romantic meeting. If they thought some magic might strike again, they were right. Ida and Rufa were girlish friends, though mature women, while Blake and Philby had in common the membership of the Spies Club. Blake's mother came too, with Philby, ever political, going out of his way to charm her. Ida privately referred to her as 'Mutter' because of her accent, which amused Rufa.

The mother-figure held strong sway in Russian society and her approval of Philby's painstaking if facile gallantry set a pattern of acceptance for the others, though Rufa thought him to be jowly and flabby-faced. At 59 years of age, he was more than twenty years her senior, well-weathered with the strains of his many-sided life. He had more in common in life experience with Mrs Blake than with the object of his desire. Still, ever the optimistic adventurer, he took extra care over his appearance and advanced his suit on Rufa, in ploys which she later recollected with bemusement. Not previously close to the Blakes, Philby later secured an invitation to be part of a Dacha-party in order to be in her company. Having shown off his considerable culinary skills which were amply laced with alcohol, he found himself trapped with Blake's mother as Rufa retired for the night.

'It was difficult to get to sleep with Kim and Mutter jabbering away non-stop just the other side of my bedroom wall. They were speaking English, which I could not understand very well at the time, but I did hear my name. Finally they called it a night.

As the house fell still, I heard a squeak and the door swung open slowly. In the pitch dark I could only make out a little red dot of light cautiously approaching my bed, like something out of a bad dream. The dot turned out to be the tip of Kim's cigarette. He lowered himself gingerly on to the edge of my bed and announced solemnly:

"I am an Englishman"

"Yes of course. You are a Gentleman" I replied.

"I am an *English* man" he repeated stubbornly

"That's wonderful" I said, dredging the English words up from my spare schoolgirl vocabulary. "Tomorrow, tomorrow...".

That seemed to do the trick and he wandered slowly away, carefully closing the door behind him. He could hardly have had time to get back to his room before I heard the now familiar squeak of the door and the little red dot reappeared. We went through the same routine:

"I am an Englishman..."

"Tomorrow, tomorrow"

Two seconds after he closed the door a second time, it swung open yet again. Without waiting, I said, "tomorrow", doubling up with laughter'.

The following day she was intrigued to see a made-over Philby. 'Serious and smartly dressed, he bore no resemblance to the 'Englishman' of the night before...' From such a comic transformation, the relationship blossomed. Rufa now saw '...a powerful, well-shaped head, a classic profile, thick silver-grey hair and bright blue eyes...'. They met regularly on return to Moscow. Within months she had moved in with him and they married the following December. By all the accounts of those who knew them, Rufa provided a loving and patient support for Philby, helping him stave off despair as infirmity caught up with him.

Still, and for all his Good Samaritan endeavours, Blake found Philby 'a closed shop' in terms of intimate friendship. Part of Philby's senior position within the Club of Spies was to suggest how the English-speaking fugitives might be presented to the outside world: to this end, he edited Blake's memoir — *No Other Choice*. Like his own, it is fulsome on the ideological motives, though significantly sparse on operational detail (Blake says their ingrained training prevented them both from even discussing operational matters). Though initially friendly because of their shared defector background from SIS and enhanced by the Blakes' match-making, the two spies fell-out over a photograph involving another of Philby's sons.

Kim had earlier facilitated his son to make a documentary film on his father in Russia. On a return visit, his son was among a party whom the Blakes entertained at their Dacha, during which he took still pictures of the two spies and their new wives. Afterwards Blake asked Philby to ensure the pictures would not be published, out of concern for Gillian's situation. According to Blake, Philby promised to accede to his request but *The Observer*, prominently published them as a coup — 'seen for the fist time together — the spies in Moscow...'. Blake was annoyed: 'At that time, I had done everything in my power to prevent publicity. My sister had refused very lucrative offers for family photographs, even my mother when she received my first letter posted in Cairo was offered £15,000 for it by a newspaper. All my concerns were for Gillian and my sons in England. So when the pictures of us at the Dacha were published I did not hear from Philby again...'.

'He could have apologised or maybe explained that it was out of his control, but he wasn't that kind of man. Never apologise, never explain — he was an English individualist and apologising did not come into his way of living. So I did not see him again, until his funeral, when I went to pay my respects...'.

(3) Donald Maclean — *HOMER*

Of all the members of the Spies Club, Blake had, as mentioned, an affection for Lonsdale, a deep respect for the

Krogers and for Donald Maclean an unqualified admiration. Maclean, high-minded son of a onetime Education Minister in a British Government, had been recruited at Cambridge via Philby and like him had suborned his own career to that of the Comintern. A serious Socialist, he had been instructed like Philby to leave the Communist Party. He had wished to become a teacher, being passionate about education as a function of 'liberating the masses'. Instead, he had been directed by Moscow to join the British Foreign Office, where his commanding appearance and lively, classical intelligence gave him swift upward mobility. Towards the end of the war he was in charge of the American desk at the Foreign Office and later posted to Washington, where with the aid of Philby and other penetrative agents he was able to inform Moscow of the Anglo-American development of the Atom Bomb. Collating Maclean's political intelligence with technical information from the Rosenbergs in America, from Melita Norwood and other sources in Britain, including another key Cambridge agent, Cairncross, the Russian scientists were able to fast-track their own manufacture of atomic weaponry, to the consternation of The West. However, as seen by Blake, such 'a balance of power' preserved the Soviet State — and its expansion — in the post-war tensions, when by 1951, America came close to using atom bombs on North Korea (Blake, remember, had been recruited in Korea, when the American B-52 bombers flattened peasant villages as a prelude to an ultimate atomic strike, had not wiser counsel prevailed)[*].

And so, seventeen years on from 1951, Blake (DIOMID) in Moscow gets to know Maclean (HOMER). Like the others, Maclean had great difficulties in adjusting to the rigours of Russian life, but in Blake's view, he had the strength of character to overcome the day-to-day problems. He spoke Russian flawlessly and applied himself vigorously at the Institute for International Relations. Like Philby and the notorious Burgess, the strains of the double-life had left

[*] See Chapters Seven and Eight.

their mark. Maclean had recovered from alcoholism, despair and mental breakdowns but kept his communist faith intact.

Blake told me: 'In spite of what he saw around him, he continued to believe, as I do, in the ideal of Communism. He believed it had to be worked towards, that it would take a more evolved type of human being to bring it about — a moral sense in more people that it was achievable. Unfortunately for him, the Russia he had fled to was ruled by an aged coterie of men whom he regarded as unwilling to give up power and whose privilege he saw as copper-fastening their hold on power, through means which were kept from the majority of the population. He regarded them as senile and corrupt and out of touch. Because he was passionate about politics and was a tremendous worker he wrote many enlightened papers which he hoped would influence the leadership to diffuse the arms race, to accept change and to move towards democracy. But he never ceased to believe, he never lost the faith…as a person, he was the finest type of human being, considerate for others and always willing to help a colleague. In my own case, he gave me much good advice and helped me come to terms with my life here…I was very close to him until the end, when he lived alone, looked after by a faithful housekeeper. Unfortunately he did not live long enough to see the changes…'. After Maclean's; funeral in March 1983, Blake, one of the chief mourners, wrote: 'He looked younger, very peaceful and almost majestic in death...he was a good and just man, a true English gentleman in the best sense of that term'.

Among the limited cortege at the cemetery where he was cremated were Blake and Philby, survivors of the faith which had brought them to a lonely vigil in a Moscow cemetery, paying their respects to a comrade in espionage, a member of the Spies Club whose disillusion they also shared. They could not have foreseen that within another decade or so 'the changes' they all so strongly wished to improve Communism would become in fact, the destruction of Communism and of the USSR. The empire which had lasted seventy odd years and which defined the political temper of the 20th century broke up in such a remarkably short time as to take historians and the standing armies of intelligence services by surprise. For all their vaunted multi-billion dollar budgets and tradecraft, for all their investment in the double-dealing and information gathering, and in spite of the satellite surveillance systems which CIA boasted could record the conversations of Politburo members inside their cars in Red Square, none of these agencies saw how The Union of Soviet Socialist Republics would implode upon itself with such terrible haste.

'The Evil Empire' collapsed more quickly, and with less bloodshed than had accompanied the disintegration of any empire of similar magnitude in the course of recorded history. By then Kim Philby was dead — and honoured in his passing — by a system itself in terminal decline. And by then, too, George Blake, who had kept his counsel when others were profligate, was heading into his seventies, well weathered in the arts of survival.

CHAPTER TWENTY-TWO

BOURKE — THE DOWNWARD SLOPE...

As George Blake in Moscow was settling into a new life in the early 1970's with marriage, a child and the companionship of The Spies Club, Sean Bourke in Ireland was having a very different experience. Whereas Blake sought privacy from the media, Bourke revelled in it. Whereas Blake had inner resources of character, bolstered by religious beliefs, Bourke believed in little beyond his ability to cause mischief. Even that waned in a city of lackeys and loungers, where the boulevardiers of Baggott Street, absorbed in their own anarchy, found his notoriety to be a one-day wonder, now that he had actually come to live among them. He came to painfully realise that few cared about him and the majority avoided him. The welcome to the 'Oirish' lad who had tweaked the Lion's tail faded into bemused tolerance.

Even journalists tired of him, their attention directed to the war on their own doorstep. By the early 1970s, Ulster became the focus of media attention, with an attrition of murder and mayhem that the South found itself ill-prepared for — unable to contain the Catholic refugees streaming across the border, looking for support from a 'Republic' that claimed the North as integral to its own territory. The southern Government of the Fianna Fail 'Republican Party' splintered into pro-and-anti IRA factions. The Fianna Fail party, which had hitherto hitched its pedigree to the armed revolution against British rule in 1916, claiming itself to be the lineal descendant, now found itself impaled on the spit of history. As a sovereign government about to join the European Union it could not overtly arm the Republican guerrillas in Ulster who claimed kinship with the Party's anti-British roots. Neither could it summon sufficient international clout to bring Britain to discuss the future of an All-Ireland State. As a result the pubs of Dublin seethed with rumour of underground funding for the IRA, typified by one Party deputy in The Dail: 'What we need is bags of guns!'.

Into this maw of conspiracy Bourke occasionally dipped, finding his welcome short-lived. For all his own belief in his Irishness, he had lived over half his adult life in Britain, which had given him a different accent and mannerisms and by the same token, made him 'a stranger at home'. His years in the RAF and his connection with Blake rendered suspicion among the guerrilla plotters. He fared no better with criminals, who gave him welcome in proportion to his spend. He kept dangerous company and may have been suspected by Gardai of concealing monies from a bank robbery, which were found in the apartment block where he lived. He was also charged with possession of a pistol. The pistol had been provided by a Marxist group within the IRA when Bourke pleaded that his life was in danger from British Intelligence whom he claimed had organised a 'maverick group' in Belfast to abduct him across the Border, into the British Jurisdiction (how did he know?). He heeded the advice of his lawyer to stay out of gaol, but he found 'straight' company a strain.

He found himself relying more and more on his own company. Again, he fell back on the prison routine, rising early to prepare his breakfast, being scrupulous in his housekeeping — and like in the prison hostel — walking to buy the paper. A neighbour who knew him when he lived in an apartment block by Sandymount Strand recalls seeing him on long walks by the southern foreshore of Dublin Bay, bracing himself against the wind that blew in from the Irish Sea — and from the coast of Britain, where increasingly, too, his thoughts strayed to a past life.

Sometimes, drunk, he telephoned Scotland Yard, inviting officers from the escape investigation to visit him in Dublin, as he could not come to London, much as he would have liked. One said: 'I did not think it would be prudent for a British police officer to be in Dublin then — there was strong anti-British feeling over Ulster. No way Sean could keep it a secret if I had gone. I invited him instead to come to Scotland Yard, where his old Humber car was still in the garage and as it was his property, he could have it...He enjoyed the joke...'.

Michael Randle visited him and found him bored. Bourke had put on weight from drinking and appeared at a loose end. There was no food in the kitchen so they went for a meal. Although Randle resented the pointed use of names similar to their own in Bourke's book and had many unanswered questions about his behaviour in taunting the police with messages while they were on the run after the escape, his politeness got the better of him and he refrained from confrontation. He did, however, raise Bourke's allegation that Blake intended to have him killed in Moscow, pointing out that Bourke had not actually heard the threat, but had surmised it. They parted more in sorrow than in anger.

Around that time Bourke met a young woman. Margaret had come with her parents to Ireland and was completing her second-level studies. After her parents returned home, she opted to stay in the care of a Dublin Family. A teenager, in love with many things Irish, she found Bourke entrancing. Her host family, taking seriously their role in *loco parentis*, became concerned at the relationship. She was frequently distressed as Sean stood her up on dates or was otherwise cavalier. Someone who knew her recalls 'Then he would phone — all would be well again. She was head over heels in love — I doubted she knew extent of his notoriety'. In spite of the family's concern, a headstrong Margaret continued with the relationship. He made regular visits to Limerick, frequenting The Munster Fair Tavern, across from the cemetery where mourners traditionally 'drowned their sorrows' after a funeral. It was in his own parish, frequented by men whom he had known as boys but were now visibly the worse for wear. Some, like him, were survivors of Daingean Reformatory and gaol terms, or had been neighbours when he grew up in Bengal Terrace. Others were unemployed or in casual labouring work. Of some whom he remembered as boys, he was shocked at the rigours of the years between — heavy smoking and heavy drinking, long stretches of being without work, had ravaged both face and character. Others had internalised the horrors of beating and buggery and were damaged in their self-esteem beyond redemption. After one painful encounter with a former inmate, an angry Bourke said the man had not recovered 'from being fucked-up by the bastard Brothers.' [*]

Some were alcoholics, but when, in an excess of generosity, Bourke picked up the tab for an evening's drinking, he felt both good and rewarded for his endeavours. His periodic arrival from Dublin meant 'drinks on the house' singsongs and good fellowship. Joe Malone, a childhood friend from John the Baptist school, where Bourke had been sent as a bad boy from the Christian Brothers, remembered Sean from the school band — 'a big cheerful curly headed fellow — banging the drum about the yard...'. Sean liked to be reminded of those schooldays and of the times when they ducked into the cinemas without paying, of imitating Errol Flynn on the big screen, of forays into the nearby countryside, of shitting upon the hapless milk woman, of selling empty jam jars for a few pence before graduating to stealing full ones from the freight wagons on the far side of the graveyard. Though Malone escaped reformatory, those escapades had landed Bourke in Daingean, beginning the long march to Borstal, the Scrubs and Moscow.

Truly, Home was the Hero. The survivors, old before their time, recalled those carousing evenings of good fellowship in The Tavern for me. None had a bad word to say about Bourke. During those times in Limerick, which was an unemployment 'black-spot' in the mid 1970s, his generosity extended to paying debts of drink and gambling, to keeping households in food, to giving a 'start' to a man out of gaol or paying a rent arrears or buying a reprieve from punishment beatings by those to whom 'debt was owed'. He had a deep pocket. Though he had managed to get through earnings of £10,000 within the first year of the publication of *The Springing of George Blake*, he afterwards sought regular advances, usually of £5,000 against the following year's royalties. It was to become a pattern of borrowing from his publisher.

---

[*] The Oblate Order of Religious Brothers, which ran the reformatory.

More than the money, he fulfilled an exalted version of himself, some realisation of the script in the head, by helping his boyhood friends. He was, in one throw, their Robin Hood and Prince Charming, the local boy made good, home with the booty. He appears at this time happy, for one cannot underestimate what money meant to many of The Tavern regulars. Since Independence from Britain, Ireland had failed to sustain its population with work or housing. For men lucky to have work, a wage hardly lasted the week: married labourers had large families; the Catholic Church outlawed contraception. If you came from The Tavern side of their city, the work was short-lived. Sean's generosity filled a real need[*].

Limerick was heavily divided on class lines, with a few staple industries providing a good living for owners and managers — the rest could, in a popular phrase, 'shag off to England'. The Church muted politicians in the privacy of the confessional and humbled opposition outside it. For Bourke — sober — it all smacked of the very control he had found in Russia — a comparison with which, in his cups, he regaled listeners. The confessionals in Catholic churches, he opined, were like the cells in the Lubyanka, from where information went to the Central Committee of the Communist Party, just as it did from the confessionals to The Vatican. Exchange the Consistory of Cardinals in Rome for the Praesidium of the Central Committee and you have a painless exchange of power between Russia and Ireland — indeed The Irish Politburo was already in place, made-up of the Cardinal, the Fianna Fail Party and the GAA[**].

As one image borrowed another, these riotous evenings, spontaneously theatrical, went on until the early hours, though testing the patience of the proprietor. Sometimes, it ended on a musical note, as Bourke, having held the soap-box

---

[*] Out of a population of three and a half million, about a million-and-half, including young children and the old, lived on subsistence. Source: Political analyst, Michael McInerney, to author 1975.

[**] Gaelic Athletic Association.

to an audience whose attention he had lubricated — and not wishing to cast a damper on the proceedings — launched into the song he had sung to Blake across the wall of The Scrubs on walkie-talkie, while planning the escape *'I'll walk beside you to the Golden Land...'*. He had a sweet tenor voice.

However popular he was among his own, in the city at large he was treated with suspicion. Attempts to rent an apartment failed when landlords became aware of his identity. He fared no better when he retained an estate agent to find him a place to live. He felt himself slipping again into despair and clung to the idea of another book to give him a purpose. The London publisher agreed an outline synopsis of a sequel, which would describe his earlier life in Daingean, then RAF and Borstal, with pen pictures of inmates and 'screws' in the Scrubs. He made a draft of early chapters, but kept falling from the typewriter into pubs. To avoid temptation, he sought a place in the countryside and through the good offices of a rural community was given a cottage to rent in Co. Limerick. He worked for weeks there on the manuscript, penning harrowing accounts of Daingean, but again found the isolation numbing and made regular treks into the city for pub company.

On the phone to Margaret, he heard that the baby she was expecting was stillborn. He left quickly for Dublin to share Margaret's grief. But he was back again in a few weeks and into the familiar routine of carousing and story telling. There was, too, a continuation of the obsessive behaviour, a repeat of the need to have an enemy which had seen him send the bomb to the policeman in Crawley, later turn against Pat Pottle and eventually believe that George Blake was plotting his execution. Now, as he tried to settle in Limerick, the local Establishment, which had denied him a place to live, became the focus of his anger. He wrote lengthy letters to the *Limerick Leader*, castigating the 'filthy hypocrisy' of his native city, its church-going 'craw-thumpers' and class distinctions. When, for legal and business reasons, the paper declined to publish his tirades, he turned his ire on the proprietor, naming him in pamphlets, which he printed with the skill of a onetime editor of the Scrubs magazine. Sometimes, to keep his pen and vitriol intact, he went about the city with copies to show his friends of letters he had sent to enemies.

Other prison-learned skills were put to good use to gain a roof over his head. A derelict stone mill in Little Gerald Griffin Street, which had belonged to his father, was restored with his skills as a bricklayer and plasterer. The old mill was an imposing relic of Limerick's 19th century status as a grain exporter; grains of wheat were in every crevice. He had been brought up in its lofty interior before moving to Bengal Terrace. Now he set about renovating it with a new passion. According to a friend, Bourke's restoration was 'immaculate'. 'He really worked on it with loving care. We cleaned the place out, then Sean scrubbed down the stone walls, repaired floors and put in the electrics — all care of Her Majesty's tuition'.

On assignment for a Sunday newspaper I met him in Limerick. He asked me to meet him at a hotel near the railway station; a Georgian building that had seen better days as one of the city's hostelries for commercial travellers. Now, the reception area was unattended and some of the Bourke entourage went frequently behind the bar counter to serve themselves drinks. He was in raffish company and although it was early evening, a lot of drink had been consumed — he seemed to have some sort of 'tab' running at the bar. The interview did not get off to a good start, because one of the party insisted I was not Kevin O'Connor.

As I had a year earlier come to Dublin, having spent my adult working life in London, the confusion was understandable, as another journalist of the same name, also from Limerick was more familiar to those who questioned my identity. My namesake had not worked abroad, whereas I had been out of the city since my late teens. My namesake had gone to a different school and we had followed entirely different paths in journalism. The more reasonably I tried to explain the co-incidence of these divergent paths, the more excited became the inebriated inquisitor. Farce teetered on the brink of tragedy. The drunks went into a huddle, one detached himself and the door was locked as he left. 'Get the gun, the gun — this fucker is a spy, he's come to get Sean...' shouted the one to the ceiling and the other returned with a jacket over his arm.

I claim no credit for 'grace under pressure' as the situation was so surreal. I was made to sit in a chair while the man with the jacket menacingly and unsteadily loomed above me. If there was a gun and it had gone off, others would have been injured, as he was incapable of aiming...some hurriedly cleared a space behind me in the line of fire. I was subjected to a series of questions about the geography of Limerick, the locations of schools and churches (but no pubs) and eventually calmer counsel prevailed when another of the interrogators, through an alcoholic haze, said he knew my brother. 'Ahh...your Flann's brother that went away, now I have you...', after which Sean, who had observed the charade with interest, agreed to be interviewed. He spoke of the difficulties of settling back into Limerick, of his contact by phone with Scotland Yard, of not knowing what became of Blake. What I remember most is how keen he was to talk of his daughter, who had a few months before been born to Margaret (I did not know then of the death of the previous infant). When the interview was published, I did not inquire about its impact on the members of the hotel star-chamber. I was not to meet Bourke again for a further three years, but I gleaned that in spite of efforts to concentrate upon his second book, the work ethic eluded him. As did gainful employment, once the old mill was restored. He embarked upon various vendettas, as was his wont, upon personalities in the city whom he perceived to be enemies. Such obsessions engaged him for months, involved voluminous correspondence to the target of his ire, to the local newspaper and to the sundry acquaintances of the target. Coherent in their initial reasoning, becoming incoherent with vitriolic abuse, the letters remain in the files of Limerick lawyers to whom they were entrusted by those who received them and thought it prudent to lodge them for legal protection.

There were other escapades, more prank than dangerous. A mock attempt at a bank hold-up landed him in the Garda station, where he was let off with a caution. A partnership in the ownership of a boat, intended for deep-sea fishing voyages, pace Hemingway, ended in recrimination. As the regular carousing continued in The Tavern, one of his cohorts, Toddy Long, who could career out of control, was barred by the owner. In that alcohol–based culture being 'barred' amounted to a dreadful sentence of deprivation. Bourke entreated for Toddy to be re-admitted. When that failed, he cajoled, offered bribes, and promised 'good behaviour' — if his friend could be re-instated. The owner was adamant — no dice. Toddy had received many warnings. A barring order was the ultimate sanction that a publican invoked to keep good order in his house. He would not relent.

Around that time Bourke found a focus for his energies that accorded with his view of life. A fledgling politician in Limerick, Jim Kemmy, possessed of a severe Socialist conscience, impacted upon local affairs with stinging criticism of the Church-State alliance, of the 'cronyism' of the local political establishment and the racist views of the holder of the Labour parliamentary seat, Stephen Coughlan. Jews and Maoists were among Coughlan's targets and Kemmy vigorously opposed him in public debate, sometimes being physically threatened by Coughlan supporters. Bourke was quick to defend Kemmy, with a withering line in invective, which recognised Kemmy as a product, like himself, of the city's turbulent history. Like Bourke and thousands of others who had taken the emigrant boat to work in Britain, Kemmy's consciousness had been honed abroad, but with the addition of extensive Marxist reading in the British Library. But Kemmy was no dilettante. A stonemason by trade in a city of brick and limestone, Kemmy's family roots were deeply embedded in Garryowen, an enclave of traditional skills, close to Bourke's own district. An open, humane man, Kemmy had little resources to confront the Establishment, so he founded a newsletter, which garnished a cadre of devoted supporters.

Bourke offered his services, as writer and typist for Kemmy's manifestoes, published in the *Limerick Socialist*. To criticise the Catholic Church was a dangerous activity in the Ireland of the 1970s, embarked upon by only the brave or foolish, as the tentacles of Catholic power reached into all corners of life. Kemmy and Bourke were unflinching in their attacks, blaming the Church-State conspiracy for the abject poverty visible in the city, for the ban on family planning, for the cosy conspiracies, which allowed the local merchant class to prosper with impunity, immune to prosecution for importing contraceptives and porn magazines. Bourke's memoir of Daingean saw light of day in *The Limerick Socialist*, as did the early work of other Limerick writers who would come to prominence. Bourke also wrote of his uncle 'Feathery' and the miser's penchant for amassing property from the sale of scrap, while living in penury in an elegant villa overlooking the Shannon. He wrote, amusingly, too of his boyhood friends and their peccadilloes of language and behaviour, including a portrait of Toddy, barred from drinking in his local pub. He took avidly to his publishing — a role he had notably enjoyed as editor of the Scrubs 'house' magazine. He provided monies for transport and posters during local council elections in which Kemmy sought to wean away votes from the Labour Party, damaged by the antics of Coughlan. He became a supporter of Kemmy, having found an anti-Establishment personality to which he could hitch his talents (as he had, years before, adopted Blake as a cause).

Kemmy and Bourke did not have an easy relationship, as Bourke seemed incapable of sustaining a friendship without bouts of rancour. But Kemmy was made of stern stuff, had an innate sympathy with Bourke's background and admired his skills as a writer and raconteur. As Kemmy recalled: 'He made friends slowly, but fell out very easily. Our friendship was often fragile, but it persisted in spite of him trying my patience. I think I understood him to some extent — he couldn't live at peace with himself. I often tried to analyse it and put it down to the brutalities of Daingean...and some things that he could never talk about…there were times when he thought he was going mad with some terrible anger inside…so I made allowances for that, and I think he appreciated that too, though we never discussed it…'.

The drinking binges increasingly deranged Bourke. After one massive bout, he surrendered voluntarily for treatment to St. Joseph's Psychiatric Hospital, the 'mad' building of his youth. But unable to take the reality of the wards, he broke over the wall and was found by police directing traffic outside another of the street's landmarks, the gaol, then a high-security place for paramilitaries. Refusing to be re-admitted to the mental hospital, he was lodged in a Garda cell.

Jim Kemmy recalled: 'It was a lovely Saturday summer evening when I got word about seven o' clock that Sean was in a cell. I was very unhappy about it, as I was going off to have a few drinks at the end of a week's work. The picture of Sean being in prison on such a lovely evening was more than I could stand, so I went to the police station. The Sergeant on duty wasn't very cordial to me. He was reluctant to let Sean into my care and asked could I guarantee he wouldn't get into trouble again. I told him I couldn't guarantee that I would be alive in the morning, but that if he let Sean out I would see that he was taken back to hospital, that I would escort him back myself. Rather reluctantly, he agreed. I went to the cell, it was very sad to see him thrown down like that, lying down in filthy surroundings and it wounded me terribly, pained me terribly. I couldn't tell you how deeply I felt and how shocked I was to see poor Sean thrown down on the ground, lying in vomit and filth and indescribable things "Come on Sean," I said, "We're going out of here". He perked up immediately and came with me and he was cheerful to the Sergeant and passed a few wisecracks. I marched him down to St. Joseph's Hospital. He came in a very docile way. He didn't make any protest; he went straight into the hospital and into an observation ward. I felt terrible sorry about it all, to see poor Sean locked up for the night…institutions all his life and now in another one...he was badly damaged and really didn't care anymore...'.

When he was released from care, he made another strenuous effort to beat the booze, aided by medication. He went for long walks into the Clare hills, overlooking the city. Sometimes a dog accompanied him, borrowed in his ramble past a farmhouse, but always returned to the owner. He had brief moments of peace, but intense loneliness inevitably gave way to the need for company of his own choosing. The visceral hatred of 'ordinary' lives, the need to have some enemy in his sights sabotaged by inability to distinguish between friend and foe, led to another fatal mellowing of resolution and brought him back to those boyhood friends who were usually in pubs and usually the worse for wear. Joe Malone remembered him 'coming down from the hills, full of new plans to finish the second book, to make a new life. He showed me a bank confirmation of £10,000 from the film director Alfred Hitchcock as a down payment on the rights of a film of the escape. He repaid some small loans, including £100 to myself, though he didn't owe me quite that much...but he needed to make the big statement and swore he would not handle a cheque-book again as he reckoned he had spent about £40,000 of the book's royalties by then...so he preferred to run-up a tab in my pub...and of course the old cycle started again '.

His drinking exceeded two bottle of brandy a day as he became a familiar figure in the markets area of the city, where pubs opened earlier to facilitate suppliers from the countryside delivering produce to the city's hotels. Bourke was to be found waiting outside these market pubs as they opened, already much the worse for wear but determined to continue the sprawl of sensation to which he had become addicted. It was not only the chemical surcharge of the alcohol that he needed, but also the changed state of consciousness — inward elevation in which desire and denial merged and he became a happy human, at benign peace with the world.

That was his inner view. Outwardly he was sloppy, slovenly and angrily offensive to his friends, into whom he barged in alcoholic affray, a cutting comment at the ready. In alcoholic haze, he was vulnerable too. At times, he was found lying in laneways, robbed. And yet, days later in painful sobriety, he was consumed with self-disgust. Joe Malone recalled him retching over the toilet, sticking his fingers down his throat to make himself vomit and swearing never, ever to drink again. It was a vain promise: the disgust and vomiting were many times repeated.

With the highs and lows of the depressive, he could be galvanised from misery into elation by some outward event. The boat for deep-sea fishing was one, letters to the *Limerick Leader* another, canvassing for Jim Kemmy yet another. Getting Toddy re-instated into The Tavern became a saga of obsession, which resulted in the ban being lifted, on condition that Bourke would keep Toddy under control. It was agreed during one of Bourke's fits of sobriety and he celebrated in fitting style. He drew up a florid document from which he read of Toddy's re-instatement, in the manner of a heraldic knighthood. He hired one of the city's famous bands to march a mile of the road leading up to the pub. The band played rousing military airs past the landmarks of the 'bad, the mad and the dead' with Toddy as Grand Marshall leading them to a finale by the pub and the cemetery. Then the band, onlookers and the curious, piled into The Tavern for drinks and carousing — paid for by the Pied Piper. It was another, periodic 'finest hour' which his ego needed.

The death of 'Feathery' provided another. Sean had been curious about his uncle since returning to Limerick and regaled cronies with tales of his meanness. 'Feathery' showed no inclination to be hospitable to Sean — or to any other of his nephews on their return to their native city. When Sean made overtures and visited the jumble shop in the market from which Feathery operated his extensive property interests, the old man ordered him out. On a later visit Sean pointed out the derelict electrical wiring and offered to repair it. When this was reluctantly agreed to, Sean bought cables and fixtures and re-wired the more dangerous parts. The materials cost about £2, but when Feathery insisted on paying (without asking the price, as Sean told it) a pantomime ensued with Sean refusing payment and Feathery insisting, until the old man put his hand into the deepest recesses of his soiled Macintosh and pressed a shilling on Sean — just the right amount for him to give currency to the tale.

On the old miser's death in 1973, no will was found, which gave the lawyers a field day on the various competing claims. It would take many months before Probate could be administered and the estate disbursed, not least because of the need to establish that the deceased had no natural-born offspring alive. In his later years, Feathery went on cruises abroad, playing the part of a landed Irish merchant — but rumours of romances with wealthy American women had to be nominally investigated and lengthened the time at which the estate could be disbursed.

While such delays were not to the liking of the potential inheritors, there was little option but to wait. Patience was not one of Sean's virtues, especially when the extent of Feathery's estate was calculated in the market pubs, near his own abode of The Mill. Sean kept meeting tenants of his dead uncle, often paying a few shillings a week for a slum property, who wondered to whom should they now pay their modest rents. With some astonishment, he realised his uncle had owned entire streets of cottages and stretches of warehouses, amounting at 1973 prices to over £250,000[*]. Meantime that grand Victorian gate-lodge, situated next to the substantial lands of the Catholic bishop, was going-a-begging. As he saw it, he would in time be entitled to his share of it, so why not move in now to establish squatter's rights. Who knows what condition it might be in by the time the lawyers settled?

He was also deeply troubled by his failure to complete his second book and rationalised that a change of location from the city centre might work some magic that would keep

---

[*] At 2002 prices, about 3 million Euros.

him out of drink's way. Occupying the villa would bring him north of the river, a mile or so away from his usual pubs. He would, he told friends, be among the hoi-poloi of Limerick, class enemies whom he despised — but also between two bishops, as the Protestant bishop was on the other side of the property from the Catholic prelate. Paraphrasing Wilde, he opined that to lose an uncle and gain two bishops smacked of good fortune — but he would only steal apples from the Catholic Bishop. True to form, he invited friends for a ceremonial cutting of the lawn. He made no secret of his pleasure in asserting his rights to his uncle's inheritance and was duly photographed by the local paper, scythe in hand, as he cut down the long grass in front of the imposing property.

In the early hours of November 25th, 1973, less than a month after the photograph appeared, a bulldozer tracked in the driveway and proceeded to demolish the gate-lodge, leaving only a few bits of walls upright. The roof was torn off, the internal walls knocked down and the building reduced to rubble. According to his friends, Sean promptly went to the local IRA and bought some weaponry, perhaps with a view towards self-defence, or perhaps for retribution against those he suspected. Rumours, both predictable and exotic flew around the city. Bourke had created many enemies for himself — near and far. Nobody was prosecuted in connection with the destruction of the villa, nor did Bourke ever use his gun. He was not physically violent or aggressive and the anger, once again, for the main part, turned inward.

CHAPTER TWENTY-THREE

BOURKE—UNDER AN OPEN SKY...DEATH AND DESTRUCTION

The White House was a pub in the city centre, on the corner of O'Connell Street, not far from the hotel where I encountered the episode with the gun and the interrogation to prove my identity. By the mid-1970s Bourke was a regular, sometimes seen buying a bottle of brandy and emptying it into a pint glass which would be drunk in a couple of hours. The pub suited his evening moods, as it was frequented by the city's standing army of artistes — writers, actors and painters. Anyone in need of 'intellectual conversation' might be rewarded after contributing to the discourse or buying 'rounds'. On the walls of the White House were framed portraits of writers, with extracts from their works. Robert Graves had spent part of his childhood in Limerick, when his father was associated with the garrison, and there was an incident in the mid-seventies when the venerable litterateur, raking the cinders of childhood, visited the White House and a regular, knowing of a historical enmity between Graves and Pound, deftly turned Pound to the wall as Graves entered, in case he should take offence. The local poet was sufficiently versed to know that Pound's broadcasts for Nazism in the last war had earned him the undying hatred of Graves, author of *Goodbye to all That*, a classic memoir of World War One.

Offences of a more parochial kind were regularly taken in the petty vendettas of the White House. A remark heard out of turn could turn into a saga of ill-will extending over many months. The poets, particularly, were given to fits of jealousy if another entered with verses recently published. But compared to other pubs, the company was lively, the whiskey was matured in wooden barrels behind the counter and in winter the mellow glow from an open coal fire made the pub a 'home from home'. The novelist Michael Curtin recalled seeing Bourke comfortably gazing into a lager glass full of brandy — 'He often drank alone, unless drawn into conversation by a remark sufficiently banal or perverse to engage his interest'.

Frequently Bourke would pen an abusive letter to someone he believed had wronged or slighted him. One individual stood accused of making unkind remarks after Bourke left his company. Bourke committed his thoughts to paper but it is unclear if the letter was ever posted or was merely to impress his own friends.

In that letter Bourke recalled their encounter as 'One of your few deviations from the well-trodden, safe itinerary which you normally pursue on your breezy, ostentatious flits through dirty Limerick', Bourke listed the hearsay remarks, as (1) 'Of course Sean Bourke is not really accepted in Limerick, is he...?', (2) 'He gets lampooned, doesn't he?', and (3) 'Sean is older than me, you know...'. In a closely-typed three-page letter, Bourke engaged in a discourse on what it meant to be 'accepted'. 'By whom?', he asked, 'Surely not by the mental defectives inhabiting the sad little village called Limerick?'.

It was a vintage piece of Bourke invective, though given the misplaced craft that went into it, probably another example of his failure to shape his second book. To adapt his own analogy, he was 'pissing in the wind' with such targeted ire, when he could have been addressing his own writing demands. There were many such letters — on other targets of his anger — which Jim Kemmy refused to print in the *Limerick Socialist*, leading to a falling-out between them. Bourke found an alternative audience by copying them to his pub friends, as a latter-day pamphleteer of the taverns. When Kemmy complimented him, all was forgiven — until the next time. Bourke sought praise and approval from his· peers — when not forthcoming, he was easily provoked to nastiness.

Around this time I encountered him in the course of a radio programme. Crime and social deprivation were two linked and persistent issues of local concern. Bourke was on the panel and made some incisive points. But as the discussion progressed he became angered by the very predictability of the contributions from others, until he lost his cool and hectored us with a piece of life history: 'I was born in Limerick because at the time my mother and father were going together, there was no television — thank Christ! And if Limerick were to sink into the sea under the weight of its own dirty, filthy hypocrisy, I would not shed a tear, Mr Chairman — (shout) and the world would be a better place for it!'. He departed with the office typewriter under his coat, which was retrieved from a pub across the way by the studio secretary.

There were other such escapades, more foolhardy than criminal, such as passing a note to the driver of an armoured bullion van, inviting the disbursement of £10,000 under threat of being shot. Luckily, both driver and police saw the funny side afterwards — no charges were brought. The carousing in the more tolerant pubs and hotels continued, with practical jokes and charades. When the local agricultural show awarded a prize for cabbage growing to a man with a similar name to 'Toddy Long' whom he had successfully reinstated in The Tavern, Bourke sent a fake letter from the Revenue Commissioners to his friend accusing him of 'concealing undeclared income'[*].

As Kemmy noted, 'He liked to lead sing-songs and make people he thought less gifted than himself the butt of humour — but could get very narky when encountering his own intellectual equal'.

These interludes apart, he was drifting until the General Election of 1977 gave him a purpose. Having attached himself to Jim Kemmy's political fortunes, as the only candidate with whom he could identify, he promised '...a telephone and typewriter and pile of stencils...I will make a good 'field office' for the campaign and take some of the work-load off your Headquarters...'.

The challenge appealed to him, as Kemmy was an outsider for a Parliamentary seat. For as long as anyone could

---

[*] Shades of Bourke's previous forgeries, including the letter from 'five prison warders' which sparked the *Daily Sketch* coverage of the Scrubs prison magazine. See Chapter 14.

remember, the constituency's five Dail places had been divided between two Fianna Fail, two Fine Gael and one Labour seat. The two majority parties were essentially Catholic and conservative. They acquiesced with the State's ban on divorce, contraception and abortion. But as the election came closer, some in the local Establishment feared that with 'the times a-changin' — riots and civil commotion in the North, a move towards liberalisation in the South — Kemmy would get some support. A new class influenced by European-wide radicalism, albeit a decade before, meant a rump in search of a seat. Kemmy fitted their mood for change, having publicly confronted Steve Coughlan's defence of local racists and IRA-killings in the North. The city had suffered badly from the kidnap by the IRA of a Dutch industrialist, Tiede Herema, and the closure of a major employer, Ferenka, while the Catholic Confraternity, which called thousands of men to nightly prayer, was seen as Right-wing in legislative matters affecting what the Left regarded as 'private morality'.

Kemmy, on the other hand, was agnostic, anti-IRA and opposed to the Catholic Church's intrusion into health matters. He was, in effect, challenging the prevailing views of Official Ireland (adherents of Official Ireland, with the right political connections, flagrantly flouted most laws). A reprise of Kemmy's career and the political culture he was trying to change is worth citing to show some of the forces at work when he resigned from the local Labour Party and set up his own political party — the Independent Socialists.

Bourke joined this breakaway group, bringing his skills as writer, pamphleteer and debater. It had about forty members, meagre funds and little access to the wider media. Its founders had left the Labour Party because of its failure to expel Coughlan over his silence on the shooting-up of a Maoist bookshop in the city, his support for Republican paramilitaries in the North and — in a city where Rugby football was another religion — his support of the Springboks visit to Thomond Park, the holy grail of Limerick rugby (as the radicals saw it, Springboks were not welcome while South Africa maintained Apartheid. Sports fans, on the other hand, looked forward to a hard, tough match against a legendary team).

It took no little courage — and some obstinacy on Kemmy's part — to pursue that agenda (I happened to be in his company when he was threatened by IRA supporters). That those issues mattered to a handful of left-wing activists said much for the shift in the political culture. Traditionally Limerick voters were conservative, rarely looking beyond jobs and housing. Any politician who delivered those — and was seen in the local media to do so — would likely be returned at General Elections. Coughlan was very much a parish pump politician. Indeed he boasted that he put local issues before national concerns. A tally of his parliamentary questions showed most to be about sourcing factories in his constituency[*]. Kemmy, by contrast, made a platform of national issues.

Coughlan, returned in four elections and twice a Mayor of the city, tentacled his influence into the working-class areas by dispensing favours, mediation and jobs (as a boy I remember being caught up in a torchlight procession to his pub, as the word went out that 'Stevie is elected' — it usually meant free drinks for the men of the parish). Not surprisingly, he boasted 'I am Limerick'. In that context he was described as a 'backwoodsman' by a new intake into the Labour Party during the early 1970s, when he sided with IRA killings in the North and attacked 'money-lenders' among the poor, which was seen as a reference to the city's history when Jewish immigrants from Eastern Europe — who lived by lending money — had been driven out of the city by men from the Catholic Confraternity.

Against Coughlan's record the breakaway Socialists fielded Jim Kemmy as their candidate, appealing to a younger, less hidebound electorate. It was to this group that Bourke lent his skills as typist, stencil-cutter and financier, giving Kemmy £200, the largest donation which the fledgling

---

[*] *Steve Coughlan* —Thesis by Patrick O' Gorman, Mary Immaculate College, Limerick, 1985.

candidate received. All that Coughlan stood for was anathema to Bourke, who in his own right was as prolific a dispenser of free drinks. Equally, Bourke liked to hold forth on history — a passion shared by Kemmy who in the pages of the *Limerick Socialist* had excavated a socialist history, obscured by the frenzied Nationalism that had become the official orthodoxy since the declaration of Republic in 1948 — a year incidentally in which the local authority decreed that low-cost housing would be given only to families with eight or more children.

Kemmy's scholarly forte was local history, unrivalled among his political competitors, amassed from years of book collecting. One piece of original research proved unexpectedly damaging to his campaign. The magazine ran a serial on the Limerick Soviet of April 1919, when workers in the city refused to pass blockades set up by the British military in the hunt for fugitives who had shot a policeman. As the War of Independence was intense and the military feared a mass insurrection in the city, work permits were issued by the authorities to control population mobility. In response, workers refused to attend factories, and a Soviet was declared which sought solidarity with the Bolshevik Revolution of 1917 in Russia. A class war ensued, banks and business were boycotted, currency printed and public buildings occupied. It may have seemed a comic episode to the Crown administrators in Dublin and London, had there not been a fortuitous influx of international press into the city, covering a transatlantic air race. As one of the staging posts for re-fuelling was in Limerick, on the Atlantic coast, the air competitors had to seek permission from the 'Limerick Soviet' to re-fuel — a stand-off which garnished international coverage.

The significance was not lost upon a British cabinet in Whitehall, dealing as it was with insurrection in Ireland, mass unemployment of former soldiers in Britain from the Great War and a rash of similar Soviets and strikes across a Europe riven by hunger, unrest and the promises of Bolshevism. When the Officer Commanding military forces in Limerick,

Brigadier-General Griffin, was ordered to bring the Soviet to an end, he did so adroitly — by standing down his soldiers from confrontation with the strikers and having tea with the Catholic Bishop of Limerick. The outcome was a letter from the Bishop, read in the city's churches, to the effect that the strikes were causing great hardship to business and families, with an assurance that the military blockades would be lifted — should the Soviet end.

As most of the Commisariat were devout Catholics, the Soviet was dissolved, with a limp declaration of defiance.

When Kemmy published this reprise of a revolutionary drama, more than fifty years afterwards, it was to have unusual electoral resonance, with an uncanny re-run of one dramatis persona. The Catholic Bishop of Limerick, Jeremiah Newman, alarmed at Kemmy's avowed anti-Church stance, was prevailed upon to endorse an alternative candidate. Mick Lipper, a respected Labour activist and former Mayor was endorsed by the Bishop and was added to the ticket when it became apparent that Kemmy might poll well. The ecclesiastical approval received wide local coverage, in newspapers and potently from church pulpits. On Polling Day, 16th June 1977, priests ferried elderly, church-going voters to the polls.

In the event, Lipper won the seat and Coughlan's political career nose-dived, with some bitterness, it may be said, at what he saw as the Bishop's intervention in reducing both his own and Kemmy's vote. Kemmy polled 2,333 first preference votes, about a third of the amount needed. Though he was naturally disappointed at not being elected, his supporters were heartened by the figure as a solid base upon which to build a political future. For Bourke it had been a sobering experience. He had gone 'on the dry' for the five weeks of the campaign and showed himself to be a model worker in designing elections posters and literature. 'Bourke worked with religious zeal' according to Joe Kemmy, campaign manager for his brother. The forces at work in the city and the manipulation of Bishop Newman by business interests confirmed his antagonism to the local Establishment.

He told Kemmy: 'I knew you would not make it Jim — and even if you had, the proletariat of this country do not deserve you — they are more reactionary than Stalin and will do what the Church and boss class tells them...'. Ever the optimist, Kemmy was grateful for Bourke's adherence and privately saw it as a bonus that he managed to 'beat the booze' for the duration of the campaign. But once it was over, Bourke went on a bender that lasted days, having promised in a pun on the escape to which he owed his notoriety, 'a massive breakout'. He kept his promise.

When he recovered he continued to make a nuisance of himself, in embarking upon further vendettas against real or imagined targets. The local newspapers received letters on subjects ranging from the grammar of their reporters to the spelling in street signs. There were more spleens against individuals, often not printable. But he also wrote finely-tuned character sketches of people he met in the streets, in hospital beds and in doss-houses. He was, in his trawling of the by-ways, a kind of latter-day recorder of the under-class of a city caught, as he saw it, between the medieval and the modern. By the same token, his fellow-feeling for those who died in the city workhouse with no possessions, generated a continuing anger, causing him to rail against Church and State with venom, while ignoring the very real advances made across a wide range of supports — in social welfare and jobless benefits (such State largess was given as much to bring welfare up to the British levels in the North as it was for concern for the underclass).

His own relating to the 'wounded and the maimed' was genuine fellow-feeling. By the late 70s, the prolonged abuse of his health through alcohol showed itself in increased weight gain and bouts of depression. After being lodged in the psychiatric hospital he wrote to thank Kemmy, adding that 'I know for definite that I suffer from temporary insanity under the influence of drink. There is nothing I can do about this...'.

Frightened by his own demons, he gave the oft-told promise, 'My only hope of survival is to cut down on the drink as much as possible, for I know I can never give it up completely'. The darkening isolation of his own life — often appearing for weeks unwashed and unkempt, in contrast to his previously dapper dress — brought home the slide into desperation. Outside in the wider world, meanwhile, the people whose lives he had influenced were settled into stable, every-day living. The conspirators in England, while active in radical causes, were also absorbed in family life, as was Blake in Moscow.

He seemed not to have advanced into adulthood or gained the maturity that comes upon most people in their forties. In lifting from George Blake a life sentence he had imposed a sentence of notoriety upon himself. Though he had desperately wished for such infamy during his years in Britain, he gave vent to his feelings that returning to Ireland had put him in another kind of prison, immersing him in an extended theatre of alcohol. In November of 1980 he told the journalist Arthur Quinlan that he would like to return to England. 'I plan to cross the border into Northern Ireland and surrender myself to the British authorities'. Citing the document supplied by the British Attorney-General during the failed Extradition hearing in 1969, he claimed he would be charged with the lesser offence of 'aiding a prisoner to escape' and with remission for good behaviour might serve about two years. 'I would use it to dry out — after all, some people here disappear into a monastery to cure themselves. I would dry out in gaol'.

Always media conscious, he had the satisfaction of seeing it reported in the international press. British newspapers contacted him to ascertain the time of his 'surrender'. He promised a public crossing on what he called Ireland's 'Check-Point Charlie' but when it came to being on the other side of the border, he backed off and funked the act. Within weeks he was back foraging on familiar rutting-ground, though now increasingly seen as a figure of fun. He seemed to have learned little from his need to provide journalists with 'copy', and was not above hinting that in time he would reveal further 'secrets', to the extent of naming prominent Left wingers in Britain who had financed the escape. Indeed, he could be profligate with such innuendo, playing a cat-and-mouse game of suggesting likely candidates whose high profile generated by the CND marches of the 1960s might put them 'in the frame' of an investigation.

Periodically he was visited by reporters from the British Sunday papers, some of whom did attempt to nail down names, though as far as we know, Bourke implied rather than stated identities. It must have been a nervous time for the English conspirators, reading these renewed speculations and of some concern also to Blake in Moscow, who was probably appraised of them.

He was also running low on funds and wrote to local auctioneer, Pat Kearney, that he wished to put his ancestral home, The Mill on the market. He devised his own sales prospectus: 'A three-storey building with solid two feet-thick stone walls. A total floor space of 1,500 sq. feet, plus private parking for four cars...a few minutes walk from the city centre, with all facilities laid on — electricity, running water, indoor toilet...there is a wide, strong door fitted with two Chubb locks and a Yale lock'. Mindful that his notoriety might be off-putting, he emphasised that the property 'had no connection whatsoever with the Estate of the late uncle, Feathery Bourke. This building was put up by my grandfather, who left it to my father...I have been occupying the building for the past five years'.

Although Kearney was one of the city's prominent property dealers, after five months on the market there were no takers. Bourke wrote again in July 1980, offering renting instead of purchase. Conscious of the public profile he held, and how it might mitigate against business, he was at pains to assure Kearney that he was '...out all day, climbing the Clare hills, to that white dome and back, seven days a week — doctor's orders and already nearly two stone gone'. When it became obvious he was unlikely to have a rental income and with drastically diminishing royalties from his book, published nine years before, another idea festered.

He would leave Limerick and decamp to Kilkee by the sea — a watering hole on the Atlantic coast which was a traditional resort of city people during the summer. Off-season it was wind-lashed and eerie and suited his mood of re-making himself in a harsh climate. An acquaintance, Patrick Clancy, lent him the family caravan, parked on Percy French avenue, named after one of Bourke's favourite song-writers. Clancy was also a singer of note and between them they had many times given full voice to French's compositions and Bourke had theatrically conducted many a pub chorus during the munificent days when his pockets were full.

Now he was, as he put it, for the 'Leaving of Limerick' to seek peace in Kilkee and finish 'this long delayed book of mine'. He moved there in January of '81, when the climate was harsh, testing himself against the elements and delving into his many periods of penal service to make the caravan homely. He was a scrupulous housekeeper and washed and laid out his clothes like regimental kit. He could hardly have chosen a worse month for a new beginning and was intensely lonely. The local population was in hibernation until the Spring. He was also badly broke. Kemmy, whose political fortunes had gained in the interim and had exchanged a stone mason's salary for a parliamentary one, again came to his rescue with regularly mailed subsidies.

Even so, much of that was spent on alcohol: in the pubs he came to know some locals who emerged at evening. He made strenuous efforts to reduce his alcohol intake, going for long walks against the gales that whipped inland from the Atlantic ocean, all the way, according to local legend from Cape Horn. Or as he poetically put it in a letter to Kemmy:

'Here, the trees and bushes lean permanently at angle of 45 degrees towards the north-east in deference to the ferocious gales. The order of the day is, "*Shannon, Rockall, Bailey, gale force seven to eight increasing severe gale nine later, storm force ten to eleven in places, visibility poor*". I will shortly be making a quick sprint down the street to post this letter, coat collar turned up, head down, top half of the body parallel to the ground'.

He assured his benefactor he would make a special trip to vote in another upcoming election, outlining the geography of the route to the polling station in Limerick. He was full of chatty gossip about his brothers in England, to whom time and distance intensified his affectionate feelings. Having balked at the surrender option, he would only see them now on their visits to Ireland, which were fleeting. Like millions of immigrants over the generations, they had largely made their lives in Britain, and Ireland was a country to which they returned only periodically. His letters from Kilkee show a clear seam of isolation — stranded and bewildered that life had cast him up on a gale-battered coast in his mid-forties. Where had the promise· gone? What price now the adventures, the mischief, the derring-do? During storms, when the caravan shook with gales coming in over Hook Head, he cowered in a promenade shelter, appearing to type his book. To a few intimates it was clear he was beyond making progress — the typing was some desperate shadow-boxing, a mimicry of a talent in decline. But to others he put on a show of bravado, writing in March '81 to Kearney, that he would be in Kilkee for about another five months: 'If the second book is only half as successful as the first, I shall be coming to you to buy a house!'.

Gradually he became known to the townspeople. To the clientele of one pub he was a quiet companion who responded only if spoken to and did not impose himself on their company. A chemist, John Williams remembered him as polite and with a cheery take on world affairs. A caravan park owner, Larry Collins, sometimes stopped at the Marine Hotel for an evening drink and saw him at the counter, where he appeared content with his own company; 'I did not join him because he drank whiskey in large amounts, which made him an expensive man to drink with — but he was always polite and friendly. I noticed him taking home a bottle of whiskey, apparently he woke about three in the morning and had to have a drop to go back to sleep'.

Another saw him regularly typing in one of the beach shelters, and understood he was working on his book. Sometimes he borrowed a dog and went for a return walk to an adjoining town of Kilrush. He sweated profusely during those sixteen mile hikes in vain effort to keep his weight down and possibly, too, from 'cold turkey' as Collins knew the walks to be more frequent when he was money-less. It was a tough time. He felt his brain sozzled, which frightened him: sometimes he appeared badly 'in the rats'. He was not a well man, had ballooned in weight and seemed to be in deep distress.

To the town librarian, Mary Hynes, 'He did not look after himself — he was so far gone, he did not bother to eat. Some charitable women fed him a good meal from time to time. But he was always a gentleman — he borrowed books and had a word for everybody here. Some people took him to their hearts but he did not want to be a burden on any one person. I think he was very lonely...'.

He could, however, engage in worthwhile conversation. A teacher found him stimulating company, with a humorous take on world events — indeed during those months there was much in the changing global scenario that might have provoked his risible reaction. The Queen of England's distinguished art advisor, Sir Anthony Blunt was revealed as the enigmatic 'Fourth Man', part of the Apostles ring within the British intelligence services who had helped protect the embedded Russian spies. It emerged that Blunt had been granted secret immunity fifteen years before, in the security trawl after the flights of Burgess and Maclean, escaping prison in return for 'co-operation', an explanation which must have rung an ironic laugh from Blake in Moscow.

Much else in Blake's adopted home was coming apart at the seams, with 80,000 Russian troops being humiliated by Mujahideen mountain fighters in Afghanistan, which was a guerrilla force funded in joint SIS/CIA operations. Premier Brezhnev was presiding over what would become known in

Russia as the 'years of stagnation' having cowed the Politburo and taken supreme power to himself, while in England a sharp return to the Right saw Margaret Thatcher sell off industries which had been nationalised by Labour governments as she empowered a new state selfishness. Across the old Empire, the union flag continued to be hauled down with celebratory regularity, though the replacement regimes were of dubious integrity and some — such as Zimbabwe (Rhodesia) and Iran (formerly Persia) — would impose dictatorial rule more oppressive than any previous 'white man's burden'.

At home in Ireland, meanwhile, governments had leaned towards the European model, since seeing the values — and valuables — accruing from membership of the EC. Nearer home again, in the General Election of June 1981, Jim Kemmy ascended into his place in Dail Eireann, as Bourke saw it, being 'the Independent Member for Limerick'. Kemmy was among a handful of non-aligned deputies upon whose support the Labour and Fine Gael government depended. Led by Garrett Fitzgerald, a 55-year old politician of academic mind, it sought to liberalise antiquated laws on health and welfare, previously stagnated by Catholic Church intrusion. The Coalition promoted dialogue with all the warring parties in the North, which continued to drain much of the South's energies, in coping with the spill-over of continuing civil unrest and paramilitary violence. But it found itself exceedingly strapped for cash, as rampant inflation and soaring interest rates of 25%, combined with the relentless IRA bombings, to frighten both foreign and native investors.

That summer, Bourke journeyed to Limerick to vote for Kemmy and returned to Kilkee, 'hiding from the Limerick hordes down for their annual wash' as he put it. In spite of local charity and Kemmy's continuing subventions, he was desperately short of cash and heading into a bleak winter. So was the country, in the fiscal sense. With scarcity of jobs, youngsters leaving school looked again to the emigrant route. As one put it in a radio interview: 'I wake up in the morning and its a litany of people killed in the North, factories closing in the South — and what is government talking about? — contraception!'. Kemmy, put into the Dail by Limerick voters on a radical platform of reduced taxation and increased family benefits (funded by tax levies on banks and land speculation) found himself increasingly out on a limb.

He had been crucial in placing the Coalition in power. Though courted by Fianna Fail, Kemmy did not think Charles Haughey fit to govern in a democracy and so aligned himself to the uneasy political marriage of his former party, Labour and the Right-wing Fine Gael. 'Better the devil you know' was his holding position as the Coalition tussled with trimming the country's runaway debt which by the end of 1981 was running at £1,000 million. It was clear to even the most sanguine of analysts that relief for the underclass would not be available in the impending budget of the new year. The Finance Minister, John Bruton, made clear his determination to reduce State debt. He was viewed somewhat narrowly by many on the left as unsympathetic to their needs. A view likely to have been influenced by Bruton's perceived personal circumstances as a wealthy landowner.

For Kemmy to withdraw support might lead to the return of a Fianna Fail government lead by Charles Haughey, a hate-figure of the Left because of the 'whiff of sulphur' which lingered about his dictatorial persona since his acquittal on charges of illegally importing arms twelve years before and a feeling that he was personally bank-rolled by powerful financial figures. As Haughey was also known to take a keen interest in the political loyalties of senior Army and Garda commanders, the prospect weighed heavily upon Kemmy of facilitating the access to power of such a personality, should he withdraw support for the Government. Yet, in that bleak winter of 1981, he found himself increasingly at odds with a government whose budgetary intentions were described as 'harsh' and 'hair-shirt'. He was, in a phrase, caught between 'a rock and a hard place'.

He was also under strong pressure from his supporters in Limerick, the hard-core of defectors from Labour, who would not easily stomach penal taxation on beer, tobacco and clothes. It was a time of severe penury for bread-winners and especially for single-parent families, who formed a gathering pressure upon the welfare system. Even standard families were among the most highly taxed in Europe, being docked thirty per cent of their weekly income at source, while struggling to repay twenty per cent on their mortgages, leaving little leftover for basics. Second cars, foreign holidays and wine at meals were for the privileged and that 'golden circle' of tax-evaders who, as would later emerge, banked millions offshore in cavalier flouting of the laws. For most, making ends 'meat' was a poor joke. In that context, Kemmy had little option, having already presented his 'shopping list' of reduced taxation on working people as the price of his support in the Budget vote.

The usual media speculation on the actual contents of the Budget predicted a 'hit' on basic commodities. It was accepted the country was close to financial bankruptcy, after years of Fianna Fail profligacy, characterised by the personal high-living of Haughey. Now the Right-wing Fine Gael, in pact with Labour, though only seven months in power, seemed set to increase taxes on drink, cigarettes and petrol — all soft ways of raising revenue, rather than confront the powerful lobbies of banks and big business. As Kemmy bitterly saw it, the Budget was likely to squeeze PAYE workers, the weekly earners whose tax-take at source provided the bulk of government income. In meetings with Fitzgerald, he had been promised a higher tax take from the banks, but the Right had riposted that increased taxation on them would ultimately lead to foreign takeover of native industries, while Big Business warned that improving welfare benefits would remove the incentive to work. In the days before the Budget, Kemmy felt he had lost the argument.

Although he presented his 'shopping list' of remedies, he had received no consolation from Garret Fitzgerald, a politician Kemmy viewed as more inclined to talk at him than to listen on this matter. Accordingly, there was much speculation that he might not support the Budget votes, which if lost, brought Government resignation. The Independent

Deputy for Limerick found himself pursued by media, trying to glean his intentions. One reporter ensconced himself in the hotel room next to Kemmy, and listened at the door to his telephone conversations with his mentors in Limerick. He was in a gloomy mood as he entered the Dail Chamber that morning of 27th January — a mood deepened by hearing that Sean Bourke had been found dying on the roadside in Kilkee. He would say later that the death 'cast an omen over all that followed'.

In the event, the Budget Debate became a terse affair, with some concessions to Kemmy through increased taxes on banks (not as much as he wanted) and improved welfare benefits. Across the wide range of family costs, however, there was no respite. A hike in purchasing tax on clothes and shoes was compounded by ending milk and butter subsidies. Most families, already stressed, would find day-to-day life much more difficult — with jobless numbers peaking during one of the coldest winters on record. Butter and milk would cost about a quarter more, while the hits on drink and tobacco, while welcomed by health lobbies, would, as Kemmy saw it, penalise working men's habits. As the Finance Minister droned on through the afternoon, explaining how his new sums would reduce the national debt, watchers in the crowded galleries saw Kemmy doing his own sums — and gleaned he was far from happy. So did Taoiseach Garret Fitzgerald.

The withdrawal of food subsidies and tax on children's shoes were the last straws for Kemmy. As the deputies filed upstairs towards their respective voting lobbies, on the drink increase, Kemmy sat in his seat, apparently unmoved by Fitzgerald's promises. 'The Patrician pleading with the Plebeian' was how an observer saw them, as The Taoiseach tried to convince Kemmy, who stared moodily down at his own calculations. Sensing the drama, the Opposition deputies stopped above them and theatrically shushed Fitzgerald to silence, sending him scurrying back to his Prime Ministerial seat. 'The Fianna Failers sniggered at Fitzgerald and he jumped back...grinning like a guilty schoolboy' wrote the sketch-writer of *The Irish Times*. Kemmy rose, mounted the steps and entered the 'No' lobby. The government fell by one vote.

It was late evening and within minutes Fitzgerald was arranging to formally advise The President in Phoenix Park to dissolve the Dail. Afterwards, in the melee of media interviews, Kemmy said that the Government's mistake was to take him for granted: 'I kept them in power with my vote and then I withdrew it. I had to bite the bullet. I could not face back to my Limerick electorate if I had voted for a tax on children's shoes. We have rampant inflation, nearly 150,000 without jobs, working people were suffering... . They expected me to weigh in behind them, they did not know the realities of life'. As explained afterwards by Fitzgerald, he had reasoned with Kemmy in the Dail Chamber to modify some of the impositions, but could not reduce the new tax on clothes and shoes. *The Irish Times* reported that the Government's refusal to exempt children's wear from the proposed 15% VAT was due to their belief that 'this could have led to a situation where some women with small feet could have bought their shoes cheaper than their children who had larger feet'. Twenty-one years on, it seems about as bizarre an explanation for the fall of a Government as any in the history books.

The day before these political upheavals, Sean Bourke had set off on a walk, when he suffered a massive heart attack about ten past five in the afternoon and was found dying on the roadside in Kilkee on the 26th January 1982, not far from the library where he was a well-liked visitor. He was seen to stagger and fall over. According to Larry Collins who arrived soon after, he was breathing heavily, 'fighting very hard to live — breathing very hard'. Two doctors gave him energetic attention. Recognising the signs of heart failure, they kept him warm, moved him indoors on a stretcher, pumped his chest and applied other medical aids for about two hours, until he was pronounced dead. His body was removed to the County Hospital, where a post-mortem was undergone, which showed standard symptoms of heart failure. One of the doctors told me that given his knowledge of Bourke's career, he had particularly looked for evidence of malicious interference, but found none.

Margaret was in France and broke down on hearing the news, deeply distressed at the loss of a person whose life's pain she understood more than most. She had never faltered in her devotion to him, in spite of his wayward ways. As mentioned, Jim Kemmy heard about Sean's death on Budget Day and after a long, tumultuous day, during which his voting terminated the 22nd Dail, he journeyed to Limerick to attend the funeral next day. The body was brought from Ennis to Limerick, the cortege moving along the street of 'the mad, the bad and the dead' that Bourke had traversed as a boy. A small procession of people followed the hearse to his burial in a sparse plot close to the graveyard gate and afterwards — as Sean had made them promise — they repaired to The Munster Fair Tavern and 'drank his health'. He was a few months over forty-seven years of age.

CHAPTER TWENTY-FOUR

OUTING THE CONSPIRATORS

All Sean Bourke had in his pockets, when his effects were logged by the local Gardai, was one pound and four pence. When Kevin Bourke put the money in the church poor box, it may have appeared a closing sum to a life which had seen more than its share of elation and misery. However, ripples continued to wash the ebb-shore of the political pond. After his burial, some of his friends wondered if Sean might 'have been seen off' by some espionage agency, either settling a score or uneasy at what the deterioration of his later years might reveal. As Joe Malone put it, 'I had the impression that Sean never told as much as he knew. But towards the end he was desperate for money — who knows what he threatened?'

It was not a route I was keen to follow, not being forensically equipped to examine such possibilities. Maybe, too, such a scenario smacked of conspiracy theories. In writing this 'dual biography' of individuals caught up in the Cold War, one has to err on the side of caution, discounting the cinematic imagination of a Le Carre or Greene. However, as this work neared completion, I remembered the feelings of his friends and address now the suspicions, voiced all of twenty-one years ago.

Two years after Sean's death I made a radio documentary[*] about the escape and retraced his last hours. The doctors who attended his collapse on the roadway in Kilkee saw his general condition as having familiar symptoms of a heart attack, a diagnosis confirmed by other doctors who performed the autopsy. There was nothing to question the official conclusions, as written in Sean Bourke's death certificate. Cause of death: acute pulmonary oedema, left ventricular failure — coronary thrombosis, certified. In the spate of speculation afterwards, Jim Kemmy was of

---

[*] *A Death in January*, Kevin O'Connor, RTE Radio, Dublin 1984.

similar view: 'Bourke had wrecked himself with drink over many years. He never looked after his health...I think he died of natural causes.'

What espionage agency would have wished him dead? British, American or Russian? Applying the standard tests of 'Motive, Means and Opportunity' one could construct a hypothesis for all three services. The paranoid suspicion, common in Southern Ireland, that the long arm of 'perfidious Albion' might have stretched to Kilkee was considered. The British agencies certainly had the technical means and could have drawn on their scientific resources at Porton Down and elsewhere to provide a mechanism for assassination that would be difficult or impossible to detect. Means and opportunity — yes, though motive seemed doubtful, on the grounds that the Security Service had more pressing engagements during the early 1980s than to eliminate Sean Bourke, regarded simply as a 'petty Irish criminal' who had made much of passing opportunity. The Blake escape was well in the past. During the 70s and 80s, both SIS and MI5 were preoccupied with KGB and the IRA, tackling them across a broad frontier and no motive was apparent for them to deal with Bourke.

The Americans? Means and opportunity, yes. Motive — unlikely. Although CIA was still heavily engaged with anti-Soviet activity in 1982, the officer cadre most resentful of Blake's role in the Berlin Tunnel during 1956 had more potent targets in their sights, with many of them, anyway, being close to retirement.

Which left KGB, which certainly had the means and opportunity — but motive? Activity by Russian agencies seemed as unlikely as by the others. Unless, as mooted by one close friend of Bourke, to protect the English conspirators, out of gratitude for their help — and against their knowledge — even though they were not communists or fellow travellers. But the leading conspirators had as actively criticised the Russian government and KGB activities as they had their own governments. And by 1982, eleven years after the publication of Bourke's book, in which he had restored the passages obscured in Moscow laying clues to their identities, there appeared no imminent threat of prosecution.

However, because KGB had murdered many of its enemies abroad, it is worth mentioning that its secretive 'active measures' section of First Chief Directorate replicated heart attacks in liquidating targets. The operation was usually sub-contracted to an Eastern European section of KGB, using Bulgarian methods of poisoning. The Bulgarian secret service developed a poison, Ricin, a multiple refinement of castor-oil seeds, to kill the emigre writer Georgi Markov in London in 1978. Working for the BBC World Service, Markov had been an unrelenting critic of East European Communism, especially as practised in his home country and regularly broadcast the realities of life there on the BBC's Bulgarian service based in London. On Westminster Bridge, near his work place at Bush House, he was bumped into by a man with an umbrella near a bus stop, apparently accidentally.

Before he died with symptoms of heart failure, he recalled being stung by the umbrella. The Metropolitan police laboratory were able, with the aid of SIS, to hunt for — and find embedded in Markov's leg — the pin-ball which discharged the Ricin from the tip of a spring-loaded umbrella — a pellet so tiny as to be barely visible to the naked eye. None of this may be relevant to the death of Bourke, other than to engage with the speculation.

The espionage historian, Christopher Andrew, citing as a source, onetime KGB officer Kalugin, writes that '... on the instructions of Sakharovsky, the head of the FCD[*], Bourke was given before his departure a drug designed to cause brain damage and thus limit his potential usefulness if he fell into the hand of British intelligence[**]. Bourke's premature death in his early forties probably owed as much to KGB drugs as to his own heavy drinking.' (Bourke did not die in his 'early forties' but at 47 years while his massive drinking for twelve years beforehand considerably shortened his life).

---

[*] First Chief Directorate.
[**] As noted in chapter 18, Blake thinks this unlikely.

Research for radio documentaries brought me into contact with some of the boys, now men, who had been among his companions in Daingean. They confirmed the buggery and beatings endured at the mercy of the Oblates of Mary Immaculate. I was able to use his own account as written for the *Limerick Socialist* and to bring it to a wider audience — along with the actual tape recordings made across the wall of the The Scrubs as he and George discussed the detailed planning.

Some weeks after the broadcast I received information on Sean's visitors in the weeks before he died, including that of a journalist from a Sunday newspaper in London. He confirmed he had met Sean, apparently seeking to identify the English conspirators and so make a story out of revealing their identity — sixteen years after the escape. When I met him in London, he told me he did not have sufficient evidence, legally, to make the story 'stand-up' — but directed me to the person he described as the 'leg-man' on the police investigation into the escape, one Rollo Watts.

Watts agreed to meet me at his office near Sloan Square, where he worked for a security firm which advised on anti-terrorist measures across a wide range of political ideologies. He was interested to hear how Sean died and seemed genuinely regretful of his death. Even at that distance, he was aware of the mark left by the Irish borstal upon the man who had once been his quarry but who — 'wiv a little bit o' luck' had eluded him 'course it was the Jesuits that did for him...' he said knowingly. 'The Oblates', I said, but a minor detail — Ireland was awash with religious orders whose names he could not be expected to know. He reminisced about Sean phoning him and inviting him to Dublin after the failure of the British Extradition warrant. Hardly safe for a Scotland Yard officer in Dublin then, he felt, so he offered instead Sean to come to London and fetch the car, 'still in the police garage...' Both enjoyed the joke.

An amiable ex-Chief Inspector, Special Branch, he ranged over the logistics of the escape and the back-up organisation. 'Course we were onto Sean straight away —

and knew some of the others soon after — one was a teacher married to a teacher — from up the Midlands I think — perfectly law abiding people who were doing good in the community. Why prosecute them, when the big fish had got away...they were not your average 'effin-and-blindin' villains who it was our job to catch...good people in their own way, doing good in the community...'. He recalled the decision not to prosecute had come from a higher level...someone in the Home Office, he thought. As our conversation progressed, he predicted future trends in international terrorism, saying that as a journalist I should look to where the action was likely, 'Arab terrorism, that's the coming thing — groups like Holy Jihad, you should be looking at them...'.

In that he was prophetic, though it was his comments about the conspirators that I, in turn, would have professional cause to remember. Although Sean's demise incurred a media recall of the escape, it was mainly a cursory account, written from library cuttings by busy obituarists. The identities of the conspirators appeared safely consigned to the files of the Security Service. Michael and Anne Randle had moved to Bradford in Yorkshire, when Michael obtained a fellowship in Peace Studies at the university, while Anne resumed her nursing career. Both were busy with jobs, family and local community. Pat Pottle and Sue (whom he did not know before the escape) had returned to London from Wales and ran an antiques store. Pat continued his printing work for peace movements.

It seemed their past was behind them, in the legal sense, though an ever-widening circle of peace activists knew of their secret history. But by January 1989, around the seventh anniversary of Bourke's death, the *Sunday Times* embarked on a closer look at the 'Michael Reynolds and Pat Porter' of his book and the logistical support of anti-war crusaders in the escape. The newspaper's interest had been sparked by the author Montgomery Hyde, a former SIS officer, whose book reviewing the escape was published towards the end of 1988.

Looking at other prisoners who were in The Scrubs during the early sixties, Hyde claimed that the 'Reynolds' and 'Porter' of Bourke's book were not their real surnames, but were aliases for two who '...helped organise the civil disobedience at Wethersfield RAF base in December 1961, for which they were imprisoned from 1961 to 1963.'

Hyde stated they were members of the Committee of 100, which the philosopher Bertrand Russell had formed in a militant split from CND. Pat Pottle was known as a onetime secretary to Bertrand Russell and had been sentenced over the demonstration at Wethersfield RAF base, which housed USAF nuclear bombers — as had Michael Randle. Both had also come to public notice over protests against American and Soviet military incursions. It did not take a genius to make the connection from the Reynolds and Porter in Bourke's book to the Randle and Pottle in the files of newspapers.

Moreover, Bourke had mischievously laid a trail, describing 'Michael Reynolds' as someone with a mother from Dublin and a father from London.

Bourke's description of how he travelled to Michael's home — 'I got out at Camden Town and walked to the house.' — was accurate, as they lived in nearby Kentish Town. Descriptions of 'Pat Porter', including his flat in Hampstead, clearly tallied with anyone who knew Pat Pottle. Taken with a smattering of other leads, a novice player of *Cluedo* would have scooped the identities quickly. Trawling through the further hints by Hyde, and talking to former members of the Committee of 100 to verify dates of demonstrations, journalists were soon on the doorsteps of Pottle and Randle. So, by 1989, after an interval of 23 years, their names were firmly in the public arena as having been involved in the escape of George Blake.

Faced with concerted media investigation, Michael and Pat considered their options, most pertinently the likely effect of exposure on their immediate families. As Randle wrote: 'Anne's situation at work was more difficult than mine. I at least was working in surroundings where political issues were constantly debated, and controversial views held...Anne, in an NHS hospital among people with a very wide range of political views, had no idea what to expect.' There was also a joint concern that exposure would damage the peace movements to which they were committed, as some of the coverage implied them to be communist sympathisers or straightforward agents of KGB. As both of these suggestions were totally untrue, the possible damage to the independence of Randle's work on Peace Studies with Bradford University had to be considered as well as their own credibility within the peace movements.

Eventually they informed *The Guardian* newspaper of their position — they would neither confirm nor deny the implications of Montgomery Hyde's book or explicit accusation in the *Sunday Times* which named them as assisting in the escape of Blake.

They asserted they never had any dealings with the espionage services of any state, but had campaigned against the nuclear war preparations of both East and West. The statement failed to halt continuing media interest and after formal interviews with the police in London, they decided to withdraw from further comment and to write their own version of the escape and to take the consequences. Their reasoning was that the media would not go away.

Meantime, a right-wing group promised a private prosecution if the Crown failed to act and 110 Tory MPs signed a Commons motion to pressure the Attorney-General to prosecute. Randle and Pottle decided a book, jointly written, was the opportunity to set the record straight and put their involvement in the context of the 1960s and the tensions of the Cold War. They were aware that such a true account would invite prosecution and possibly gaol — a prospect neither wished and of which their families were fearful. They went ahead, jointly reviving memories of dates, times, conversation and documents written shortly after the events.

In the wake of their book, published in the spring of 1989, the predictable happened. *The Blake Escape: How We Freed George Blake — and Why* was a thorough, detailed corroboration of Bourke's narrative, told with the all-too-human tensions and black comedy of the conspirators waiting in Kentish Town to hear either from Sean — or from a police knock on the door. It filled out the wider picture from another point of view, the POV as it is known in screen-writing, the angle of the English conspirators. It gave a first-hand account of hiding Blake in various London places, the stress on sympathisers providing shelter and the strain upon their own patience as they realised that Bourke, in his volatile way, placed them at continuing risk of discovery. Indeed, at times living with Bourke was more of a problem than hiding Blake. For students of English politics, their book also provided a coherent account of the anti-war movements and the genesis of street protests which had affected public debate on Britain's nuclear alignment with America during the 1960s, when the country's rulers floundered in the wake of the Suez debacle. The authors mapped a lineage of dissent, from current civil disobedience back to conscientious objectors during the war and forward to what the philosopher Bertrand Russell regarded — in spite of then minority support — as the future triumph of reason and humanity over war-mongering. Citing civil disobedience as factors in gaining votes for women in Britain and rights for Negroes in America, their apologia explained why they campaigned against Nuclear bases — and how they ended up in Wormwood Scrubs where they met George Blake, whose 42-year sentence for spying the authors declared to be savage and inhuman.

Blake's sentence led them to evaluate the work of Western espionage services, in which they took a starkly different stance from the usual crop of writers on the subject. They cited evidence that MI5 had conspired against their own elected (Labour) Government and that President Truman had become fearful of CIA interference in policy making. They included records of SIS activity against President Nasser of Egypt and murders and attempted murders organised by CIA of foreign political figures, whose polices were deemed hostile to American interests and the long involvement of CIA in undermining liberal movements in South American countries.

A mere week after the book's publication the authors and Anne Randle were arrested and questioned. In the event, only the two authors went forward for trial, being indicted at Bow Street in July 1989 and released on bail to appear at the Old Bailey in August. Michael Randle was described as a university lecturer in Peace Studies and Pat Pottle as an antiques dealer. They were charged with aiding Blake's escape, with harbouring him as a fugitive and with assisting him to evade capture — offences ranging in penalty from five to two years. If found guilty on all three counts, they faced a concurrent sentence of about five years, or nine years if sentenced in sequence. Also, confiscation orders were placed on the values of their homes and on the likely earnings from the book, which meant they would be penniless if they were found guilty.

With its echoes of the sensational Blake escape during the height of the Cold War, the impending trial of the conspirators attracted international attention, with peace groups and individuals in 18 countries petitioning against the trial. Some came from inside Eastern Europe, remembering Randle and Pottle's solidarity during groundswells against Russian rule and in particular their bringing to international media notice both the military repression of a country and the imprisoning of dissidents within the Soviet Bloc.

However, their lawyers succeeded in getting a High Court hearing — to stay the criminal trial — on the basis that the impending Crown prosecution, 23 years after the offence, was an 'abuse of legal process'.

To add another personal contact with the story, on reading of that application, I informed their solicitor about my interview with Rollo Watts. I balanced journalistic protection of sources against the severe sentences and financial ruin facing Randle and Pottle and the fact that Watts was retired when I interviewed him. I agreed to be called as a defence witness, furnished an affidavit and was duly cross-examined on its veracity during the hearing. By then other Special Branch and security services personnel had been ordered to appear, following the judge ruling against the Home Secretary's wish to prevent them being questioned. In court, Rollo Watts denied he had ever met me, said the words used in my affidavit were not of his usage and denied he had discouraged prosecution. But as the men's lawyers succeeded in having Watt's former superior, Arthur Cunningham attend for cross-examination, it became clear that Watts had been instructed to evaluate the clues in Bourke's book in 1970, had made the connections to Randle and Pottle and had suggested that a 'prosecution would amount to a persecution' as the men were not criminals but usually law-abiding citizens of worth to the community. After much legal debate, legal precedent was set when an M15 officer, speaking from behind a screen said a file had been found confirming Watts' report, and the view, as communicated to the Home Office, was that no prosecution should occur as 'the big fish had got away and there was no point in going after the little fish'.

In spite of that evidence, the judge ruled that in 1970 there was no evidence that would stand up in a court of law and refused to stay the criminal trial. Whereupon the men's lawyers asked for — and obtained — a Judicial Review of that decision. In November 1990, two High Court judges delivered the Judicial Review, in which they outlined the political background and the legal arguments for and against prosecution. On the plea of unfairness because of faulty or fading memory after 24 years, they ruled that the defendant's book showed, on the contrary, all too clear a memory, being 'a barefaced chronicle of giving aid to a spy'. On the submission that this was a cynical prosecution, because in 1970 there was a decision not to prosecute, the judges (surprisingly!) held that reasoning to be unsupported by the evidence of witnesses. They were also satisfied that in 1966 or soon after there was nothing to suggest that the police knew who had helped Blake escape. Accordingly, a long period of delay between the commission of an alleged offence and prosecution was not itself a reason to stay the proceedings as no unfairness was caused to the defence.

With appeal dismissed, the trial opened in the Old Bailey, in Court No 1, where Blake had been tried all of 25 years before, now with his two helpers, Randle and Pottle in the same dock. This time, though, there was no secrecy. As the trial progressed over ten days, it became a legal cause celebre, having already made some kind of legal history by (a) a High Court judge halting the criminal trial on the day it was due to begin — to hear the Abuse of Process plea and (b) the production in court, on judges instructions, of files from Special Branch and MI5.

Further unusual procedure was set by Randle and Pottle calling each other into the witness box to establish for the jury their individual credentials as conscientious objectors to war, activity for which they had lost their liberty numerous times.

Among their character witnesses was Jan Kavan, a leading activist in the movement which recently overthrew the Czech communist government, who warmly praised Randle for the risks he took in smuggling resistance literature into the country after the Soviet invasion — and then on video came a recording of George Blake (unrepentant communist) who spoke to camera of the escape, confirming their roles. 'I never had any doubt in my mind that they acted purely out of humanitarian motives...indeed I had to explain to the Soviet authorities who these two men were...they were never at any time in contact with the Soviet authorities.'

Other unusual tactics followed. Michael Randle took the court through the evolution of the English legal system and a function of juries in sometimes finding defendants innocent when the charges were clearly malicious or politically motivated. He cited cases when juries had acquitted hungry peasants on charges of sheep-stealing, when the only sheep belonged to the landowner who kept the peasant hungry. He told the Old Bailey jury of a 17th century case of Quakers charged with unlawful assembly for preaching on the Sabbath in nearby Gracechurch Street. When the jury refused to find them guilty, the judge had ordered the jury locked-up until they changed their minds. He raised a rare laugh from the jury, who followed his arguments intently, when he said: 'I'm not suggesting that if you bring in 'not guilty' verdicts, His Lordship is going to lock you up...!'

On the last day of the trial, Pat Pottle gave a summing-up address, in which he claimed they were in the dock because, among other pressures, '110 MPs signed a motion calling for our prosecution...Your task would be a lot easier if this were a simple case of guilt or innocence, but it is not. It is a case of right and wrong. It is a case of politics, a case of how governments lie, cheat and manipulate, and then cover their tracks in a smokescreen of official secrecy...this is a political trial. A political decision was taken in 1970 not to prosecute. When we were publicly named in 1987, it came as no surprise to the police: they had known since 1970...The accepted theory about George's escape was that it was organised and carried out by agents at the KGB. That was embarrassing to British intelligence, but at least they could argue that KGB was an organisation with limitless resources. What would the revelation that a petty criminal and two peace activists had carried out the escape do to our relations with our allies? It was better that the world continued to believe that the whole thing was organised by KGB rather than the Lavender Hill Mob. The judge has ruled our reasons for freeing George to be irrelevant. I disagree with the judge. The idea of a jury system is that you can look at the whole case, not just the legal mumbo-jumbo. You are 12 independent people. Unlike most judges you exist in the ordinary world of everyday life...Common sense must tell you that our reasons for helping to free George from prison must be relevant...

The moral indignation about George's work for the Russians is something I completely agree with. But moral outrage is only genuine when applied to both sides. Have our values become so perverted that we only claim moral outrage at the other side's activities and not our own? What George did for British intelligence and KGB was wrong — we have never tried to justify it nor whitewash it. But espionage is a dirty business, where rumour becomes fact and fact becomes

318

fiction. The individuals involved in it are exploiters and in turn are exploited. Even when caught they can still be used as international pawns in a game, some to be swapped, some to be given immunity, and the unlucky ones left to rot in prison. No one who supports this kind of thing can hold their heads up high.

What did George do that sets him apart from other spies uncovered at that time? He was not really British, was he? Not of the old school, not one of us. Deep down, he was a foreigner, and half-Jewish to boot. He was never part of that privileged undergraduate set at Cambridge in the 1930s. Not like dear old Kim [Philby]...or dear old Anthony [Blunt].

A secret trial, a vicious sentence of 42 years, a secret appeal — is this democracy in action? Is this open justice? Are we not becoming the very thing we condemn? George was no threat to you, me, or our children. He had been caught spying for the Russians, just as they had caught people spying for the west. His usefulness was over, his spying activities at an end. What purpose was served by giving him such a sentence?

Yes, I helped George Blake escape. I did it for purely humanitarian reasons. I think we were right to do so. I would do it again. I have no apologies to make and no regrets. I will finish by quoting Bertrand Russell: "Remember your humanity; forget the rest" '.

Convinced by the weight of the defendants' arguments — and unusually for a London jury, disregarding the judge's guidance to convict — they found them Not Guilty. The media had a field day, with editorials and debates on the functions of juries and legal arguments as to how their powers might be curbed. 'A bad day for Justice' said the next day's lead editorial in the *The Daily Telegraph*. 'Escape into Pantomime', said *The Guardian*. The two men, meanwhile, were feted by their supporters and free to get on with their lives.

CHAPTER TWENTY-FIVE

A SHOCK TO THE SYSTEM

Within minutes of arriving at Sheremetyevo Airport in the summer of 1992 I realised I was entering into the territory of a beaten people. Compared to the bright lights and commercial energy of Western airports, this 'gateway to Moscow' was as gloomy a cavern as I imagined it during the Cold War. Glimmerings of the future came from the facade of a duty-free shop being built by an Irish airports company. As shop-fitting expertise was not available in Moscow, the company flew out its own construction and retail personnel. Within months they had built the shops and trained a Russian workforce in such strange mechanics as smiling at customers and stocktaking with profit in mind. Aer Rianta secured the contracts because of their experience with the Soviet state airline, Aeroflot, at Shannon.

During the early 1980s, with a world-wide fuel shortage wrought by Arab insistence upon less exploitative prices from the West, the Soviets increased oil production from their Asian satellites. With longer-haul jets and improved payloads, they needed a mid-Atlantic re-fuelling depot. The Russians had surplus fuel, but encountered resistance from the Anglo-American cartel. In a deal done between Aeroflot and Shannon International Airport, the Irish traded landing fees for aviation fuel, which was shipped from Russian ports to the Shannon estuary, stored in the airport and sold onto Western airlines already rationed. The Irish resisted secret pressures from British and American governments, as advised by CIA and SIS, and gave ground space to the Russians. The deal worked, enabling Shannon to have a fuel supply independent of the Anglo-American monopolists of Shell, BP and Esso.

With the Shannon facilities secured, Aeroflot extended its frequencies from Moscow via Shannon to Havana, to New York and to the Southern hemisphere. Encouraged to further deal-making by the urgent advent of Perestroika (new Russian economic policy), Aer Rianta was offered contracts for retailing in a host of former Soviet locations — hence the few bright lights of the capitalist future, peering through the gloom of Moscow airport. Notably failing however, to illuminate the entry points, still controlled by military. After as many checks of travel documents as seemed designed to keep three separate sets of border guards employed, one penetrated out into daylight — and into poorly maintained roads and motor traffic that belched heavy pollution. The wide six-lane highway to Moscow was so heavily potholed and so spasmodically grid-locked as to present as formidable an obstacle to a land invasion as the Russians had to Hitler's advance in 1943.

But this was 1992 — if this was where the Free World had met the Evil Empire in armed conflict, they would have abandoned the highway and skirmished in the fields alongside. But even as that piece of amateur war games took shape in my mind, we passed the large concrete sculpture of a tank trap, marking the ground where Hitler's advance foundered. My guide, an 'old Moscow hand' said it had fresh flowers on it always and my eyes misted as I thought of the supine servants of Communism who perished in the Great Patriotic War and for whom there would be no monument. Not even, in most cases, in the memory of their offspring. Official amnesia had rendered them as invisible as if they had never lived — though new access of historians to the archives would yield numbers so immense as to become a ghostly pall over the Cold War.

Even then, perhaps, only in the minds of sentimental outsiders like myself, trying to make connections between the iron past and the fluid present. I was to find everywhere the confirmation of my companion's advice: 'There are no 'experts' on modern Russia — only varying degrees of ignorance'. It became a mantra as I booked into an apartment block with the fold-down bed rented out by the occupant whom I was told 'had gone to live with relatives'. The hangover of 'suspicious foreigners' still deprived Moscow of the hundreds of small hotels which every capital needs for trade. The shortage meant that families already cramped, earned a month's wage from a few days letting to the influx of foreign businessmen lured by deals in the 'new' Moscow. A cock crew in the morning as I looked out onto a sanded square with hens, chickens pigs and dogs — farm companions of a generation whose grandparents had been summarily uprooted by Stalin from a collective and dumped in the middle of Moscow.

'These are country people who still keep their ways' I was told by an Irish businessman who had been among the entrepreneurs from the West who had taken to heart the official invitation to engage in 'joint ventures' with Russians, part of Michael Gorbachev's rushed attempt to save the tottering system from outright collapse. Capitalism — the long derided enemy — had been invoked to underpin Glasnost and Perestroika — the dual catch-call of Openness and Rebuilding of the entire Soviet system. Since Communism had officially closed down two years before, the economy was in crisis in the place most visible to judge it — on the streets. 'Sell everything' Gorbachev said, so makeshift kiosks adapted from railways wagons sold food, family heirlooms, saints' icons and vodka, while the State shops had dust-sheets on their obsolete goods. And on the streets, too, the quick-brush strokes of that first visit coloured later judgments, as the businessman, from a rural Irish background, told of his own visits outside Moscow where he had seen miles and miles of fields of potatoes rotting — because there was no money to pay workers and no transport to get them to the cities.

'Outside of Moscow, there is little work done. Since State salaries are now so irregular, people don't bother to work. The miners have not been paid for months'. An astute survivor of Soviet life in crisis, he provided an entertaining commentary as we visited the mandatory sights of Moscow, beginning with the McDonald's restaurant with its lengthy queues — longer than for Lenin's tomb and joined the entrance for dollar customers (the other for rouble currency).

The tall and strikingly handsome waitresses spoke of their ambition to get to America. One had trained as an aerodynamics engineer, another as a physicist. No work for them now. Working as a waitress in McDonalds, they felt, would prepare them for America.

In the Arbat market, within sight of the Kremlin, the emblazoned insignia of the failed Soviet state was on sale at knockdown prices. Giant red banners that had been emblems of Party offices in far-flung regions were being traded to tourists. The larger, embroidered ones, I was told, might have been brought by train and mule many thousands of miles by travellers fleeing local famines and civil wars. The colours that had deluded them for generations at last held the promise of currency on arrival in Moscow. Discarded by war-lords who had replaced Party officials, their scroll-work no longer respected, the lurid banners that had replaced religious icons in the 1920s now went as wall-coverings to Western buyers who could only hazard at the depth of passions they had aroused or the amount of blood spilt for their bloody colour. The sellers, however, had felt the swing of Communism's illusions from hope to repression and suffered no pangs in parting.

These Lenin-embossed emblems had swayed over the largest political systems of our time. By the end of the 20th century, more of the world's population claimed adherence to Marx than to any other system of governance. Now Marx's venerable moustached head, graffiti-splurged, lay in a junkyard alongside other tottered totems — Dzhersinski, Stalin, Bulganin, Khrushchev — all crow-barred from plinths in the upheavals of recent years. Officially reviled in that 'revisionist' way peculiar to Russian leaders, their fallen features retained the historic impact which had been venerated by generations of idealists from the West — from Rosa Luxembourg, through the Rosenbergs to Philby and Blunt and Blake. Equally, they had mesmerised intellectuals from Sartre to Shaw in pursuit of a theory whose practice by Stalin and Ho Chi Minh must rank among the great political conjuring acts of our times.

Seeing the emblems and banners piled in the Arbat streets said more to me about the collapse of Communism than the rush to political analysis — Communism's icons reduced to decorative garbage. As the stalls were also piled high with discarded uniforms of deserters from the Soviet army, naval and air force, one quickly saw how the collapse of military might had made redundant the red banners. Or the collapse of the Red Banner had made redundant the military might. Over the Kremlin flew the red-white-and blue flag of the newly formed Russian Federation, the 'old flag of Mother Russia' as described to me proudly by Yuri Luzhkov the Mayor of Moscow and apparatchik to Yeltsin. Moscow was then in the throes of another seismic seizure of the body politic. Yeltsin and Luzhkov were pitting their power against the revived opposition of the 'Old Stalinists'.

The Mayor had provided strong-arm support for Boris Yeltsin the previous summer against a group of conspirators, called 'counter–revolutionaries' by their supporters but described as 'second-rate managers of a bankrupt shop' by the businessman who had seen the failed revolt on the streets. Seeking to stop the break up of the USSR and reverse history, the conspirators had put Gorbachev under house arrest in his Dacha and attempted to storm the Beli Dom, (White House) of the new democratic parliament. Their conspiracy — a litmus test of the fledgling democracy had failed to gain either popular or military support. Tanks 'attacked' the Parliament from military depots near the Kremlin but KGB had ensured they had no ammunition (I was later to learn that CIA was also active in 'monitoring' the situation). After skirmishes and the deaths of students, the coup had been repulsed by Yeltsin and his armed cohorts.

Yeltsin's power had been strengthened by his epic — and theatrical — defence of the Parliament and the fortuitous presence of a CNN camera crew. The conspirators had jammed the state radio and TV, but CNN from its vantage point in an office above the conflict was using satellite. A year on, with the conspirators awaiting trial, Yuri Luzhkov controlled Moscow and remembered those who had stood by him. During the failed coup, hundreds of foreign businessmen clogged the airport in flight, fearing seizure or Siberia. The Irish had stayed — repaid by Mayor Luzhkov with the bounty of further, extensive retailing contracts.

It was to one of those outlets that I repaired with my businessman guide. Although the Irish Pub, as a catering brand, proliferates throughout the globe, it was then a novelty to Muscovites and heavily patronised. The Shamrock Bar was tucked into a corner of the Irlanksi Dom (Irish House), which dispensed, through fourteen check-outs, all the glittering goods of The West. Fridges, washing machines, video recorders, power showers and microwaves were being wheeled out the doors like there was no to-morrow — not surprising, given the unstable politics on the streets and starvation in the countryside. The spirits of Turgenev and Tolstoy, I thought, must be revolving up there in the ether around the red stars that still hung over the onion spires of the Kremlin, becoming neon-lighted like a slice of Broadway.

'This place is full of spooks' said my guide. He meant a group of white-shirted men from the American Embassy in the Shamrock Bar and not the graveyard of the statues. Then, unwittingly, he asked if I had heard of George Blake, the KGB spy and before I could flounder for an answer he dropped his voice to inform me that the said elusive person had been seen in this very place, 'He comes in on a Saturday, buys Irish tea and reads the papers'. (Blake was somewhat disconcerted later to hear of that gossip). In the bar, I met an army officer from Ireland who was assigned to the EC mission of famine relief. He told me that military personnel from European countries' joined their Russian colleagues on Sunday for a 'fun-run' in Moscow — during the week they supervised the dispatch of EC-funded meat which had been released from storage and shipped to feed starving Russians (he said most of the Russian butchers were drunk in the factories where the beef was packaged — the women did all the work). I was to meet some of his colleagues later and hear a conversation between a former Russian signals officer and a former RAF Nimrod pilot, in which they discovered — by agreeing map coordinates on the bar table — they had targeted each other above some distant border of the USSR.

In other piquant bar encounters, a mild-mannered American lawyer told me he had an office in the Kremlin. He was negotiating rights from the city council to rent sites on major roads for advertising hoardings, previously not allowed. He commuted monthly to his home in Maryland, via the Shannon re-fuelling stopover and did his shopping at the duty-free. Another American loudly hectored the bar staff to 'hurry up for Christ sake, can't anybody show these Ruskies how to pour Guinness'. He was, he said, looking for prospecting licenses for oil. Nearby — and warily, some tall former Irish army personnel would not be drawn on their business, but I gleaned they were purchasing Russian aircraft parts and been visiting 'closed cities' of missiles manufacture. 'They are acting as middle-men for the Americans' said my businessman guide, who apparently knew such things.

I had looked forward to meeting George Blake since sending him a play about the escape which had been performed the previous year. He had responded with interest, which encouraged me to ask for a meeting. Leaving my guide I telephoned an intermediary and was given another number. Blake came warmly on the line and suggested a meeting outside a hotel, where — to the minute — he emerged from the passing pedestrians. We journeyed to another part of the city. Over the next few hours I partook of his family hospitality, joining Ida and son Mischa in a meal. Afterwards we spoke quietly for hours in his own rest room, with tabernacles of the Russian Orthodox Church and medieval religious icons ranged on the walls above. The bookshelves held volumes of history in Russian, Dutch, German and English. The room exuded tranquillity and the aroma of incense, but the bookshelves recorded the sufferings of the Nazi Holocaust, the Stalin Terror, the Berlin Blocade, the American bombing of Korea.

That record was manifest in the books, which he had in some cases marked with slips of paper, reflections of his private journeys through those public times: *The Cambridge Modern History, Official History of Holland during World War Two, Conflict in World Politics,* Anthony Sampson's *The Arms Bazaar* and *Anatomy of Britain Today. Memoirs of Harold MacMillan* and *The Life of Gladstone* kept company with books about his fellow travellers Philby and Vassal, along with the bound doctorate of Donald Maclean, *British Foreign Policy since Suez* ('I liked and admired him').

Clearly he kept in touch with Britain's evolving history. I had little doubt that he had read thoroughly the volumes on his shelves. We ranged over many aspects of East-West politics, the turmoil in Russia, the failure of Communism. 'It has never been really tried' he said. 'Perhaps it needs a new type of human being to bring it about, one of high moral character. But one must not be too harsh on its failure, though one might be on those who purloined it...it will have many stages to go through... . But I do believe a more evolved or elevated human being will bring about an end to conflicts, to oppression'. As to the current chaos, the collapse of the Soviet Union, he elaborated on the logistical difficulties of administering an enormous expanse of many races and territories and the inherent failure to mesh such conflicting cultures to the control of Moscow.

He granted the failure of Centralism, once an iron tenet, in the face of changed expectations wrought by media and information access. He conceded that the break-up of the USSR was similar to the withdrawal of the European empires witnessed in his own times — France from Asia, Belgium from The Congo, Spain and Portugal from South America, Germany from Africa. He spoke tellingly of the retreat of the largest empire, Britain, from all of those continents. The advent of technology should in theory have made it easier to control the far-flung colonies — especially by a Europe whose development of 20th century technology from aircraft to rockets, from the telegraph to the television, had advanced mobility and communications. But the energised pressure for independence had out-swung the means of control — the spirit had overcome the flesh. The end of the Century was marked by the End of Empires, we agreed.

To borrow a communist cliche, man was born free but was everywhere in chains — but often exchanged one set of chains for another, usually of the home-made sort. We ranged over the anti-colonial movements which Russia had aided, in Africa, Asia and South-America, provoking American subversion of democratically-elected leaders during the Cold War. But was not Russia now acting like any fearsome imperial power in Chechna, then beginning to be disturbingly reported in the Russian media with all-too-familiar rituals of atrocity by Chechnens, provoking counter-terror by Russian troops. He appeared wary of criticising Russian foreign policy, (perhaps with his pension in mind?) wearily reaching for Shakespeare to justify the war. 'Were twere done, twere well it were done quickly'. He asked particularly about the decline of Sean Bourke and was curious about the details of his demise. 'I was very sorry to hear of his death, because I owe him everything'. For a while he was lost in private thoughts, then — indicating this home and family 'I owe him my freedom, so I cannot think badly of him — he gave me life'.

I returned to Moscow during 1994, to make a series of television documentaries on the 'changing' Russia. There was more poverty visible on the streets and also more prosperity — more fur coats passing more beggars. The papers told outright of civil wars in Georgia and Chechna. The Baltic States, Estonia, Latvia and Lithuania, had formulated their own independence, so far without bloody strife. There was tension and much negotiations over control of assets — barracks, airlines and vast tracts of state properties. The Balkans, however, which had sundered when the grip of Tito's iron fist cast off its mortal coil, broke bloodily into 'ethnic cleansing' and sectarian massacres. The Ukraine had seceded, taking with it the bitter folk-memory of Khrushchev's mass murder of its small farmers who had failed to meet targets of grain production. That territory, in common with other regions, would not likely again become subject to Russian control, under whatever guise.

A few miles away, along the new West End of Moscow, there were more neon lights, advertising signs and the fight was not for the soul of Russia but to queue at the new supermarkets.

Near the Ministry of Defence, curiously modelled on Britain's similar ministry in London, in the evening, convoys of soldiers were drawn up in carriers, battle-prepared: tall guardsmen had replaced the regulars to the entrances. 'What's happening?' I asked the onetime signals officer from my previous visit. 'Oh nothing much, maybe another coup, that is all...'. We passed darkened troop carriers, with only murmurs and the clink of gunmetal to indicate armed tension. We went to another recently opened Irish bar, this time replete with Western-style bouncers in Armani suits. It was not hard to glean the function of burly, suited men at the door — I was told they kept 'order from unruly elements' in return for a percentage of the turnover, which again curiously, was fixed at 12%.

The bar in the Irlanski Dom was busy with food, drink and gossip. Westerners seemed more attuned to talk of another coup than Russians who shrugged resignedly. Rumour was traded against rumour — an Irish construction crew had been clearing rubble from an underground railway line that was not on the Metro map and apparently linked The Lubyanka with an exit near Bibliotecha Lenina, the vast grey library building near the Kremlin. Apparently the Irish crew had been hired because as foreigners they would not appreciate the significance of the work — in fact they copped it quicker than most. Wafting from group to group, I met white-shirted American lawyers, some of whom said they lived in Virginia, which any student of foreign policy would know was within the commuting belt of CIA at Langley.

A few tables away, were two men from an American Aid agency, whom my signals officer said had brought in a supply of radio transmitters to help the pro-Yeltsin forces maintain communications when the Moscow phone services had been jammed by the Stalinist conspirators. Moving to a group of young German businessmen I asked if they felt any hostility because of the awful things done by the Nazis to the Russians in 1943.

'Feel my belt' said one jokingly. I encountered a pistol butt. 'Walther PK' he said just as amiably. It was that kind of evening in that kind of bar. When I recounted it to George Blake, in what had become another of our regular meetings, he was both amused and serious. The chaos which had replaced discipline troubled him, but he held hope for the future: 'Maybe not in our time, but the brotherhood of man will come'.

He cheered up at the prospect of the St. Patrick's Day Parade, then an improving feature of Moscow life, bringing floats, bands and gaiety to streets that previously had seen only military parades. The Western business companies encouraged their staff to don fancy dress and paid for the Cossacks horse troop to march. From Ireland had come its most famous band, the Artane Boys' Band, whose pennants were red-white-and blue, which happened to be the official flag of the CIS, Confederation of Independent States, which had replaced the USSR. Among those on the reviewing stand outside the White House was Mayor Yuri Luzhkov and a few Government ministers, a traditional Irish gaiety replacing the old solemn row of Politburo figures in hats. One minister arriving late, jokingly asked if it was another coup and was told, with an edge to the reply, that no coup is secure until the counter-coup is defeated. Interviewing Mayor Luzhkov later, among minders in suits and shoulder-holsters, he wagged his finger at me when I remarked that the colours of the Artane Boys Band were the same as those over the Kremlin — 'But Mother Russia is older...' he said and I did not feel inclined to disagree (he was right).

Seven months later, the counter-coup whose ingredients we smelt smouldering, flared into fire, as crowds protesting at Yeltsin's 'dictatorial' control of Parliament marched towards the Beli Dom. Waving the red flags of old Russia, it was initially good-natured, calling Yeltsin a traitor to 1917, as they linked arms and broke through a police cordon — and then the shooters came out and it became an armed counter-revolution.

A group of dissident deputies within the parliament had stored guns and communications equipment and attempted to take the building, while another guerrilla group stormed a television station, to announce a 'peoples' coup. The world saw the tanks driving down Kalinina from the Kremlin, just as they had in the failed putsch three years before. Only this time a lesson had been learned — the tank commanders were not given their ammunition until they aimed their guns firmly at the Beli Dom, home of The Duma, Russia's democratic assembly. Within hours it was ablaze from incendiary shells, the resisters shot or arrested and the building stormed by troops loyal to Yeltsin. The fragile experiment in parliamentary democracy had survived another test. On the streets, however, organised crime and protection rackets increased.

An old man in the snow...

The Moscow that I returned to in the winter of 2001 differed startlingly from the beaten capital of ten years before. There were new hotels near the airport and the route to the city was punctuated with hoardings of universal prosperity. The Washington lawyer was presumably counting his royalties as Sanyo, Microsoft and Ericsson signposted the route to Moscow, where had been the memorials to the defeats of Napoleon and Hitler and the glory of Stalin. There were no fresh flowers on the tank-trap, though some lingering respect for the uncounted dead — or money delays — had left the fields un-built around it. Glimpsed through forests were new ranch-style houses of the new money of the new Russia, more like the outskirts of Las Vegas.

Nearing the city, the roads sped with BMW and Mercedes rather than lumbering Ladas and Zils. Some of the 1930s apartment blocks, once satirised as 'new repressionist style' had their sculptures of cement-muscled workers concealed under giant banners promoting holidays in Florida. Ulitsa Tverskaya, once a long artery of baroque apartments that reflected the squat Politburo faces that paraded every October above Lenin's tomb, was transformed into a lure of retail stores, restaurants, bars and nightclubs. Yet along this wide artery the tanks of another coup would have driven to the Kremlin, as would the advance parties of Western invasion. Hard to believe how recently it had been targeted for blasting by missiles, had I not been the summer before in Lake Tahoe in the Nevada mountains and seen the entrance to the underwater silos that had, in secrecy, housed the ICBMs aimed at Russia.

Were it to happen now, America would destroy some of its own imperial outposts. McDonalds had grown from one to twenty-five outlets in Moscow, Microsoft computers were in widespread use by the Russian civil service. The Kremlin was being re-wired for Internet networking, gift of CIA which had signalled the electronic end of the Cold War by freeing-up their most potent secret communications system, the Internet, for world-wide use. CNN was available in the hotels as were domestic services, some with hard-hitting debates on Yeltsin and his abilities — or lack of them. CNN, which had evaded jamming by the inept conspirators ten years before because of its satellite signal, had played a crucial role in informing Russian and Western opinion in the decade since the abortive coup. The network was now available in millions of Russian homes and in hotels and workplaces.

Underground, by The Kremlin walls, glitzy shops replaced what had been a Soviet command-and-control post during the Cold War. Instead of a bunker for Nuclear Strike (the annihilation of millions), lay the newly-marbled avenues of the global future — glittering shopping malls on three levels, devoted to the luxury goods of the West — limousines, fur coats, over-priced suits and women's designer fashions from the capitals of Europe.

On a Sunday it was packed with young Russians, well-dressed, better fed, as much in thrall to 'retail therapy' as their Western counterparts. Under Red Square, where their obedient parents and grandparents had walked with respectful ceremony, they ambled eagerly for the illusions of commerce. A walk away, Lenin's tomb, once a required ritual for honeymooners, looked abandoned, its high-stepping guard abolished. Its militarism was no longer deemed inspirational to an upcoming generation. A Lenin look-alike made dollars posing for tourists. In this winter, too, more people died from exposure on the streets, about 300 in two months. The Salvation Army had been expelled because of the 'army' in its title and since the collapse of police controls about a million homeless had arrived in the capital from the regions, no longer needing the official passports to live in Moscow. Many were not equipped to survive in a city where retailing and computer skills were more in demand than old-fashioned physical labour.

In and out of all of this manoeuvred the new 'revolutionaries in suits', the businessmen and fixers, the bankers and contractors, the wheelers and dealers with their armour-plated cars and bodyguards with machine-guns cradled on their laps. All this within walking distance of The Lubyanka, where I imagined the ghosts of the executed haunted the deep basements that had spawned terror across a continent.

The Pushkin Museum still commanded queues for a poet they had imbibed at school. A short distance away, more baroque buildings housed out-offices of the FSB, inheritors of KGB. Lingering as a tourist, one could see the unmarked cars coming-and-going in the same way they trekked out of SIS on London's South Bank or sped down the avenues near the Ecole Militaire in Paris. Empires may be disintegrating but the spies charted their demise, as they had their creation (*The Moscow Times* reported on a week of exchanges between FBI and their Russian counter-parts, Federal Security Service in a countryside location. Apparently the Americans were taken aback as the Russians concluded the banquet by letting off pistol volleys above their heads).

When I telephoned George Blake I was greeted as warmly as ever. As it was snowing heavily and pedestrians were being killed every day by blocks of ice falling from buildings. I offered to set off early and make my own way to his home — a journey of some intricacy for the visitor with many Metro interchanges — but he insisted on meeting me part of the way: 'If you go into the Taganska Line at Tverskaya Station, change at Lubyanka for Komsomolskaya on the Circular Line — travel in the last carriage to Prospekt Mira and wait for me'. As ever, he was punctual and we greeted each other like old friends. He had become frail since our last meeting, during the walk to his home I noticed him relying on his walking stick to negotiate the sludge as we trudged along with the locals, often having to walk on the road as the footpaths were impassable. He was feeling the winters more and complained that the streets were not cleared of snow as regularly as before.

During the walk we caught up on each other's family lives. He asked after a niece who on a University tour from Dublin had brought him the script of the play (when contact was difficult). His son Mischa had married and had a son, so he had grandchildren in his two adoptive countries. His English sons visited regularly and he grew more fond of them each time. We spoke of Michael and Anne Randle and of Pat and Sue Pottle and of people rather than of politics. As we trudged through the snow, the years seemed to fall away through the Moscow gloom. Part of me was living with this book, trudging with a survivor of three wars — The Nazi War, Korean War and the war responsible for our meeting, the Cold War.

Over us hung serial connections. Although Sean Bourke was dead a long time, Limerick had come into his life again, through the marriage of his English son James to a young woman from the city. His son by Ida, Mischa and his wife had attended that wedding in Limerick, a visit unlikely to have happened during the Cold War — and later his new daughter-in-law and her family had been his guests in his country dacha. 'I like them very much'. Nearing his apartment block, we negotiated building skips filled with rubble: 'The neighbour below us is re-furbishing in what I believe is called Euro-style...there is a lot of banging — it's been going on for a year now'. I got the impression he was a bit bewildered by the lavish lifestyles encroaching upon his previously quiet world. It did not surprise me that Ida had taken a break to visit the Dacha, to cope with another new problem — she was installing stronger locks and paying for local inspection, as it had been broken into — unheard of before.

He was clearly saddened at the reports of the massive, organised theft of State properties and resources and the crime and fraud in the cities, probably having informed knowledge through his seniority in KGB, but as ever held onto his belief of a better world to come. We sat, as we had before, in his chapel of books and icons and had many cups of lemon tea, ranging over the events of his life. He asked if I thought his book was 'not sensational enough' and when I agreed he said he had suppressed some things out of respect to his former colleagues in SIS. 'I did not want to rubbish them, the way Philby did, all espionage is difficult, only those who do it can appreciate how difficult it is...'.

No Other Choice had sold over 200, 000 copies in the Soviet Union, but he had not been paid royalties. Would the monies make a difference? He said yes, very much — his pension went up every year, 'but only by a little and things are so much more expensive now...'. But the Dacha, provided by the Russian Government was 'for my lifetime'. I sensed a weariness at how some things had turned out, as he recited the old mantra that Communism, as he believed it, had never been really tried. Still, he had no regrets...five years in the Scrubs, loss of wife and young family whom he dearly loved. He sighed — no, he would not have wished things to have turned out differently, as it had already been ordained by God.

'How?' I asked, 'in what manner?'. Calvinism was a very extraordinary dogma, he said. God, before creation of the world, decided in His infinite wisdom who was going to be saved and who not — decisions made in His sovereign pleasure. The consequences are this: whereas other religions believe one can earn Salvation because of good works, the Calvinist believes nothing can save one, except God. Therefore, because they know they are saved, Calvinists are constantly checking their life — not in order to be saved, but to confirm they are saved... . He sighed and we fell into silence... .

CHAPTER TWENTY-SIX

THE END OF EMPIRES

May the Circle...

In the autumn of 2002 I stood outside the forbidding walls of Daingean Reformatory in the Irish midlands. Little of its structure had changed during the half-century since Sean Bourke and thousands of other boys had been imprisoned there. The high fortress walls, presciently similar to the walls of The Scrubs gaol in London, loomed gloomily above us, the moss-laden limestone weeping with the damp of midlands mist. Nearby ran the canal. Escaping boys ran along its path, in the belief it led to Dublin.

They did not get far, as local police, routinely responding to alerts, drove a mile or so along the road and waited by a canal bridge, confident the runaways would appear in their sights, to be returned within the walls.

A local man pointed out the buildings visible through the heavy iron gate — the living quarters of the priests and brothers, the chapel, the gardens in which the boys tilled produce. It was eerily derelict now, used to store public monuments; a graveyard of religious statues and artefacts, some going back to Ireland's time under Empire. When the British left in 1922, the vacuum of their departure was filled by the progenitors of the new State, a formal alliance of the Catholic Church and revolutionary politicians. A strict regime of censorship and church power was imposed. Priests, gunmen and ideologues ruled the old roost with a fervour that saw divorce outlawed, lands requisitioned and large estates broken up and given to small farmers. Many of the old aristocratic mansions of the Anglo-Irish were taken over by the newly enthused religious orders. In the case of Daingean, what had been a military barracks and then an industrial school with a statue of Queen Victoria inside the iron gates, had been given to the Oblate Order of Mary Immaculate, brothers and priests bound to the religious life.

Inside that main gate, where many a boy had arrived with fear in his heart, could be gleaned the walkways where priests strolled reading their breviaries, in breaks from coping with the 'filthy scum' of the ramshackle state that was Ireland in the 1940s.

If the ghost of Sean Bourke hovered over that forcing-house of his character, it would look down also upon an Ireland much changed since his death in 1982. The Church-State alliance which he hated had sundered under the weight of a new liberalism wrought by the prosperity of joining Europe and becoming less a British satellite. Another generation had fought — and won — the battle against Catholic fundamentalists in matters of lifestyle, health and welfare, driven also by the need for the Southern Republic to appear more secular in wooing Northern Protestants as part of the peace process. The military conflict in the North had entered another cessation — though the people there remain much damaged by the conflict. The latest phase had lasted nearly thirty years and health surveys showed high levels of mental stress.

In the South, the revelations of physical and sexual abuse of minors by Catholic clerics in schools and institutions were investigated by a series of State-backed enquiries. Almost every week during court terms, greying and penitent former priests and brothers were pictured in handcuffs going to gaol. A board set up to compensate the abused, mostly living abroad, expected to pay out over E40m, forcing some Catholic orders to sell off extensive lands and others to put property assets into trusts beyond legal reach. Two bishops had resigned in recent years, in matters relating to sexual morality, church attendances were falling and vocations sparse — all adding to the rapid erosion of Catholic power. The Spiritual Empire of Catholic missionaries, which teachers promoted as an antidote to British imperial values appeared to be heading into the same twilight. By contrast, Bourke's native city, Limerick, embarked upon an urban renewal which removed much of its old poverty and made it to visitors a glittering city on the Shannon, though it was superseded as the third city of the Republic by Galway. Crime, of a ferocity well removed from his boyish pranks, remained doggedly a blight upon its image.

...be Unbroken.

Pat Pottle, of the English conspirators, died in October 2000. He had settled in Wales with Sue, as they continued their joint interest in country life, antiques and left-wing literature. The obituary in *The Guardian* recorded his formidable career in anti-war activity, his role in the Escape and recalled his speech from the dock delivered to a jury which found him 'Not Guilty' of a charge to which he pleaded Guilty (with Honour!). I attended his memorial service in Conway Hall in London, traditional meeting place of the English Left and as such regularly monitored by MI5.

What the Security Service report made of the occasion might someday make for curious reading, as the Sunday afternoon turned out to be a joyous celebration of Pottle's life. The mosaic of his activities was stitched together by speakers, who recalled his organising abilities in the peace marches of the 1960s, his physical bravery in travelling to oppose the Greek Colonels' military junta in their own country and his consistent opposition to militarism of the Right or Left. Most of the attendees were of his generation, aged about late fifties and into sixties, with their affection for his memory undimmed by either the harshness of the Thatcher years or the pragmatism of New Labour. Many had the lean, tanned faces of people who walked in the countryside: they had learned early to walk with purpose. Having trudged through many an anti-Nuclear march in formative years, some were now active in anti-globalisation campaigns. Some were upholstered by jobs in academia or media, others showed the stress of lives at the gritty end of the social services in Britain's decaying inner cities. For many, lives spent as poorly-paid teachers or nurses or probation officers — props to the social services —had left their idealism undimmed even as it had taken toll on their energies.

Some had with them the younger offspring of second families and some of the men, at sixty, hoisted fretting infants of new unions onto their shoulders, to be part of proceedings which the children would hardly remember but which, in the mysterious ways of political ideology, might yet imbue them with dissent from the conventional order. Among the gathering, it is likely, were those who had supplied the safe houses which had harboured Blake and Bourke from October to December, all of thirty-five years before.

For most, the years in between had not been unkind and they sang with revivalist fervour a medley of folk and protest songs from the 1960s — *We Shall Overcome, Down by the Riverside, May the Circle be Unbroken.* As the songs and stories bonded their joint and several pasts, some had tears in their eyes for their histories and for an era gone.

As they harmonised in full voice I felt the presence of a lost England, given vent by a moment of pure theatre as a broad-shouldered young man addressed them. Introducing himself as James Blake, son of George, he said he had come at the suggestion of his father, to thank those who had harboured him all those years ago.

'My father is deeply grateful to you all, he sends his good wishes and condolences to Pat's family. And for myself, it is much more pleasant to visit my father in Moscow than to visit him in Wormwood Scrubs. Thank You...'.

For some, even now more misty-eyed, it was suddenly a rainy October in 1966 when they were all younger. Their comrades had been anti-war protestors, their political enemies were the fragmenting empires of colonial powers. They had marched, week after week, trudging to protest outside nuclear bases where American and British bombers exercised notional flight-paths over Russia. Some had been in gaol for those marches, others had lost jobs or had promotion stymied or had a discreet file slipped to an employer by the Security Service. The world seemed a perilous place then, with talk of four-minute warnings, nuclear shelters and Russian troops at the gates.

Since those heady and formative times for radicals, and to an unknown extent because of their influence, the political world had changed completely. The flags of many empires had come down across the globe, most startlingly in the disintegration of the USSR, which imploded from within rather than by attack from without, though its economic energy had become depleted by the drain and strain of the Arms Race with America. The consequences of the collapse are both so proximate and so far-reaching as to be not fully understood, though within a decade the West would have cause to urgently examine the vacuum of power created by the demise of the USSR. For the purposes of this saga, it is relevant to record that CIA and SIS gradually wound down their considerable monitoring of, and active operations against, Soviet targets in Asia, specifically in Afghanistan, where in 1992 the long armed rebellion against Soviet rule ended with the capture of Kabul. As both the Russians and West withdrew, a consequence was the growth of the autocratic Taliban who in turn nurtured Qaeda al-Jihad militant cells, worldwide, in a protracted conspiracy to attack the West. As some Arab countries, intent on 'exporting' radical Islam, exploited the new regime in Afghanistan, last skirmishing ground of the Cold War, there emerged a leader as charismatic and cunning as were his forerunners in intent, Hitler and Stalin. Under the leadership of Osama Bin Laden, backed by a coalition of Arab nationalists, attacks upon Western targets shook the democracies and alarmed them into limiting their own liberal values.

Nurturing resentments among populations displaced by the demise of empires brutally created by European powers in Arabia, Asia and Africa, Bin Laden and his inner circle exploited the profoundly felt alienation of millions in former colonies. The collapse of the Soviet Union extinguished the centre to which many Marxist states had looked, for both ideological 'guidance' and, as importantly, for military and economic support. In some cases a political void was filled by the growth of the largest mass movement to replace Marxism — Muslim fundamentalism.

Using equipment abandoned by Russia and the West, Qaeda al-Jihad (Al Quaeda) created a world-wide system of secret cells to launch guerilla war upon the West. It was, in conception and execution, similar to the anti-imperial structures created by the IRA in the 1920s in Ireland, by the Nazis in Germany in the 1930s, by Irgun in Palestine in the 1940s and the Mau Mau in Kenya in the 1950s, by EOKA in Cyprus, by Algerians to gain independence from France in the 1960s — a syndrome replicated by ethnic groupings in Africa and Asia towards the end of the Millennium. The net effect then was to bring about the End of Empires by bomb, murder, arson and shock — or as was perceived by the victims, by outrage and terror. As militant movements sharpened groundswells for independence, eroding the imperial will to stay, the political result in most cases was the same — prevailing powers sued for peace by surrendering territory.

A similar strategy seems to be that adopted by Qaeda al-Jihad, demanding ancestral redress in those Arab territories upon which America, France and Britain hold military bases or patent political leverage by economic influence. Since the early 1990s, the movement had demanded Western withdrawal from parts of Arabia, Africa and Asia (including Israel from Palestine) and their replacement by Muslim states. The failure of Western powers to prevent the protracted massacres of their co-religionists during the break-up of Yugoslavia was well noted among the recruiters. 'Always the Muslims, always the Muslims' said a local political leader to me in North Africa during the NATO strikes over Bosnia, months after the massacres. 'Too little, too late' he concluded as we watched on television the belated relief of Kosovo and the emaciated Muslim prisoners staring through the barbed wire in camps of 'ethnic cleansing', so patently a replica of the Holocaust. His weary vocal reaction was a tiny part of a much larger pattern of radical

Muslim reaction. Al Quaeda embarked upon suicide attacks, mainly against American military bases and embassies.

Throughout the closing decade of the millennium, these attacks escalated to the 1998 destruction by explosives of American embassies in Nairobi and Dares Salaam and the astonishing co-ordinated aggression upon mainland America during the long day of September 11, 2001, when Muslim militants launched four aerial attacks, using civilian aircraft to dive-bomb targets in New York and Washington D.C. The resulting murders of over 3,000 civilians forced the US government onto a war footing. CIA and SIS, having wound down their Soviet-Asia operations appeared deficient in warning, though KGB, through its continuing presence, had an inkling. As claimed by President Putin to the British Government, his own Asian service had weeks before predicted from Qaeda al-Jihad... 'something serious, long in the planning'.

What was provoked by September 11 drastically changed the balance of global power, as America and Britain embarked upon forming a world-wide Coalition Against Terrorism. In the wake of what became known to Americans as '9/11', many states, recently independent found on their doorsteps hastily-arrived emissaries from their former rulers, this time more supplicant than demanding. Even as the old empires were dying, a re-alignment emerged under the Coalition Against Terror. The Americans wooed Russia with increased IMF loans and removal of trade embargoes in order to install troops and listening posts in Uzbekistan and Kazakhstan previously off-limits to US military. Pakistan was given a billion dollars and promised non-interference with its Nuclear programme. On territories adjacent to the training camps of Al Qaeda-Jihad, Britain revived its listening posts to crank-up support from India, Egypt, Saudi, Somalia and Yemen. It meant, as was afterwards indicated by British Foreign Secretary Jack Straw, much eating of humble pie. Resentments over unfinished imperial business, mainly economic, had to be acknowledged before those countries agreed to use their defence and intelligence services in covert hostilities against Al Qaeda.

Dormant sinews of imperial power were revived by diplomacy and real-politik, as Prime Minister Blair urgently hurtled half-way around the once imperial globe to convince leaders of the imminent scale of the extremist Muslim threat. Against this scenario, a concentrated war in Afghanistan, fought mainly by American and British troops (shades of Korea) rooted out The Taliban which had trained the attackers on America. As in any conflict — from urban street riots to frontal assault — when man is pitted against man for survival and gain of territory, there will be disregard of a term recent in international politics — 'human rights'. The American-backed allies, the Afghan Northern Alliance, newly-armed and funded against their internecine enemies, The Taliban, replicated the tactics of previous imperial wars, whereby a native force acts on behalf of an outside power, in hunting down indigenous 'enemies'. It was no different for Al Qaeda suspects in the months after 9/11, as independent reports confirmed.

As the diverse nationalities of the captured guerrillas revealed, Qaeda al-Jihad had fermented connections with the legacies of many empires. It had recruited Chechen veterans of that ten-year old war, where oil interests and drug cartels were a sub-text for the Russian destruction of cities and populations. It recruited from obscure wars in Yemen and Indonesia, in territories long abandoned by European powers. Qaeda al-Jihad cited American and British military support for Israel's takeover of Arab lands, as far back as the Palestine Mandate of 1948, when a British Government sought to lighten the burden of collective guilt over the Nazi Holocaust by promising Jews worldwide a permanent place of refuge.

Unfortunately for world peace, this apparently benign move was enforced with disregard for millions of Palestinians who suffered enforced displacement from their ancestral lands. As rapidly emerged in the interrogations of Bin Laden's foot soldiers (potential bombers of Western cities), their leader had drawn his recruits from a wide casting through the twilight of European empires, from Iran to Saudi to Somalia to Nigeria — states where withdrawal had been replaced by radical Islam.

The net effect, by the end of 2002, was that America — the superpower with a near monopoly of the new technology — had become re-installed as the New Empire across former colonies who found themselves contingent to the extremist Muslim threat. The old empires went and a new one came into being. Whether in time Islamic fundamentalism will erode America and its values the way other resistance movements eroded other empires is at this stage conjectural. The states which do not comply with American demands to limit or destroy their nuclear and biological weaponry face sanction or war. As before, many of those present in Conway Hall to remember Pat Pottle were on the streets again, prepared to oppose their country going to war alongside America.

The irony is that the United States is also an actively immigrant country, from its annual intake of a million immigrants keen to become 'Americans'. This feedstock of labour, crucial to its strength, comes mostly from refugees from the old empires and dictatorships, from the failed fascist and communist experiments of the 20th century. They come from the repressive regimes of new Islam and from the poverty of old Hispanic Americas. A very large proportion are from the former states of the USSR. People, as ever, will vote with their feet for their own well-being — the migrant senses the pastures which will best sustain the future family.

By the end of 2002, the European Community agreed to consider membership of nine former States of the USSR, which a mere fifteen years before had appeared arm-locked to Moscow. Mobilised with EC passports, these citizens of an enlarged Europe will range freely over an enormously expanded community created from the Schuman Declaration at the end of the last war — a market motivated to subdue old imperial rivalries and so prevent a repeat of the horrors they inflicted twice in the 20th century. In an expanded Europe, at least, democracy, however cumbersome, has replaced the empires which exacted such costly havoc in human lives — but the legacy of those empires in other continents has yet to be resolved.

In November 2002, George Blake received the ultimate public recognition in Russia. State television devoted an hour-long documentary to his life and times and exploits.

Although privately honoured previously with many decorations, including the Order of Lenin and the Order of the Red Banner, this media profile marked official gratitude of his long-term devotion to the socialist experiment. The banquet and speeches which followed are likely to have been approved by Russian President Putin.

In Ireland, social workers, police and probation officers, protested, once more, over the lack of policy and facility for young offenders. A former President of the Prison Officers Association said 'There is no open facility for young offenders and its a damming indictment on the government'.

The criticism had been made many times, reflecting the frustration of those charged with dealing with young offenders. Without a policy of care and containment, many let loose by the courts — or banged into adult prisons for a brief stay — became the ruthless criminals whose spate of murders in the early months of 2003 alarmed the country. One could only imagine the ghost of Sean Bourke, looking down on his uneasy homeplace, as its citizens cowered behind locked doors, afraid to venture into parts of their city, the no-go areas of vicious vendetta. Burning of houses, and bodies found tortured, stabbed and shot were a regular occurrence. What price now, I imagined him cackling of the power of the once-vaunted Catholic church to stem the tide of anarchy. As indeed I had imagined his departing spirit gloating over Dail Eireann, that other centre of deluded power, on the day Jim Kemmy brought down a government when they taxed children's shoes: *I that went barefoot to the school gates — beaten for being both poor and late. Good man Jim, you showed them. I'd love to think you thought of me then, when you walked into the NO lobby — that it was your parting gift. In the finest parliamentary tradition, of course! My spirit lifted, soared up and away, to some kind of peace. Revenge is sweet. Goodnight old comrade and goodbye...*

ACKNOWLEDGEMENTS AND SOURCES

Personal knowledge is an advantage when embarking upon a biography of two people as diverse as Blake and Bourke. Knowing Sean Bourke, before and after The Great Escape, proved highly useful when I had to weigh the balance of my own judgments against the public record — in trying to fit odd pieces to the mosaic of a life that was made up of chameleon colours and some deceptions.

Similarly with George Blake, a professional spy since his teenage years, trained initially by the Dutch Resistance, then by the Secret Intelligence Service of Britain and — concurrently for about nine years — subject to the discipline of the Soviet Intelligence Service. To know more of that life brought me through the sweep of 20th century history, through three wars — Second World War, Korean War and Cold War.

Accordingly, I read much on the connection between espionage and politics. Dr Christopher Andrews's many works are rich in detail, if, in my view, deficient in glossing over SIS-sponsored killings. He is less reticent about the Russian service and I gained much insight from his collaborator, KGB defector Vasili Mitrokhin in *The Mitrokhin Archive*. More useful for understanding how SIS was a law unto itself is Stephen Dorrill's *MI6 — 50 years of Special Operations*. However, no printed record is worth as much as personal interface. With Blake, I used the bounty of many meetings in Moscow to probe light upon previously dark areas. I sensed the 'religious' zeal that was the more potent for being less visible. He was helpful, trusting me to honour his reticence about his first family in England whom he felt had borne the brunt of difficult times during his conviction as a Russian agent — and later escape — at tense times during the Cold War. In return he rewarded me with insights into his life in Russia.

Building upon those interviews, I then re-visited their own published accounts. Inevitably — and for all their apparent honesty — they lean towards some significant omission. Bourke denied he sent the bomb to the policeman in Crawley, though he did, while Blake is curiously bland about the fate of Western agents he betrayed — he denies deaths, but given KGB policies of the 1950s towards traitors, one might be reasonably sceptical.

In sifting the personal from the political I found very helpful the advice given to me by an eminent historian: 'Read the books, walk the land, listen to the accounts — somewhere in between is the truth'. Pursuing that shifting, elusive goal brought me into the wider political context of the times. By 'political' I mean not only how people are governed, but the beliefs they inherit from both family and society — the ultimate arbiter of behaviour. I found it therefore necessary to make mental leaps into the past, to discard present assumptions by immersing myself in newspapers, libraries and conversations.

For Bourke's childhood I found useful the early chapters of *The Springing of George Blake* by Sean Bourke, amplified by my own interviews, as well as his printed account in the *Limerick Socialist* and the recollections of Bourke's twin brother Kevin and of Joe Malone, who shared a boyhood with him. Eoin O' Kelly conducted able research on aspects of Limerick life. Bourke's time in London coincided with some of my own: I could readily relate to the realities of immigration and to the class and political landscape of Britain during the 1960s. For Blake's boyhood, I relied on *No Other Choice,* amplified by interviews in Moscow.

On the world war of 1939-45, there is a mountain of references, Jacques Legrand's *Chronicles of the 20th Century* provides insight into the daily lives of people — the poverty, uncertainty, Anti-Semitism and failed leadership — which made inevitable Europe's march to war.

The Cold War, spawned by another bout of political weariness in the aftermath of those horrors, was mainly fought by the espionage services of the Great Powers. Again, there are a multiplicity of books, from the general to the specific. For my purposes, one stands out: *Battleground Berlin,* which pierces to the centre of the Cold War, as seen by those who daily skirmished along the frontier. Two of its (three) authors are — David Murphy, then Head of Anti-Soviet section of CIA and Sergei Kondrashev, Lieut-Gen. KGB.

The Korean War also has many standard references. Blake's harrowing survival of the forced marches when captured in Korea is corroborated in telling detail by a little-known account by an Australian missionary: Fr. Philip Crosbie's *Three Winters Cold*.

Of both men's time in The Scrubs, I drew less upon their books and more upon extensive interviews with them and other inmates, including a visiting tutor. While contemporary newspaper accounts indicated a perfect escape, the actual black comedy of the enterprise as seen from the perspectives of Michael Randle and Pat Pottle revealed hazards not known then to Blake and Bourke in *How We Sprang George Blake — and Why*. Of their time in Moscow, Blake's book is sparse on KGB detail, while Bourke's is self-serving but useful on his emotional turmoil. I needed to read Ruffina Philby's *The Private Life of Kim Philby* — to appreciate how lost amid real Communism were Stalin's Englishmen.

Other Russian works confirmed their isolation, notably *The Philby Files* by Genrikh Borovik. As for Bourke's own attempt to regain his lost childhood by returning to Ireland, I drew on my own professional encounters with him over twelve years and on the records in both print and broadcasting — 'the first draft of history'. Bourke's final sallies back to Limerick and Clare could not have been understood without the help of many — notably Joe Kemmy and Larry Walsh and their archives of Jim Kemmy's letters and the magazines he edited: the *Limerick Socialist* and the *Old Limerick Journal*.

I would also like to record my gratitude to the RTE Sound Archive for their generous co-operation.

Finally, the chapter notes are for the specialist while some of the sensitive information which helped my overall understanding of the saga remains within the discretion of those who gave it. Kevin O'Connor, Dublin, February, 2003.

CHAPTER NOTES

Chapter 1

'...the natural, primary and...' 'The State acknowledges that...' Bunracht Na hÉireann, (Constitution of Ireland) 1937.

'...Remember the bull, John...' 'Toora-loo, a loo, aloo...' Interview with Kevin Bourke, Ayr, Scotland, September 1987.

'If ye won't learn...' Information to author.

'Sean was hiding under...' 'You got a penny...' 'Errol Flynn, The Count...' Interview, Ayr, Scotland, September 1987.

'She was sitting up...' *The Springing of George Blake*, Sean Bourke, Cassell, London, 1970, pp 116–117.

Chapter 2:

'A school for bad...' Interviews with Joe Malone 1983, 2002.

'I hated being sent...' '...I was twelve and...' 'Brother X was supervising...' 'From the washhouse we...' *Limerick Socialist*, 1976.

'Brother Y had a...' '...I made my way...' Daingean Days, Witness to Obscenity, Part Three, Sean Bourke, *The Old Limerick Journal*, Autumn 1982, pp 26-27.

'I saw boys with...' information to author

'I knew enough about...' 'What Sean told me...' Joe Malone, interview, 1983.

'...a stack of quality...' 'Within six months, he...' Kevin Bourke, Interview, Ayr, Scotland, September 1987.

Chapter 3

'It was this thirst...' *No Other Choice*, George Blake, Jonathan Cape, London, 1990, pp 38. *

'a great reckoning in...' *As you like it*, Shakespeare.

'tall and extremely thin...' *No Other Choice*, George Blake, Jonathan Cape, London, 1990, pp 44.*

'...from the burning hell...' *No Other Choice*, George Blake, Jonathan Cape, London, 1990, pp 50.*

'Even though the Nazis...' Interview, Moscow, February 2001.

Chapter 4

'I stood on British...' *No Other Choice*, George Blake, Jonathan Cape, London 1990, pp 76.*

'The corridor where I...' *No Other Choice*, George Blake, Jonathan Cape, London, 1990, pp 84-85. *

'I was excited and...' Interview, Moscow, February 2001.

'But if the successes...' *Secret Service – the making of the British Intelligence Community,* Christopher, Andrew, Honeymoon, London, 1985, pp 486-487.

'A thousand Weimer citizens...' *Manchester Guardian,* 9th May 1945.

Chapter 5

'never before had I...'   'Often at dusk I...' *No Other Choice,* George Blake, Jonathan Cape, London, 1990, pp 116. *

'...one cannot always be...' *No Other Choice,* George Blake, Jonathan Cape, London, 1990, pp 117.*

Chapter 6

'...a nightmare journey...the...' *No Other Choice,* George Blake, Jonathan Cape, London 1990, pp 127.*

'sporadic fire had come...' *The Guardian,* January 18, 2000, quoting investigation by AP reporter Charles Hanley, into events at No Gun Ri, 26 July 1950.

'a major of the...' *Three Winters Cold,* Philip Crosbie, Browne and Nolan, Dublin, 1955, pp 135.

'...tall for a Korean...' ibid, pp 136.

'...my gaze went sometimes...' ibid, pp 138.

'But they will die...' 'Then let them march...' ibid, pp 135.

'Don't try to escape...' Interview, H. Montgomery Hyde, Kent, 1985.

Chapter 7

'Then I will shoot...' *Three Winters Cold,* Philip Crosbie, Browne and Nolan, Dublin, 1955, pp 142.

'...used to the hygienically...' 'many had owned their...' *No Other Choice,* George Blake, Jonathan Cape, London, 1990, pp 134-135.*

'...though it is natural...' ibid, pp 135.*

'After what I had...' '...although I was their...' '...the destruction and the...' ibid, pp 141.*

'I remembered how in...' ibid, pp 141-142.*

'...would have involved us...' *The General and the President and the Future of American Foreign Policy.* Richard H. Rovere and Arthur M. Schlesinger Jr., Farrar, Straus & Young, New York, 1951, pp 244.

'It was a grave...' *No Other Choice,* George Blake, Jonathan Cape, London, 1990, pp 141.*

Chapter 8

'...a big, burly man...' *No Other Choice,* George Blake, Jonathan Cape, London 1990, pp 143.*

'...a young, fair Russian...' '...on whose utterances and...' ibid, pp 144.*

'...that somehow he agreed...' ibid, pp 145.*

'My inward struggle was...' ibid, pp 146.*

'...in exceptional circumstances, organise...' 'One would never dream...' 'I do not consider...' '...an unfortunate necessity...As...' ibid, pp 147.*

'This must have been...' ibid, pp 148.*

Chapter 9

'I hope there is…' contemporary court reports.

Chapter 10

'not overburdened with mental…' 'humane and energetic' *My Silent War*, Kim Philby, Granada Publishing, 1979, pp 108.

'…too much of the…' *No Other Choice*, George Blake, Jonathan Cape, London, 1990, pp 160.*

'…the communist delegations observed…' ibid, pp 163.*

Chapter 11

'if I told her…' *No Other Choice*, George Blake, Jonathan Cape, London, 1990, pp 164.*

' if I broke off...' ibid, pp 165.*

'Looks like Harvey's got...' 'all dangling ends were...' 'They have stopped beating...' *Mole*, William Hood, Weidenfeld and Nicolson, London, 1982.

'The tunnel was seen...' '…the tunnel provided detailed...' *Battleground Berlin, CIA vs KGB in the Cold War.* David E. Murphy, Sergei A. Kondrashev and George Bailey, Yale University Press, New Haven and London, 1997, pp 424.

'shameful underwater espionage' *Pravda*.

'So skilfully had the…' *No Other Choice,* George Blake, Jonathan Cape, London, 1990, pp 181.*

'…I passed some anxious...' ibid, pp 182.*

Chapter 12

'I got a deep…' 'Always too willing to…' Interview, Moscow, February 2001.

'If I fled on…' *No Other Choice*, George Blake, Jonathan Cape, London, 1990, pp 192.*

'Was I not about...' *No Other Choice*, George Blake, Jonathan Cape, London, 1990, pp 192.*

'I knew the game...' 'but I was determined...' 'I was in serious...' Interview, February 2001, Moscow.

'I felt an upsurge...' *No other Choice*, George Blake, Jonathan Cape, London, 1990, pp 198.*

'We don't want to...' Interview, February 2001, Moscow.

'Everyone acted as if...' *No other Choice*, George Blake, Cape, London, 1990, pp 199. *

'He spoke a lot...' ibid, pp 199-200.*

'for a purpose prejudicial...' Official Secrets Act (Amended) HMSO.

Chapter 13

'I was absent from...' 'If only I had...' Interview, February 2001, Moscow.

'...an unprepossessing figure...' *No other Choice*, George Blake, Jonathan Cape, London, 1990, pp 203. *

'His small wig, pushed...' '...busily taking notes hardly...' ibid, pp 202.*

'that for a purpose...' 'every document of importance' 'Having reached this conclusion...' 'of very great importance' 'I am told that...' 'you have said...' 'akin to treason' 'you could continue to' 'clearly be against the' 'Blake was a British...' 'Blake did not have...' 'in the public interest' 'it was very difficult...' 'Foreign Office official', Contemporary Newspapers.

'a member of the...' Dick Marsh MP, *Hansard.*

'to be punitive, to...' Court reports.

'a year for every...' *Daily Express,* May-June 1961.

'calm astuteness'   'when one looks at...' *The Crawley Observer,* December 1961.

'Bourke was taking a...' Information to the author from a reporter in Court.

Chapter 14

'Five dissatisfied prison officers' 'A disturbing letter...' 'often to be seen...' 'whitewash the crimes...' 'for dubious purposes' Contemporary newspapers.

'I think about it...' Interview, February 2001, Moscow.

'The rulers rule us...' Information to author from Brian Pottle.

'If you get the...' Kenneth De Courcey, interview, 1984.

'I'm your man' *The Springing of George Blake,* Sean Bourke, Cassell, London, 1970, pp 8.

'The Irish fear you...', 'The English assume you...' information to author.

'If I was depending...' *The Springing of George Blake,* Sean Bourke, Cassell, London, 1970, pp 123.

'...with the grand Christian...' *Limerick Socialist,* 1977.

'Christian fucking country' SB to author, Limerick, October 1966.

Chapter 15:

'*This is Fox Michael...*'Audio tape in possession of Author.

'I must have been...' 'I kept calling him...' 'I had my eyes...' 'Hurry, hurry, drop down...' 'Jump, jump for Christ's...' 'Please, Sean, you will...' Interview, February 2001, Moscow.

'I threw him the...' 'In fact, he's right...' *The Springing of George Blake,* Sean Bourke, Cassell, London, 1970, pp 170.

'Old Blakie's had it...' Information to author.

Chapter 16:

'I was no longer...' 'It was clear that...' 'The basement was actually...' 'a half-caste for the...' Interview, February 2001, Moscow.

'mystery of the pink...' 'flower pots as signalling antennae' Contemporary newspapers.

'For an instant in...' *No other Choice,* George Blake, Jonathan Cape, London, 1990, pp 246.*

Chapter 17

'...glinted in the pale...' *The Springing of George Blake,* Sean Bourke, Cassell, London, 1970, pp 231.

'I have been in...' ibid, pp 219.

'I had not realised...' Interview, February 2001, Moscow.

'The big fish had...' Information to Author, London, 1984.

'We had too much...' 'Sean was too much...' 'Our positions were completely...' 'Sean's desires clashed directly...' Interview, February 2001, Moscow.

'...I liked everything that...' *No other Choice,* George Blake, Jonathan Cape, London, 1990, pp 255.*

'Every town in every...' *The Springing of George Blake,* Sean Bourke, Cassell, London, 1970, pp 264.

'How would they do...' 'They would allow me...' 'The only thing at...', ibid, pp 270.

'five years on porridge' Interview, February 2001, Moscow.

Chapter 18

'At the height of...' *The Springing of George Blake,* Sean Bourke, Cassell, London, 1970, pp 274.

'All this Secret Service...' ibid, pp 273.

'You know, I can't...' *The Springing of George Blake,* Sean Bourke, Cassell, London, 1970, pp 286.

Chapter 19

'I had never worn...' 'I woke up one...' *News of the World,* 1 September 1968.

'and where would an...' 'good Englishmen' 'with £1,000 from friends' 'not give a damn...' 'The KGB did not...' *World in Action,* Granada Television, 23rd October 1968.

'great delusions of grandeur' '...stride into my room...' *The Springing of George Blake,* Sean Bourke, Cassell, London, 1970, pp 250.

Chapter 20

'an amateur effort' 'as surprised as the...' 'University-educated...persons of conviction' 'I am not a...' 'I wanted to be...' RTE Radio, October 1968.

'had rendered much of this...' 'would it truthfully express...' ' had sent the bomb...' 'give me immense pleasure' 'God is the type...' ' I believe in God...' 'If Ian Paisley asked...' 'your real motive had...' 'yes it is fair...' Contemporary reports of Bourke's extradition hearing.

'My honourable Queen's Counsel...' Information to author.

'connected to a political...' Court reports, contemporary newspapers.

'Holy Jaysus, Ireland's only...' 'Fur-coated Paddies' 'I suppose none of ..' ' and you certainly cannot...' 'Protestants join this Catholic...' 'Little Irelanders' 'Sinn Fein — Me Fein' 'only time he got...' Go back to England...' 'you are terrified of ...' 'oh what have we...' authors recollection.

'he was absolutely over...' Information to author.

'about thirty, very slightly...' 'more vocal than Michael...' 'pretty ...practical, asking sensible...' *The Springing of George Blake,* Sean Bourke, Cassell, London, 1970.

'Any intelligent boy-scout could...' Information to author.

Chapter 21

'only the best being...' 'to see Soviet life...' 'The news from Gillian...' 'In spite of all...' 'No I never felt...' 'Even when I was...' Interview, Moscow, February 2001.

'We are just like...' *No other Choice,* George Blake, Jonathan Cape, London, 1990, pp 259.*

'I don't think he...' 'In the Scrubs he...' 'Only a great cause...' *No other Choice,* George Blake, Jonathan Cape, London, 1990 and Interview, Moscow, February 2001.*

'Kim was in a...' Interview, Moscow, February 2001.

'semi-employable pensioner dependent...' Genrikh Borovik, *The Philby Files: The Secret Life of Master Spy Kim Philby,* Little, Browne & Company, New York, 1994.

'incorrigibly untrustworthy' Information to author.

'It was difficult to...' *The Private Life of Kim Philby,* Rufina Philby, St Ermin's Press, London, 1999, pp 26-27.

'Serious and smartly dressed...' ibid, pp 27

'...a powerful, well-shaped head...' ibid.

'seen for the first time...' *The Observer.*

'At that time, I...' 'He could have apologised...' 'In spite of what...' 'He looked younger, very...' Interview, Moscow, 2001.

Chapter 22

'I did not think...' 'Then he would phone...' 'from being fucked-up by...' Information to author.

'a big cheerful curly...' Interview, 1983.

'He really worked on...' Information to author.

'Get the gun, the...' 'Ahh... your Flann's brother...' Author's recollection.

'He made friends slowly...' 'It was a lovely...' Interview, November 1983.

'coming down from the...' Interview, 1983.

Chapter 23

'He often drank alone...' Interview, Limerick 2002.

'One of your few...' 'Of course Sean Bourke...' 'He gets lampooned doesn't...' 'Sean is older than...' 'by whom?' 'Surely not by the...' Kemmy Papers, University of Limerick.

'I was born...' RTE local radio, Limerick 1977.

'He liked to lead...' Jim Kemmy, RTE documentary by author, 1984.

'...a telephone and typewriter...' Kemmy Papers, University of Limerick.

'Bourke worked with religious...' Joe Kemmy, interview, Limerick, 2002.

'I knew you would...' 'I know for definite...' 'My only hope of...' Kemmy Papers, University of Limerick.

'I plan to cross...' 'I would use it...' Sean Bourke to Arthur Quinlan, Limerick, November 1980.

'A three-storey building...' 'had no connection whatsoever...' '...out all day, climbing...' 'this long delayed book...' 'Here the trees...' 'If the second book...' Kemmy Papers, University of Limerick.

'I did not join...' Interview, Larry Collins, Kilkee, November 1983.

'He did not look...' Interview, Mary Hynes, Kilkee Feb 1984.

'hiding from the Limerick...' interview, John Williams, Kilkee, 2002.

'I wake up in...' Interview, RTE Radio, Dec 1981.

'whiff of sulphur' phrase coined by Conor Cruise O' Brien.

'cast an omen...' interview, Dec 1983.

'The Patrician pleading with...' Dail observer, Budget Debate, January 1982.

'The Fianna Failers sniggered...' 'I kept them in power...' 'this could have led...' *The Irish Times*, 28 January 1982.

'fighting very hard to...' Interview Larry Collins, Kilkee, Nov 1983.

Chapter 24

'I had the impression...' Interview, 1983.

'Bourke had wrecked himself...' Interview, November 1983.

'...on the instructions of...' *The Mitrohkin Archive,* Christopher Andrew and Vasili Mitrokhin, Allen Lane, The Penguin Press, 1999, pp 522.

'Wiv' a little bit...' 'course it was the...' 'still in the police...' 'Course we were onto...' 'Arab terrorism, that's the...' Author's recollection of Rollo Watts' comments.

'...helped organise the civil...' *George Blake, Superspy*, H. Montgomery Hyde, Constable, London, 1987, pp 63.

'I got out at...' *The Springing of George Blake,* Sean Bourke, Cassell, London, 1970, pp 175.

'Anne's situation at work...' *The Blake Escape - How we Freed George Blake and Why,* Michael Randle and Pat Pottle, Harrap, London 1989, pp 231.

'I never had any...' George Blake, on video submission to Old Bailey trial of Randle & Pottle and Interview, Moscow, 2001.

'110 MPs signed a...' Pat Pottle, shorter synopsis of speech edited by Richard Norton-Taylor, *The Guardian*, 27th June 1991.

'A bad day for Justice' *The Daily Telegraph. '*Escape into Pantomime', *The Guardian.*

Chapter 25

'There are no 'experts'...' 'These are country people...' 'Outside of Moscow, there...' 'second-rate managers of a...' 'This place is full...' 'He comes in on...' 'They are acting as...' Irish businessman to author, Moscow.

'I liked and admired...' Interview, Moscow, February 2001.

'It has never been...' Interviews, Moscow 1992, 2001.

'Were' twere done', twere...' 'I was very sorry...' 'I owe him my...' Interview, Moscow, 1992.

'Maybe not in our...' Interviews, 1994, 2001.

'But Mother Russia is...' Interview, 1994.

'If you go into...' 'I like them very...' 'The neighbour below us...' 'not sensational enough' 'I did not want...' 'but only by a...' 'for my lifetime' Interview, Moscow, February 2001.

Chapter 26

'My father is deeply...' James Blake, at Pat Pottle's Memorial Service, attended by author, December 2000.

'something serious, long in...' *Avenging Terror,* Channel 4, September 2002.

'There is no open...' *Irish Independent*, 29 January 2003.

* from No Other Choice by George Blake, published by Jonathan Cape. Reprinted by permission of The Random House Group Ltd.

SELECT BIBLIOGRAPHY

Andrew, Christopher, *Secret Service*, William Heinemann, London 1985.

Andrew, Christopher & Gordievsky, Oleg, *KGB - The Inside Story - of its Foreign Operations from Lenin to Gorbachev*. Hodder and Stoughton, London, 1990.

Andrew, Christopher & Mitrokhin, Vasili, *The Mitrokhin Archive*, Allen Lane, The Penguin Press, London, 1999.

Bamford, James, *The Puzzle Palace, A Report on America's Most Secret Agency,* Houghton Mifflin Company, Boston, 1982.

Beevor, Antony, *Berlin - the downfall*, Viking/Penguin, London 2000.

Blake, George, *No Other Choice*, Jonathan Cape, London 1990.

Block, Jonathan & Fitzgerald, Patrick, *British Intelligence and Covert Action*, Brandon Books, Co Kerry, 1983.

Boldin, Valery, *Ten Years that Shook The World, The Gorbachev Era*, Harper Collins, NY, 1994.

Borovik, Genrikh, *The Philby Files: The Secret Life of Master Spy Kim Philby,* Little, Browne & Company, New York, 1994.

Bourke, Sean, *The Springing of George Blake*, Cassell, London, 1970.

Bunyan, Tony, *The History and Practice of the Political Police in Britain,* Julian Friedmann Publishers, London, 1976.

Cahill, Liam, *Forgotten Revolution, Limerick Soviet 1919,* O'Brien Press, Dublin, 1990.

Catchpole, Brian, *The Korean War, 1950-53,* Constable Robinson, 2001.

Cookridge, E. H., *George Blake, Double-Agent,* Hodder and Stoughton, London, 1970.

Crosbie, Philip, *Three Winters Cold,* Browne and Nolan, Dublin, 1955.

Deacon, Richard, *A History of the Russian Secret Service,* Frederick Muller, London, 1972.

Dorrill, Stephen, *MI6 — 50 Years of Special Operations,* Fourth Estate, London, 2000.

Dulles, Allen, *The Craft of Intelligence,* Harper & Row, New York, 1963.

Elliott, Nicholas, *Never Judge a Man by his Umbrella,* Michael Russell Publishing, Norwich, 1991.

Farrelly, Jim, *Who's Who in Irish Politics – the Top 500,* Blackwater Press, 1990.

Fitzgerald, Garret, *All in a Life,* Gill and Macmillan, Dublin, 1991.

Grose, Peter, *Gentleman Spy, The Life of Allen Dulles,* Houghton Mifflin Company, Boston / New York, 1994.

Gunther, John, *The Riddle of MacArthur: Japan, Korea and the Far East,* Harper & Row, New York, 1951.

Gwertzman, Bernard, and Kaufman, Michael T. (Edited By) *The Collapse of Communism,* Times Books / Random House, 1990.

Hastings, Max, *The Korean War,* Michael Joseph Ltd, London, 1987.

Hersh, Burton, *The Old Boys, The American Elite and the Origins of the CIA,* Scribners, New York, 1992.

Hohne, Heinz and Zolling, Herman, *The General was a Spy,* Coward, McCann & Geoghegan, NY, 1972.

Hood, William, *Mole – the story of the 1st Russian Intelligence Officer Recruited by CIA*, Weidenfeld and Nicolson, London, 1982.

Johnson, Loch K., *Secret Agencies, US Intelligence in a Hostile World,* Yale University Press, New Haven and London, 1996.

Legrand, Jacques, *Chronicles of the 20th Century*, Hampshire, 1988.

Modin, Yuri, *My Five Cambridge Friends*, Headline Book Publishing, London, 1994.

Montgomery Hyde, H., *George Blake, Superspy,* Constable, London, 1987.

Mosley, Leonard, *Dulles: A Biography of Eleanor, Allen, and John Foster Dulles and Their Family Network,* Hodder and Stoughton, London, 1978.

Murphy, David & Kondrashev, Sergei A. & Bailey, George, *Battleground Berlin, CIA vs KGB in the Cold War*, Yale University Press, New Haven and London, 1997.

O' Halpin, Eunan, *Defending Ireland, The Irish State and its Enemies since 1922,* Oxford University Press, 1999.

Penrose, Barrie & Courtier, Roger, *The Pencourt File*, Harper and Rowe, NY, 1978.

Philby, Kim, *My Silent War*, Granada Publishing, 1979.

Philby, Rufina, *The Private Life of Kim Philby*, St Ermin's Press, London, 1999.

Porter, Bernard, *Plots and Paranoia, A History of Political Espionage in Britain 1790-1988,* Unwin Hyman, London, 1989.

Powers, Thomas, *The Man who kept the Secrets, Richard Helms and the CIA,* Alfred A. Knopf, New York, 1979.

Randle, Michael & Pottle, Pat, *The Blake Escape, How We Freed George Blake and Why,* Harrap Books, London 1989.

Ranelagh, John, *The Agency - the Rise and Decline of the CIA*, Weidenfeld and Nicolson, London, 1986.

Rositzke, Harry, *CIA's Secret Operations: Espionage, Counterespionage, & Covert Action*, Reader's Digest Press, 1977.

Rovere, Richard H. & Schlesinger (Jr.), Arthur M., *The General and the President and the Future of American Foreign Policy,* Farrar, Straus & Young, New York, 1951.

Smith, Robert, *MacArthur In Korea: The Naked Emperor,* Simon and Schuster, New York, 1982.

Stafford, David, *Churchill and Secret Service,* The Overlook Press, New York, 1997.

Thorne Jr., C. Thomas and Patterson, David S., (Editors), LaFantasie, Glenn W., (General Editor), *Foreign Relations of the United States,1945-1950, Emergence of the Intelligence Establishment,* Department of State, Washington DC, 1996.

West, Nigel, *MI5 – 1945-72 – A Matter of Trust,* Weidenfeld and Nicolson, London, 1982.

Whelan, Richard, *Drawing the Line - The Korean War 1950 –53,* Faber & Faber, 1990.

Wise, David & Ross, Thomas B, *The Espionage Establishment,* Jonathan Cape, London, 1968.

Woodward, Bob, *Veil: The Secret Wars of the CIA 1981-1987,* Simon & Schuster, London, 1987.

Wright, Peter, *Spycatcher*, William Heinemann, Australia, 1987.

INDEX

Abwehr, 36, 40, 43, 47, 52.
Aer Rianta, 320, 321.
Aeroflot, 224, 320.
Afghan Northern Alliance, 344.
Al Quaeda, 342, 343.
Alexandria, 29.
America, see United States.
Andrew, Christopher, 47, 259, 309, 347.
Andropov, Yuri, 231, 232, 262.
Angleton, James, 124.
Anti-Semitism, 32, 348.
Ark Royal, HMS, 36.
Armistice Day, 27.
Atomic Bomb, 59, 68, 83, 87, 89.

Baker Street, London, 35, 116.
Balkans, 54, 58, 328.
Bannister, Captain R.J., 108, 166.
Behar, Albert, 14, 27, 39.
Behar, George, 13-14, 27-39.
Belgium, 33, 37, 73, 201, 327.
Bengal Terrace, Limerick, 7, 9, 12, 180, 275, 279.
Beria, Lavrenti, 100, 111.
BerlinTunnel-see George Blake.
Bevin, Ernest, 55.
Bin Laden, Osama, 341, 344.
Burns, Bishop, Patrick, 72.
Blair, Tony, 344.
Blake, Adele (GB's sisiter)
Blake, George,
    Berlin Tunnel, 116, 117, 128, 129-134,136, 137, 139, 141, 150, 150, 160, 203, 265, 308.
    Cairo, 14, 30, 31, 139, 183, 264, 269.
    Escape, 182-191.

Holland, 28, 30, 31-37, 40, 43-44, 86, 101, 110, 119, 214, 215.
    In hiding (after escape), 189-203.
    Korea, 61-91.
    Prosecution of, 154-165.
Blake, Gillian, 119, 120, 121, 122, 140, 144-148, 150, 153, 156, 214, 254-256, 269.
'Blondie', 94.
Blunt, Anthony, 112, 152, 300, 319, 323.
Bourke, 'Feathery', 11, 105, 282, 285-286, 297.
Bourke, Kevin, 11, 25, 26, 228, 231-236, 307.
Bourke, Sean,
    Childhood, 7-13, 16-26.
    Crawley, 105-109, 141, 153, 164, 165, 196, 202, 217, 348.
    Daingean, 16-24, 181, 213, 222, 275, 276, 278, 282, 283, 310, 337.
    Death, 303, 305.
    Extradition case, 209, 241-246.
    Kilkee, 298-301.
    RAF, 25-26.
    The Scrubs, 168-174.
Bradley, Omar, 87.
Broadway, Buildings, 41, 42, 51, 57, 60, 70, 97, 109, 119, 143, 145, 146, 147.
Brown, George, 211, 238.
Bruton, John, 302.
Buckingham Palace, 43, 50, 135.
Budget (Ireland 1982), 302-305.

Burgess, Anthony, 82, 88, 96, 97, 112, 115, 145, 147, 155, 265, 270, 300.

Chechna, 328.
China, 59, 68, 73, 78, 82, 83, 84, 87, 89, 99, 100, 114, 173.
Churchill, Winston, 35, 45, 47, 48, 50, 53, 55, 58, 97, 118.
CIA (in Berlin) 122-138.
CIS (Confederation of Independent States), 330.
CND, 154, 155, 192, 206, 252, 297, 312.
Committee of 100, 195, 206, 207, 226, 312.
Conway Hall (London), 339, 345.
Coughlan, Stephen, 281-282, 291-294.
Cordeaux, Colonel, 42.
Crabbe, Commander, 135-136.
Crosbie, Fr. Philip, 76, 80.
Curiel, Henry, 139.

Danaher, Jack, 180.
Deakin, Frank, 163.
De Courcey, Kenneth, 170, 174, 175, 185.
Deutsche, Rudi, 232.
De Valera, Eamonn, 7-9.
Dozhdalev, Vasili, 93-98, 204.
Driberg, MP, Tom, 152.
Dubcek, Alexander, 211, 232.
Dulles, Allen, 117.

Eden, Anthony, 136, 139, 151.
Eisenhower, President Dwight, 84, 99.
Eitner, Horst, 142, 144, 147, 148.
Elliott, Nicholas, 135, 136, 144-147.
EOKA, 137, 342.

Ferenka, 291.
Fitzgerald, Garret, 301-305.
Foot, Michael, 155.
French, Percy, 298.

Gaitskell, Hugh, 162.
Gee, Ethel, 149.
Gehlen Organisation, 142.
GOLD, Operation, 117, 129, 137, 150, 257.
Goleniewski, Lt. Col., Michal, 143, 147-149.
Gorbachev, Mickael, 260, 322, 324.
Graves, Robert, 288.
Griffin, Brigadier-General, 294.
Grivas, General, 137.

Harvey, William, 125, 134, 147, 150, 151, 155, 265.
Haughey, Charles, 302-303.
Herema, Tiede, 291.
Hollis, Sir Roger, 156.
Holt, Vyvyan, 66-67, 79, 84, 86, 87, 94.
Hood, William, 125.
Houghton, Harry, 143, 149, 207.
Hutchinson QC, Jeremy, 157-159, 165.
Hyde, Montgomery, 311-313, 352.

Inchon, 74, 75, 81.

John, The Baptist (School),16, 276.
Joint Intelligence Committee (JIC), 52, 53, 151, 155, 162.

Kemmy, Jim, 281-285, 289-295, 298-307.
Kemmy, Joe, 294, 349.
Kennedy, President John F., 128,169.
Khrushchev, Nikita, 100, 111, 122, 128, 132, 133, 135, 137, 323, 329.
Kings College (Cambridge), 57.
Kondrashev, Sergei, 112-116, 126, 132, 203, 256, 257, 262, 349.

Kroger, Helen, 156, 159, 161, 259, 270.

Larisa, 229-236.
Lecky, Terence, 147-150.
Lenin's Tomb, 322, 332, 333.
Limerick Soviet, The, 293-294.
Lipper, Mick, 294.
Lonsdale, Gordon, 149, 156, 159, 161, 163, 164, 173, 257-260, 269.
Lord, Herbert, 65, 66, 77, 80.
Lunn, Peter, 114, 116, 266.
Luzhkov, Yuri, 324, 325, 330.

MacArthur, General, 69, 73, 75, 81, 82, 83, 87.
Maclean, Donald, 69, 73, 75, 81-83, 87, 96, 97, 112, 115, 262, 265, 269, 270, 271, 300, 327.
Macmillan, Harold, 124, 151, 153, 161-165, 169, 259, 266, 327.
Malone, Joe, 276, 284, 285, 307, 349.
Mampo, 75, 76, 89, 100.
Manningham-Buller, Sir Reginald, 157-159.
Mao Tse-Tung, 59.
Marx, Karl, 14, 59, 63, 84, 90, 95, 99, 232, 263, 274, 281, 323, 341, 342.
Mary Clare, Sr., 79.
Mau Mau, 104, 342.
MAX see 'Popov, Major Pytor'
MECAS, 140.
MI5, 47, 96, 110-112, 117, 135-137, 147, 148, 154, 156, 160, 163, 164, 168, 172, 193, 207, 211, 238, 252, 259, 308, 314, 317, 339.
MI6, see SIS.
Montgomery, General, 47.
Mountbatten, Lord Louis, 207.
Munster Fair Tavern, The, 180, 275, 276, 277, 281, 285, 290, 306.
Murphy, David, 132, 350.
Mussolini, 36, 38, 45, 49.

Nasser, Colonel, 127, 136, 137, 139, 314.

NATO, 68, 78, 84, 89, 99, 154, 342.
Newman, Bishop Jeremiah, 294.
Nile, River, 29.
Normandy, 46, 47.
Norwood, Melita, 259, 270.

Oblate, Order, 16, 276, 310, 337.
Olympic Stadium, 119, 121.
Ordzhonikidze, 135.
Osborne, John, 154, 171.
OSS, 124.
Owen, Vice-Consul, 67, 79, 84.

Palestine, 342, 344.
Palestinians, 139, 344.
Parker, Lord Chief Justice, 149, 156, 159, 160, 161.
Perestroika, 260, 321, 322.
Philby, Kim, 96, 109, 124, 140, 155, 260-269, 272, 319.
Philby, Rufina (Rufa), 266-268.
Popov, Major Pytor, 122-129.
Portland Spy Ring, 151.
Pottle, Pat, 155, 173, 176, 178, 195, 197, 202, 205, 226, 237, 250, 251, 278, 311, 312, 315, 318, 339, 345, 350.
　　　　Memorial Service – *see Conway Hall*
Pottle, Sue, 251, 334.
Pusan, 71, 75.
Pyongyang, 70, 71, 74, 75, 81-84, 97, 101.

Queen Anne's Gate, 42, 43, 109.
Quine, John, 149, 152, 153.
Quinlan, Arthur, 296.
Quinlan, Monsignor, 100.

Radcliffe Commission, 163.
Randle, Anne, 155, 176, 178, 182, 192, 194, 197, 199, 201, 208, 209, 213, 226, 234, 237, 250, 251, 311, 312, 315, 334.